Faithful to the Word

The Sunday and Feast Day Homilies
of William H. Shannon

Liturgical Cycle A

Faithful to the Word

**The Sunday and Feast Day Homilies
of William H. Shannon**
Barbara Staropoli, SSJ editor

Liturgical Cycle A

ISBN 978-1-61422-833-2

*Cover Credit: "Love's Bond," sculpted by Timothy Schmalz and gifted to the Sisters of Saint Joseph of
Rochester by Monsignor William F. Shannon, is displayed near our Motherhouse Holy Family Chapel.*

Introduction

When Father William H. Shannon went to God on April 29, 2012, you would have thought he orchestrated the day himself. Maybe he did! It was a Sunday, the most important day of the week as far as he was concerned, and it was the Fourth Sunday of the Easter Season also known as Good Shepherd Sunday.

Father Shannon left a remarkable legacy. Of paramount importance in that legacy, he would consider his almost 95 years as a baptized Catholic. Along with this were his 70 years as an ordained priest of the Diocese of Rochester, NY, his 38 year tenure as a faculty member and chaplain at Nazareth College of Rochester and his loving service to the Sisters of Saint Joseph of Rochester as chaplain and honorary member of the Congregation for 65 years.

After retiring from teaching in 1982, Father Shannon turned his full attention to writing. Along with the publication of books on spirituality, a major focus became the life and writing of Thomas Merton. These works are outlined in Archivist Kathleen Urbanic's article, A Monumental Contribution: The William H. Shannon Papers in the SSJ Rochester Archive. This was written for Blessings, a publication of the Sisters of Saint Joseph, and is included as Appendix 2 at the end this volume.

Along with a full life of literary activity, there was another very important component in Father Shannon's life. He was a dedicated priest and took seriously the responsibility to preach the Word of God. During the 1960's, he took advantage of post-Vatican II workshops in biblical scholarship which were held nationally and presented by scholars like Raymond Brown. He considered this opportunity one of his major "conversions," mentioned in his remarks for the fiftieth anniversary of his ordination.

Inspired by these experiences, each week through his life, he spent time in reflection and scholarship preparing for the

Sunday homilies he would present. Those of us who knew him remember the conscientious process that occupied a significant part of the week. Before he became proficient at the computer, his desk would be piled with Scripture, commentaries, thesaurus and yellow pads filled with notes. For him, the Sunday homily was always central and his preparation for it was his most important work. His congregation at the time might have been the students of Nazareth College. Those who were awake enough on a Sunday morning received a challenging reflection of the readings. In later years, his thoughts were shared with the congregation gathered at the Motherhouse of the Sisters of Saint Joseph for Sunday Mass and many knew they were receiving a great gift in his preaching.

It is my privilege to present this collection of the Sunday homilies from Liturgical Year A. They are meant to be a prayerful companion to the Sunday readings, inspiring and deepening the call to faith through the scholarship and the insightful reflections they provide.

May the spirit and words of Father Bill Shannon continue to inspire you who reflect on them and bring you the challenge, joy and peace of the Word of God.

Barbara Staropoli, SSJ
October 15, 2016

I express my sincere gratitude to:

Dr. Christine Bochen
    Professor of Religious Studies, Nazareth College,
    William H. Shannon Chair in Catholic Studies

Christopher Daviau
    Information Technology, Sisters of Saint Joseph

Danielle Crino
    Alumna of Nazareth College, Technical Writer

Lisa Hartmann
    Assistant to Father Shannon, 2009-2012

Mary Anne Laurer SSJ
    Office for Mission Advancement, Sisters of Saint
    Joseph

Mary Anne Turner SSJ
    Director, Information Technology, Sisters of Saint
    Joseph

Kathleen Urbanic
    Congregational Archivist, Sisters of Saint Joseph

The Sunday and Feast Day Homilies

Year A

THE FIRST SUNDAY OF ADVENT

Isaiah 2: 1-5
Psalm 122: 1-9
Romans 13: 11-14
Matthew 24: 37-44

I want to tell you a story. A very brief story. You receive a phone call from a friend. "I am at the airport," she says. "I shall be with you in a little while." You respond: "Yes, do come. I look forward to your coming. Of course, we have been enjoying your presence here for some time. It is so wonderful that you have been with us so long."

Your reaction may well be: "That's not only a dull story. It's a loony one, too. How can you speak of someone coming to you, if you are already enjoying the presence of that person?"

It does seem like a bit of a problem, doesn't it? And it is. It is the problem that is at the heart of the season of Advent. It is a problem that is highlighted in the very prayer that opens this liturgy. In that prayer, we ask "that the dawn of his coming may find us rejoicing in his presence." Listen to what we are saying: "When Jesus comes he will find us already rejoicing in his presence." That is the paradox of Advent: He is coming. He is coming in the most unexpected ways. Yet we already have him.

The way of opening up this paradox is to heed the advice Jesus gives us in the Gospel: Stay awake! Wake up! Wake up to what is happening all around you. Or, as the Second Vatican Council put it, read the signs of the times. The example in the Gospel is an instructive one. The interesting thing about the Noah story is that it wasn't raining when he started to build the ark. People thought he was a bit crazy: building this huge boat in a place where there was no water. The people of his time are not accused of doing anything wrong. They just went about their daily activities – and if their society had such an institution as "black Friday," they would have besieged the local stores, pushing and shoving, looking for bargains. The point is their lives were lived at a very superficial level and they were oblivious of what was really happening. They never saw the rain clouds gathering menacingly in the sky. Noah did. He was the only one who was truly awake.

Yes, we have to be awake. We have to read the signs of the times. We live in a world where almost any time in any place things may explode. What is going to happen with Iran. Will there be war? How threatening is the situation in Pakistan? What is the significance of the fact that I can buy a shirt in the Irish shop – a shirt with the name Ireland in the front and then notice a tag which says: Made in China? There is a danger, though, in wallowing in pessimism. There are many wonderful things happening too, in our world. There are groups like *Sojourners* magazine, Pax Christi and other groups inviting a divided America to find a common ground for action. Overcoming poverty in America can become such a common ground on which a divided people may act together. We know that at the heart of the Middle East problem is not just Iraq and Afghanistan and the divisions there. It is the Israeli-Palestinian problem. What is not sufficiently known is that there is in Israel a growing movement of Israeli people called PEACE NOW. They are hoping that fruitful dialogue may lead to two states in Palestine. All over the world there is the yearning for peace, not any sort of peace, not a peace that is only the cessation of hostilities, but a peace that is based on justice and the recognition throughout the world of human dignity, human rights and human responsibility. Growing also in the world is the realization that the only way to such peace is the way of nonviolence.

Jesus' call to us, therefore, is look outward – to see what is going on in the global village to which we all belong. But looking outward will be futile unless there is a deep looking inward. Carl Jung has said: "One who looks outside, dreams. One who looks inside, awakens." The true awakening is the awakening of the spirit. Deep down beneath the rubble and sinfulness of our lives is an underground center of mystery: God's dreams for us that have so long remained unremembered. At that level of our being there is a relentless compulsion that yearns to transcend our mortality and to draw us toward the heart of God. Robert Browning in his poem on Andrea del Sarto, a 16th century Italian painter says:

Ah, but a man's reach should exceed his grasp,
Or what is Heaven for?

Is there a familiar ring about this poem? Does it remind us of some other opening prayers of the Masses of recent Sundays, where we were invited, for instance, to say: "Lead us to seek beyond our reach." Or "The love you give us always exceeds the furthest expression of our human desire." Yes, Advent reminds us that we are coded for God, that we are God-bound.

An article in the London *Tablet* tells a moving story about a Church in the Netherlands. "On entering the building, everyone would stop and bow in the direction of a white-washed wall.   It was a tradition that nobody questioned. They felt it was the right thing to do. One day the parish decided to renovate the church. They began to strip the paint off the old walls. While doing this, they discovered traces of a painting on the wall toward which everyone bowed,   but nobody knew why.

"Very carefully they peeled off the layers of white-wash. What emerged was an ancient and very beautiful painting of Christ. Nobody was old enough to have actually seen it. But now they came to understand why they almost instinctively persisted in honoring the wall that concealed the glorious work of art. The holy work of Advent is, I think, like that. It peels away the false veneer to reveal and restore, under our December anxiety and excitement, the unique masterpiece that underpins, inspires and echoes the eternal longing of every human heart." It's God's image within us.

In Advent we prepare to meet the Christ within us who is the Christ who comes to us. In Advent we live out the reality of the Advent paradox. We beg God in that opening prayer: "increase our longing for Christ our Savior."

Thomas Merton put it this way:

Make ready for the Christ, Whose smile, like lightning,
Sets free the song of everlasting glory
That now sleeps, in your paper flesh, like dynamite.
(Collected Poems 115)

THE SECOND SUNDAY OF ADVENT

Isaiah 11:1-10
Psalm 72: 1-2, 7-8, 12-13, 17
Romans 15: 4-9
Matthew 3:1-12

Many people don't quite know what to make of Advent. Even when we don't get caught up in the crass pre-Christmas commercialism, we are a bit confused about what we are supposed to be doing during Advent. We know of course about the three comings of the Lord traditionally associated with this season: His eschatological coming at the end of time; His historical coming during the reign of Herod the Great and Tiberius Caesar; His coming in grace to deepen our participation in God's life.

The problem is: how do we get a handle, so to speak, on these three comings. Some people feel that it seems a bit difficult and somewhat unreal to get all steamed up about his final coming, when we don't honestly expect it is going to happen in our time – though of course there is always the chance of our being surprised.

Others, while they realize that his coming in grace deserves our careful reflection, would say: this really isn't unique to Advent. It's something we ought to be thinking about at all times.   So, again, it's difficult to get all fired up about this coming of the Lord.

If we follow this kind of reasoning (and I am not necessarily saying that we should), we have only one option left: to turn our thoughts in Advent to the historical coming of Jesus. And I guess we have to admit that, with all our talk about the Lord's eschatological coming and his coming in grace, what is really on most people's minds during Advent is Christmas. And this is a perfectly valid, though incomplete, perspective to have on Advent. The problem is to clarify what we mean by Christmas or rather what we mean by the historical coming of Jesus.

The danger is that we tend to restrict that coming to its beginning and think of the historical coming of Jesus as primarily a birth event. This is all very lovely, full of nice sentiments and beautifully romantic.

But in a sense it misses the point. The historical coming of Jesus that Advent celebrates is not primarily about the coming of a baby, but the coming of the strong Son of God. It is about the coming of God's greatest teacher and prophet who comes with a message about the Kingdom.

The historical coming which Advent celebrates is the coming into full maturity of the one who announces the breaking into the world of the reign of God. This is what John the Baptist is talking about in the Gospel: the One who comes in the power of the Holy Spirit.

By all means let us revel at Christmas in the birth of the Child, but let us never forget that the focus of Advent is not on that Child come to full maturity and calling us to accept the reign of God in our lives. The painters of the icons got it right. When they picture the Child, he may be small but he has the face of an adult. He is God's Wisdom made flesh.

One way of distinguishing Advent from Lent is to note that Lent centers around the *preaching of the Church about Jesus,* namely, that He died and was raised by God. This is the Church's fundamental message. It has no other message. Advent on the other hand might be said to center about *the preaching of Jesus.* For Jesus comes to preach to us about the reign of God.

In saying this I do not intend to separate the preaching of Jesus from the preaching of the Church. There certainly is continuity between them. Yet though there is continuity, there is difference. *Jesus preaches the reign of God; the Church preaches Jesus, namely that the reign of God which He had preached has in Him broken into our world.*

Advent, therefore, confronts us with the need of preparing ourselves for Jesus' message about the kingdom. And His principal message about the reign of God is that it is a reign of justice. The word "justice" has many meanings in the Bible. Its principal meaning is that it is an act of God, judging on behalf of the poor and vindicating their rights against oppression by the wicked. Very often the wicked who oppress the little ones of God are not just individuals; they are also evil structures in society. This is the message brought by John the Baptist. It is the message that Jesus speaks of in his preaching: it is not only individuals, but the very structures of our society that need to undergo conversion.

If we are going to work for a society in which justice prevails, we must begin to take on the biblical understanding of justice and begin to see ourselves as instruments of God to vindicate the rights of the poor and the oppressed. The responsorial psalm is worth our serious reflection and concern. It speaks about God's time and says: *"Justice shall flourish in God's time."* Then it goes on to say:

> *God will rescue the poor when they cry to out to God*
> *and the afflicted who have no one to help them.*
> *God shall have pity on the lowly and the poor.*
> *The lives of the poor God will save.*

As we reflect on this psalm, as we hear the challenge to be instruments of God's reign, our hearts and our prayers and our actions must somehow go out to the poor who are suffering throughout the world.

Thousands of people have fled their country and are huddled in inadequate refugee camps, where many will die from the cold weather, where many have already died from the thousands of bombs we have dropped on these hapless people.

Into this picture of a dismal future, Isaiah sounds a poetic chord of hope. He tells us of "a shoot [that] shall sprout from the stump of Jesse." What is meant by this shoot that comes forth from a seemingly dead stump?

The eminent scripture scholar, Walter Brueggemann, comments on this passage. "The stump," he writes, "is any closed-off historical possibility, any place in life that has failed and collapsed and ended in despair. It is like the potted plant, dead and thrown on the compost pile, forgotten and abandoned. Isaiah's poem imagines that God can and does raise up new life where none seemed possible.

Every such raising up of a 'shoot' from a 'stump' is a miracle and it is this miracle that makes peacemaking possible."

THE THIRD SUNDAY OF ADVENT

Isaiah 35:1-6a, 10
Psalm 146: 6-10
James 5: 7-10
Matthew 11:2-11

Today's first reading is about salvation from unfreedom. By salvation I mean God's grace enabling us to overcome the things in us that make us unfree. The reading from Isaiah pictures God's grace overcoming unfreedoms that come from forces over which we have no control. The examples he gives are: blindness, deafness, the inability to walk. Isaiah presents salvation as a restoration of the freedom to see, to hear, to walk. Salvation means God overcoming the physical forces that make people unfree.

The Gospel speaks of a very different kind of unfreedom. It is the unfreedom that exists in a heart that seems to have lost the power to trust and believe, the power to hope for salvation. John is in prison; and to be in Herod's prison meant to be in darkness. But the real darkness in John is not from the absence of windows in his cell, but from the absence of light in his heart. He no longer sees where he's going or what God wants of him.

It is not difficult to see why this inner light seems to have gone out in John. After all, he had spent his whole life preparing the way for the One-Who-Was-To-Come. Now, all of a sudden it seems, he begins to wonder if his whole life has been an absurd and even ludicrous mistake. Jesus, on whom John had pinned his hopes, was not acting like the Messiah. He was not saying what the Messiah was supposed to be saying. John is forced to face the agonizing possibility that would make his whole life a question mark: "Had he picked the wrong candidate?" John found himself forced to question the very raison d'etre of his life. For, following in the line of all the prophets of Israel, he had called the people to repentance. Like all the prophets he had preached: Repent, or else. Repent or you will surely experience the wrath of God. This was classical prophetic teaching: what John expected Jesus to say.

His problem was that Jesus was not saying this. True, Jesus was calling people to repent: to mend their ways; but his call to repentance was followed, not by the classical "OR," but by an unexpected "AND." He did not say: "Repent OR the wrath of God will come upon you." His message was totally different: "Repent AND then you will be able to see the love and mercy of God that has always been extended to you."

This was not just a difference of emphasis. It was preaching that was saying something totally different about God. The prophets' message had always been "God loves you." Still it was a love that laid down condition. God will love you, but on the condition that you behave. And because human persons are often very weak, the prophetic picture of God inevitably comes out as the picture of God as a God of wrath. And equally inevitably the basic human stance toward God, in the light of that message, will be one of fear. When I am conscious of my sinfulness and weakness (and who of us is not?), then a God whose love is conditional scares me.

John had heard enough about Jesus' preaching to know that he was saying something quite different. Jesus said what no prophet before him had dared to say. He was telling people that God's love was unconditional. In Jesus' preaching there is no room for: "God loves you, if..."   His preaching was quite simply: "God loves you." For Jesus, God is Love (as the 4th Gospel will write later). Hence God could not love. And if God cannot not love, that means that God's love can never be conditional.

This is the problem John was brooding over in the miserable setting of his prison cell. Maybe he thought it too good to be true – what Jesus was preaching – or maybe his mind was so locked into the traditional beliefs about God that he was scarcely free to believe the GOOD NEWS that Jesus was bringing to people.

Notice the approach Jesus uses to activate John's freedom to change his thinking. He does not try to change his way of thinking by a command. (This is a common mistake made by authority: thinking that a command to accept something, especially if it is repeated often enough, can get people to be obedient and to change their minds. The way one thinks cannot be the act of obedience. You cannot command people what they are to think.) You will notice Jesus doesn't make that mistake. He doesn't say to John: "Look here. You must believe what I say because I say it."

No, Jesus' method of persuasion is simply to tell John to look at the facts. Look what God is doing through me among his people. Take account of your experience and the experience of others you know. Note how God is giving sight to the blind, hearing to the deaf and strong limbs to the crippled. But what is more important than all of these is that the Good news is being preached to the special objects of God's love: the poor. And the Good news is that God is Love, not Wrath.

What Jesus is saying to John is this: "All your life you have been brought up to think of God and his Messiah in one particular way. I am calling you to change your thinking. I am calling you to look at what people are actually experiencing about God. Then be free enough in your own heart to believe what you are seeing and change your thinking about God and his Messiah. Don't let that truth become a stumbling block to you just because it's new. Let the truth about God set you free."

What was John's reaction to Jesus' message? Did he accept the Good News? Did he go to his martyr's death in peace? We are not told. This is another one of those tantalizing stories, so frequent in the gospels, where we are left cliff-hanging and not informed about what happened next. Perhaps we can say that one of the reasons this story is deliberately left incomplete is that it is not just John's story; it is our story too.

The incompleteness of the story forces each of us to ask herself/himself some probing questions: Do I see that my beliefs cannot be the shadow of someone else's, but must be my own personal acceptance of God's truth? Do I truly understand that belief cannot be commanded? Do I see the need of personally experiencing God and what he is doing in the world, if I am to accept him in an authentically human way in my life? Am I prepared to accept God as absolute and unconditional Love? And if I am, what does this say about the way I must choose to live my life? What does it have to say about the way I must learn to deal with other people? With friends? With people I like? With people I don't like? What does it have to say about the judgments I have to make and the actions I have to take regarding the policies and actions of my country?

Today's Gospel leaves us with a number of questions about John the Baptist. What is more important: it leaves us with a lot of questions we have to put to ourselves.

THE FOURTH SUNDAY OF ADVENT

Isaiah 7:10-14
Psalm 24: 1-6
Romans 1:1-7
Matthew 1:18-24

There is a uniqueness about this 4th Sunday of Advent that sets it apart from the three preceding Sundays. The readings of those first Sundays call us to get prepared, to be ready for something grand and glorious that is about to happen. This 4th Sunday is already beginning to say: it has happened. The divine plan has come to fulfillment. The Word of God has been made flesh in Mary's womb. The Son of David has come, but he is not just son of David. He is Emmanuel.

The first reading is that remarkable passage from Isaiah which tells of the prophet's unhappy encounter with Ahaz, who was a descendant of David and king of Judah. The context of the reading from Isaiah is this: the kingdom of Judah is in trouble from neighbors to the north. Ahaz has it in his mind to make an alliance with the Assyrians. Isaiah warns him that such an alliance will only end in disaster. To allay the king's fears, Isaiah offers to give Ahaz a sign from God that he will be with the king. Ahaz has no need to fear.

King Ahaz, pretending piety as his reason, refuses to ask for a sign. His real reason is that he had already decided on the Assyrian alliance and did not want anyone, not even God, to prevent him from carrying out his decision.

But one does not so easily dispose of God. Ahaz will be given his sign whether he wants it or not. Isaiah pronounces the sign. It is a sign that God will be faithful to the covenant. The Davidic line will not be cut off. The sign is the promise that Ahaz's young queen, whom Isaiah calls simply a "young woman," is at that very moment pregnant with a child who will continue the Davidic line and through whom the promise of divine protection will be fulfilled.

The Hebrew word, *almah*, used here to describe the mother of the child simply means a "young woman." That is the way that Isaiah is translated in the New Revised Standard Bible: "The young woman is with child and shall bear a son and shall call him Emmanuel." The New American Bible, however, translates the passage in a way more familiar to us: "The virgin shall conceive and bear a son and shall name him Emmanuel." Clearly the New American Bible has in mind Matthew's text which explicitly refers to "the virgin" as the one who will conceive. Does this mean that it is being false to the Hebrew text for theological reasons, namely to defend the virginity of Mary? An interesting light is thrown on that question by the fact that the Septuagint, the Greek translation of the Bible, translates the Hebrew *almah* with the Greek word *parthenos* which means "virgin." And the Greek Bible was produced two hundred years before Christ and therefore long before any Christian Gospel could be written.

The New Testament happily seizes upon this rendering of Isaiah to express a new truth: namely, that, though every king of David's line embodied in some way God's promise to be with his people, it is only in Jesus, son of the Virgin Mary, that the promise is perfectly fulfilled.

But to have Mary's son be the fulfillment of the promise made to the Davidic line, he must belong to the line of David. That is why Joseph's presence in today's Gospel is so crucial. Notice that he is explicitly called "son of David" by the angel who appears in his dream. It is by his acceptance of Mary as his wife that Joseph gives a Davidic lineage to Mary's virginally conceived son. Hence her son, just as truly as the son of Ahaz's queen, and much more importantly, is called "Emmanuel."

It is with the naming of the child that the theological meaning of today's liturgy comes to its fullness. We should note that both the first reading and the Gospel conclude with a child being called "Emmanuel." But there is a significant difference. In the first reading it is Ahaz's queen who calls her son "Emmanuel." In the Gospel we are told of Mary's son: "*They* shall name him Emmanuel." This is to say that Mary's son is "Emmanuel" for all peoples, for all of us. Hence it is not Mary, but all of us who call her son "Emmanuel."

More than that: "Emmanuel" has a different meaning when applied to the queen's son and to Mary's son. Ahaz's son, the good king Hezekiah, was indeed a sign that God protected God's people. But it seems as if this is done from afar. It is as if God in the First Testament, while being God-with-the-people, is still on the other side of the human reality, not on our side. It is as if God protects people from without as it were.

The son of Mary is Emmanuel, God-with-us, in a much profounder sense. We experience God's love and care and protection, not from afar, but from within our human condition. God is with us. God is for us. God is on our side of the human reality.

What I am suggesting is that the Incarnation adds a new dimension to the Love that has always accepted us. It means that One who has always loved us with divine Love is now able and delighted to love us with a love that is truly human. This is not to say that God loved people more after the Incarnation than God did before. It is simply that God's love is manifested more clearly, more explicitly – because it is manifested as human.

If the people of the First Testament seemed at times to be crushed by a power that they could not always identify as Love, the Incarnation removes once for all the ambiguity that at times shadowed that love for the people of Israel. For now, we see that Love shining forth in a human face, in the features of the human Jesus who became like us in all things but sin.

Now we know in the deepest possible sense what it means to say that Jesus is "Emmanuel." In Jesus God is with us in all possible meanings of those words "with us": with us in the sense of being *in our midst*, with us in the sense of being *for us*, with us in the sense of being *at our side.*

What Jesus' presence among us as one of us teaches us is that Love in God is not simply a *moral quality*, that is, something God does. It is God's very *ontological reality*, God's very being. Hence God's love is not something outside us that occasionally touches our lives, Rather God's Love is like a fountain of water springing up in the depths of the divine Being and flowing endlessly through the whole of creation, filling all things with *life and goodness and strength.*

To put it another way: God's Love is a consuming Fire that purifies us. And once we have been purified of all that is alien to that Love, it consumes us so that we become as it were indistinguishable from the Fire. We find our true identity in the Fire, and in finding our identity we come to know the Fire itself.

Love flowing through all of creation, Love consuming us in its Fire – these are human words, human analogies, that try, however imperfectly, to help us understand the name – first given by Isaiah to Ahaz's son – but then given with so much greater meaning to the only one in our flesh who has ever perfectly mirrored God: the one we call Jesus-Emmanuel.

CHRISTMAS (Mass at Midnight)

Isaiah 9: 1-6
Psalm 96: 1-2.2-3,11-12, 13
Titus 2: 11-14
Luke 2: 1-14

There is a Christmas story that you may have heard in one of the many versions in which it is told. It's about the little boy who played the part of the inn-keeper in the traditional Sunday school Christmas play, attended by doting and anxious parents. According to the script the young inn-keeper had two lines. The first was: "I'm sorry, but there is no room in the inn." The second line was supposed to be: "Well, you can sleep in the stable if you like."

At the proper time Mary and Joseph came to him – weary and hopeful and asked if there was a place in the inn for them to stay. He managed his first line to perfection. "I'm sorry," he said, "but there is no room in the inn." But he never got to say his second line. As he saw Joseph puts his arms around Mary and start to walk away, the little boy suddenly improvised and cried out: "Wait! Come back! You can have my room."

Quite obviously he ruined the Christmas play. He had entered into the play so fully that it was no longer a play. It seemed to him as if it was for real. A marvelous baby was to be born and he just could not turn that Child's parents away. He never got to his second line: "Well, you can sleep in the stable if you like." He had a better idea, as love came down at Christmas into the little innkeeper's heart and he knew what love must do. What he really did was to throw away the script. It was no longer a play, but real life. And all of a sudden he was a real innkeeper, with a heart full of love.

Christmas is the day when *God threw away the script.* The script called for a mighty Deliverer who would come with power to destroy the enemies of his people. Jesus threw away that script. He enters our world as a little Child. He brings power: not the power of destruction, but the power of love: love that destroys not enemies, but enmity.

The script called for an avenging Judge who would visit divine wrath on God's wayward people. Jesus throws away the script. He comes, as St. Bernard expressed it poetically, as a Bee, nourished amid the flowers of Nazareth, who brings honey, but no sting, that is mercy, but not condemnation.

The script called for a king and surely a king ought to be born in a palace. He chose to be born homeless among the homeless, with no place for him in his world except among the poor. Thomas Merton, in somberly moving poetry, suggests his continued presence among the poor, the migrants, the homeless.

The shadows fall. The stars appear. The birds begin to sleep.

Night embraces the silent half of the earth.
A vagrant, a destitute wanderer, with dusty feet, finds
his way down a new road. A homeless God, lost in
the night, without papers, without identification,
without even a number, a frail expendable exile, lies
down in desolation under the sweet stars of the
world and entrusts Himself to sleep.
(from Hagia Sophia: *Collected Poems: pg. 370-71)*

The message of the Gospel he brought us is that we too have to throw away the script. The script which our culture writes for us calls us to comfort and complacency, to enjoyment of what we have, regardless of the needs of others. In the topsy-turvy world of the beatitudes, which Jesus gave us, he tells us to throw away the script and points us to a different way to happiness. He calls us to be poor and meek and humble. He calls us to hunger and thirst for justice and peace that they may come to all of God's people.

The script our society writes calls us to take good care of ourselves and of our needs and to find God in our own self-fulfillment. Jesus calls us to throw away that script and to find God first of all in our sisters and brothers, especially those who suffer, who hunger, who thirst for justice and peace. He calls us to share their emptiness and to find God in that emptiness.

It's not easy to throw away the script our culture writes for us. Charlie Brown realized that. In a recent comic strip, Lucy, who embodies the script of a greedy self-seeking, consumerist society, reads to Charlie Brown her gift list – things she figures to get for Christmas from her two grandpas and grandmas and eight uncles and aunts. When she finished, Charlie Brown asks her: "Where's your gift list?" "My what?' she asked, bewildered by the question. Charlie Brown walks away, muttering: "I knew it." In another strip, Charlie Brown chides Lucy for pretending that she and her brother love one another, though it's clear she is always at odds with him. "You hypocrite," Charlie Brown says, "do you really think you can fool Santa Claus this way?" "Why not?" Lucy replies, "We're a couple of sharp kids and he's just an old man." Charlie leaves them. He's sad. He hits his head against a tree and says: "I weep for our generation."

Do not weep, Charlie Brown. For something new is happening in your generation. A new consciousness is being born. A new script is being written – slowly, but relentlessly.

We have reached a point in the evolutionary process where we are beginning to see human beings and human relationships in an entirely new way. We are beginning to realize that our fate is bound up with the fate of peoples throughout the world. Whether we like it or not, we are all part of one family traveling through space on our tiny planet earth.

Our experience as a world community is teaching us that our only salvation is Jesus' call to communion, a world communion. To choose the alternative – that is, to choose separateness – is to choose disaster and destruction.

This new heightened consciousness of human solidarity draws us toward a new sense of oneness that people have never experienced before. Merton wrote: "We are already one, but we think we are not. What we have to become is what we are."

During the civil rights movement of the 1960s, Merton wrote a series of "Freedom Songs" for a young black tenor. Their theme is about this new consciousness that – despite the odds against it – is being born slowly but irresistibly. One of poems is called "Earthquake."

Go tell the earth to shake
And tell the thunder
To wake the sky,
And tear the clouds apart.
Tell my people to come out
And wonder
Where the old world is gone.
For a new world is born
And all my people shall be one.
So tell the earth to shake
With marching feet
Of messengers of peace
Proclaim my law of love
To every nation
Every race.
(Collected Poems pg. 701)

Yes, we do indeed have a new script; it's really an old one. It's the one that Jesus wrote.

CHRISTMAS (Mass during the day)

Isaiah 52: 7-10
Psalm 98: 1-6
Hebrews 1:1-6
John 1:1-18

Most of the time the lives we live are quite prosaic. We go about a daily round of work and duties that are ordinary, sometimes boring, scarcely ever even touching on the spectacular.   But if most of our lives are prose, there are certain times when what we experience is the stuff of sheer poetry.

Today is one of those wondrous times. Today's feast is poetry. For poetry is language that is more concentrated, more imaginative, more mysterious, more powerful than ordinary speech. And poetry is the only language that can attempt the telling of the momentous event we celebrate today. The poetry is all there in Luke's Gospel: the birth in a stable; a great light in the sky; lowly shepherds in star-lighted fields; voices of angels. An invitation. And, most of all, a proclamation. And the proclamation tells us that the poetry is in the Child - the Child who is Saviour.

As in all poetry, there is more here than meets the eye. More in this Child than speech can tell. More unspoken, because it cannot be said. Luke's poetic voice is tantalizing; for it both reveals and conceals mystery: the mystery of this Child. We try at times to turn the poetry into the language of theology. We say: in this scene the

Transcendent has become immanent. God has become human. But somehow on this day words like these stick in our throats: we have said them many times, yet who would dare to say what they really mean and all that they imply? Perhaps, at least today, better not to reflect or attempt to talk theology. Better just to *look* at the Child.

For that is where the mystery of this feast is to be found: in the Child. Christmas is about a Child: God's Child, Mary's Child. But it is also about the Child that is in each of us. And if we had the eyes that could pierce mystery, we would realize that the heart of the mystery is that God's Child and Mary's Child and the Child in us are really one.

Karl Barth, one of the great theologians of the past century, loved Mozart's music; and every morning before going to work on his dogmatic treatises, he would listen to a Mozart piece. Staunch Protestant that he was, he never got over his annoyance that Mozart was Catholic. Barth writes about a dream he had. In his dream, Barth tells us, he was appointed to examine Mozart's theology. Deliberately he centered his questions about the Mozart masses. But Mozart refused to answer a single question. Barth came to understand that Mozart was not a theologian and that it was not a theologian who spoke in his music. Instead, he tells us: "It is a Child, even a divine Child, who speaks to us in Mozart's music."

It is the Child in us who will be our salvation. Yes, indeed. For the child in us is our true self that is one with God. The Child in us is the innocence, the goodness, the new life in all of us that insistently, though not always successfully, seeks to surface in our lives. We have to carry the Child within us safely through each stage of our growth: through childhood and adolescence, into adulthood and old age. Indeed, we have to bring the Child with us through death itself. For if we were to lose the Child in us, we would lose our way into the kingdom of heaven. That's what Jesus said, isn't it, that to enter the kingdom, we have to become children, that is, we have to find the Child in us. No matter how far we wander into the realms of unreality, even of sin, the Child in us never becomes extinct.

For the Child in us is God's Child. Mary gave birth to the Child in a specific moment of history; but the divine birth takes place in eternity, where there are no moments or divisions. It is a birth that is complete – but wondrous mystery – is ever taking place.

A Russian writer, Andrei Sinyarsky, while he was in a Soviet labor camp, remarked in one of his writings that Childhood is the invention of Christianity. Before the coming of Christ, children had no significance in ancient society. They were without rights. They were non-persons. It was as if children and childhood did not exist. It was in the feast that we celebrate today that the Child was discovered, almost – if one uses Sinyarski's language – invented. For in this feast a Child becomes more than a Child. Here, Sinyarski says, we have a Child who is "a constant reminder that in God the Child is never extinct."

In the mystery of eternity God forever begets God's Child. God, if I may put it this way, is always giving birth to the Child and the Child is always there. For eternity is not bits of time: it has no past or future or process of change as we know it; it simply is: God giving birth to God's Child and that Child always being, never becoming extinct in God.

If it is true that the Child is never extinct in God, it can also be said, though with obvious shades of difference, that the Child is never extinct in us. Or to put it as Meister Eckhart does: "Every minute Christ is born in my soul." The paradox of Christian existence is that the Child who is always there is yet, moment by moment, being born in the depths of each one of us.

How is Christ born in us? How do we give birth to Him? As often as we surrender the falsity that may be in us, we allow the Child to emerge, to speak and act in our lives. Often we do not do this. When I suppress the Child in me, hide it, I speak with an alien voice and I act with alien hands. Yet the very falsity of my voice is a sign — to God, to me and probably also to others (at least to those who know me well) — that somewhere beneath that falsity there is the Child who has almost got lost. And I can build layer and layer of falsity, each speaking with a different voice — a voice especially suited to that layer. When these layers accumulate, I hear so many voices in myself that I no longer recognize the voice that is my true voice.

Yet we must not despair. Just as the Child in God is never extinct, so the Child in us can never be extinguished. And it is in moments such as today's feast that we must listen carefully to ourselves and to others. And if we do so we shall be able to hear, beneath all the layers of falsity and weakness and sin, the sweet voice of the Child. And we will understand that the reason the Child can never be extinct in us, is that it is our true self. It is our real identity. Or, as the Zen people say, "our original face with which we were born." And we know in the glow of today's joy, that it is the Child in us who will be our salvation.

The Child we look at on this holy feast is God's Child and Mary's Child. But it is also the Child that, from moment to moment, must be born in us. We continue to look with wonder and praise. We allow our imagination free range. For this day is a special day: it is a day of sheer poetry.

HOLY FAMILY

Sirach 3:2-7, 12-14
Psalm 128:1-5
Colossians 3:12-21
Matthew 2:13-15, 19-23

This is the feast of the Holy Family. As you hear the readings, you might think: `shucks, I could have made a better choice of readings for this feast. The first reading from Sirach: well, it has a beauty of its own, but it seems more like a "Father's Day" reading than a Family Day text. It calls us to be kind to our fathers in their old age.

The second reading is probably more pertinent to the feast. In this text from Colossians, Paul offers a portrait of a good family and does so in a rather picturesque way.

One of the daily occupations of everyone in a family is getting dressed in the morning. Paul takes this necessary and obvious part of family life and uses it as an analogy to detail the kind of spiritual clothing that a good family should dress up in.

The first spiritual garments, the undergarments, so to speak, are mercy, kindness, meekness and patience. That's a good start. Then atop these garments we are told to put on forbearance and forgiveness — two virtues that surely go well together — putting up with others and forgiving them when it is necessary. These two seem almost to be robes that belong to God that we borrow as it were from the divine wardrobe.

Once you have all these clothes on, then — Paul adds — "Over all these virtues put on love which binds the rest together and makes them perfect." One might say that just as the outer garments protect the inner ones, it is love that protects all the virtues. Love makes them work.

Then, as we go through the day properly clothed spiritually, we will be thankful to God and to those with whom we are in contact. We will want to help one another and admonish one another; and of course we will be ready to receive help and admonition from others. All this goodness filling our hearts will move us — spontaneously – to burst forth in psalms and hymns and inspired praise that will express our gratitude to God.

It's surely an idyllic picture Paul paints of the family. You don't see many families exactly like this. But I bet we do see a lot that approximate it. And it does set a pretty high goal to work toward. So I think we can say that the second reading measures up better than the first as a reading for Holy Family Sunday, though there is a bit at the end of this reading about "wives being subject to their husbands" that wouldn't work very well in most modern marriage situations. Happily, though, this part is put in parentheses that invites us to omit it.

Probably the Gospel is — at first reading anyway – the most problematic of the three for use on this feast day celebrating the Holy Family. First of all the time sequence is all mixed up. Liturgically we have not yet celebrated Epiphany and – *voila* – here is the Holy Family going off into Egypt. This is supposed to happen after the magi depart; but, liturgically they haven't come yet.

Then there is the rather odd fact that *Matthew's chief interest doesn't seem to be in getting Jesus and his parents into Egypt, but in getting them out.* The only reason he wants to get them there is that he wants to have them called out by God; and he wants to do this because he is very intent on showing that Jesus is the new Israel, just as Israel of old was called out of Egypt. Matthew twists the meaning of the text from the prophet Hosea to fit the flight into Egypt and the return from Egypt.

Thus this is a reading that serves a fundamental theme of Matthew's Gospel, but — we have to ask — what does it have to do with the Holy Family? Perhaps in our day it has more to say than we first grasp. For after all we do have a family in this story: a father, a mother and a Child. The special poignancy of the story is that it is about a family forced by cruel and tyrannical powers to flee their own land and become refugees in a strange country. Mary and Joseph with their Child seeking sanctuary in a foreign land present a contemporary picture that is ever so real and so painfully evident in our world.

We live in a world where there are countless displaced refugee families seeking shelter and sanctuary in other places because their lives are threatened in their own country. More than a million Iraqis have fled for their lives into Syria and Jordan. When later they follow their yearning to return home, they find that their homes have been occupied by others and they have nowhere to go.

Hundreds of thousands of displaced Palestinians still live in refugee camps and have not a strong voice that will speak out for them and enable them to determine their own future.

And besides the refugee families and the displaced families, there are the countless fragmented families: children who have been separated from their parents and have no place to go and nowhere they can call home. So many people living in intolerable situations, lonely, despondent, with no hope and with the memory of once fond dreams that have turned into illusions and nightmares. The only family they have is society: a society that is often cruel, that seems to have little desire to give them sustenance and shelter, much less love and compassion. They have fled to Egypt, but their destiny is never to hear the call to come back to their own homes. They are wanderers on the face of the earth. They are the family-less.

As we reflect on this Gospel, we may begin to see that — in this time of turmoil and violence — it may be the most appropriate Gospel for us to hear on Holy Family Sunday. As we enjoy the warmth and comfort that community offers us — community which is God's gift that we receive without ever earning it — we need to think of those who have no community, no family, no security, no home. They are too many for us to ignore, if we are true disciples of Jesus, indeed even if we are simply decent respectful human beings. As we strive to put on the clothing that Paul has described for us, we shall begin to sense the responsibility we have to those who scarcely even know of the spiritual garments of which Paul spoke, because they have never really experienced them.

Obviously we are talking about a gigantic problem, a global problem. It is not possible for us to determine immediately and easily what we are called to do. Perhaps the best we can say today is that, as we approach the beginning of a new year, we need to move out of our little world and become more socially conscious; more fully aware of what is going on in the world and what must be done. We need to grow in the determination that during this new year we will become involved as generously as possible in seeing more clearly what we can do, no matter how limited our resources may be.

SOLEMNITY OF MARY, MOTHER OF GOD

Numbers 6:22-27
Psalm 67: 2-3, 5, 6, 8
Galatians 4:4-7
Luke 2:16-21

Twenty-eight years ago I visited Greece. As part of the visit, I took a cruise on the Aegean Sea. One of the stops on this trip was Ephesus. Ephesus was a thriving city in New Testament times. The Church of Ephesus was very dear to St. Paul; its members were the recipients of one of his letters. Today it is a much excavated site; a delight of archeologists. Some distance from the excavated ruins of the city, it is possible to see the ruins of a very ancient church building. This building marked the place where in 431 the third ecumenical Council of the Church was held.

It was a thrill to be so close to the scene of this important Council. Thrilling to remember – and to picture – in my imagination – the final day of that Council. Records suggest that that night the people of Ephesus held a torch-light procession, in which they kept shouting *"Theotokos! Theotokos!* as they paraded through the city streets.

The reason for this jubilant display was the news that the bishops at the Council had rejected the teaching of Nestorius. Bishop of Constantinople, Nestorius taught that Mary could only be called *Chirstotokos* (which means "mother of Christ"). She could not be called *Theotokos* (mother of God). Nestorius insisted on this difference in describing Mary, because he believed that there were two persons in Christ: a divine person and a human person. Mary, he taught, was mother only of the human person. Hence she could not be called "mother of God," but only "mother of Christ."

What was at stake at the Council was not just or even primarily a title of Mary. What was at stake was nothing less than the whole meaning of the Incarnation. The bishops rejected the teaching of Nestorius. For they realized that his teaching threatened that reality. If the child Mary gave birth to, the child she nursed and cared for, was not the divine person of the Word of God, then it could not be said that the Word became flesh. For a mother gives birth to a person and if the person Mary gave birth to was only human, then it could not be said that God truly became one of us. The bishops knew that the very heart of Christian faith was at stake.

Twenty years later (451) the Council of Chalcedon completed the work of the Council of Ephesus by defining what has ever since been the framework for the teaching the Church on Christ, namely, that in Christ there are two natures, one divine, one human. These two natures are united in one divine person. Jesus Christ, therefore, the Word of God, is one divine person who is fully divine (and always was so) and fully human (at a particular time in history the Word was made flesh and thus took on the fullness of a human nature). While it is true that the Council of Chalcedon clarified further the teaching of the

Council of Ephesus, it will always be Ephesus that is linked with Mary's title as *Theotokos*.

At this point, you may want to stop me and say: "Bill, this is pretty heady stuff for New Year's Day. Keep in mind that last night was New Year's Eve and some of us are not ready for too much deep thinking so early in the morning. Well, let me tell you why I felt I had to speak about the Council of Ephesus. Today, on the western world calendar, may be the first day of a New Year; in the Church's calendar, however, it is the feast of *Theotokos*, the feast of Mary the Mother of God. This feast of Mary the Mother of God honors the oldest and the most important title of Mary. In fact, I would go further and say that it is the most necessary feast of Mary. For Mary exists for Jesus. She exists to give Jesus his humanity. That is her glory and her great honor.

Could I push even a bit farther and say that it is *the only necessary feast of Mary*? It is fine for us to honor her birth, to remember her Conception and Assumption and all the other titles a loving Church wants to heap upon her. But the title of Mary the Mother of God is the one that really matters.

Even when I say this I have to add a corrective made by Jesus himself. Remember the story in Luke's Gospel, where a woman in the crowd speaks up and says: "Blessed is the womb that bore you and the breasts that nursed you." Jesus answered: "Rather, blessed is the one who hears the Word of God and obeys it." (Lk. 11:27) Jesus

40

seems to be saying that whatever honor attaches to being his mother, being a disciple of Jesus – one who hears God's word and obeys it – is an even greater claim to honor. Apparently Jesus saw discipleship as trumping even motherhood. And remember that at the annunciation, Mary set the compass that would forever guide her life: "Be it done to me according to your word." Mother of God she was indeed, but even greater, she was preeminently the disciple of Jesus.

Mother of God and preeminent disciple – it may be that these are the only titles of Mary that we need. For sure, they are the only necessary ones. If being Mother of God elevates her above us, being disciple of Jesus makes her one of us. The Middle Ages – a time when Jesus was seen as stern judge – people turned to Mary, almost making a goddess of her. Mary was presented at times as being between God and the Church as an intermediary. I think of the inelegant, rather repugnant statement – attributed I believe to St. Bernard – that describes Mary as the neck of the mystical Body of Christ.

At the Second Vatican Council, there was initially a call for a special document on Mary. Wisely, the Council Fathers chose to include its discussion of Mary in the document of the Church. It was Augustine who said: Mary is a member of the Church, a preeminent member to be sure, but still a member.

I don't know how many of you read the office of readings in the Breviary. I always look forward to the second reading for today's feast. The reading is from a letter written by St. Athanasius to Epictetus. In it he says that "the Lord's body was a true body. It was a true body because it was the same as ours. *Mary, you see, is our sister*, for we are all born from Adam."

What beauty and warmth there is to that statement: "Mary is our sister." It helps us understand that she is one of us. It brings her near to us. I wish we would think more often of Mary – who, after all in her earthly lifetime was a simple peasant woman – as our sister.

So often the names we use in addressing Mary can easily tend to distance her from us, almost to dehumanize her. If I can use a kind of far-fetched analogy, some people at first found it hard to call me "Bill." Maybe some still do. I remember dear Sister Benedict who would manage once in a while to say "Bill" and then quickly run away. Clearly in using this analogy, I acknowledge its incongruity. I just want to suggest that some people find it difficult to say "Mary," instead of "Our Blessed Mother," "Our Blessed Lady," "The Blessed Virgin." Please don't misunderstand me. I don't want in any way to downplay the value of these loving terms people use in addressing Mary. But we must never let such titles separate us from her or distance her from us. Maybe it would be helpful to our devotion and our prayer life to address her at times by the name her mother and father gave her. Why not simply say "Mary"? She is, you see, "our sister."

EPIPHANY

Isaiah 60:1-6
Psalm 72: 1-2, 7-8, 10-11, 12-13
Ephesians 3:2-3a, 5-6
Matthew 2:1-12

At first thought Epiphany seems to be Christmas revisited.
The magi and their visit is very much a part of our
Christmas experience; yet Epiphany adds a new dimension
to our Christmas. Christmas is about the Word made flesh:
about God in Jesus becoming one of us. Epiphany is about
people coming to know that Jesus, Mary's son is also God's
Son.

For it is one thing for the Word to become flesh. It is
another thing for us to become aware that the Word made
flesh is truly among us – in Jesus. Epiphany is the feast of
the manifestation of Jesus that leads us to awareness of
his identity.

To understand how the Church arrived at awareness of
Jesus as God among us, it is important for us to realize that
the Gospels, quite literally were written backwards. By this
I mean that the passion- resurrection narratives were
written first. Then an account of the public ministry of
Jesus was prefixed to these narratives. Finally – and a good
bit later – the infancy narratives were prefixed to the
account of the ministry. Thus, there were three stages in
the writing down of the Gospel: (1) the passion
resurrection narratives, (2) the ministry narratives and (3)

the infancy narratives. That is why I say that the Gospels were written backwards.

Each of these stages involved progression into a deeper understanding of Jesus' identity. Thus in the earliest days of the Church, the resurrection was the moment when Jesus' followers came to know his identity as son of God and savior. Thus in the early preaching of the Church (e. g., in the sermons of Peter in the Acts of the Apostles) we read that by the power of God Jesus was raised from the dead and thus "made to be God and Messiah." By later ways of speaking this language is clumsy, even inaccurate: saying that Jesus was *made* God and Messiah. But it helps us to understand that it was in the experience of the Risen One that the disciples of Jesus first came to know his true identity.

But as these early disciples reflected on the mystery of Jesus, the moment in which his identity became clear to them was pushed back to the period of Jesus' ministry, in particular to the moment of the baptism of Jesus. It was at this moment, the early disciples came to realize that Jesus received the full outpouring of God's Spirit and hence they understood that he was at that time always the Beloved Son of the Father.

What we see in the infancy narratives, which was the last part of the Gospels to be written, is a pushing back of the Church's moment of Christological awareness to the time of Jesus' birth. The child born of Mary is already Son of God.

In each of these moments of Christological awareness there is a discernible threefold pattern. First there is the experience that reveals the identity of Jesus. Second, there is the proclamation of who he is. Third, there is a reaction: a reaction that is twofold: On the one hand there is acceptance and homage; on the other hand, there is rejection and persecution.

This threefold pattern appears in the resurrection narratives and also in the ministry of Jesus that follows his baptism. There are those who accept him and those who reject him. There is homage and there is persecution.

What the infancy narratives intend to show is that this pattern had been true from the very beginning. In today's Gospel Jesus is proclaimed by the magi as "the new-born King of the Jews." The magi accept him and pay him homage. Herod and the Jerusalem priests reject him and Herod attempts to persecute him.

In fact, the infancy narratives follow quite strikingly the pattern of the passion stories. In the passion narratives the secular ruler (Pilate) and the chief priests and elders of the people are aligned against Jesus. The infancy narratives paint a similar picture: Herod (the secular ruler) and the chief priests and the scribes of the people either oppose Jesus or are indifferent to him, while the magi who come from the east accept him and pay him homage. Interesting, too, is the fact that in both narratives, it is the same title that is in question. On the cross Jesus has a title written over his head which reads: "King of the Jews." This is precisely the title that the magi give to him, as they ask where the "king of the Jews" is to be born. In both instances this title is accepted by some and rejected by others.

Thus as we read the New Testament we see different instances of growth in the disciples' awareness of Jesus. In each of these moments of Christological awareness, there is an experience which issues in a deeper recognition of Jesus' identity.

Nor are these moments of growth in recognition of Jesus' identity confined to New Testament times. Throughout the history of the Christian community, right down to our own time, there have been moments of Christological experience which have deepened and expanded the Church's perception of the mystery of who Jesus is. And that will always be true. For the mystery of Jesus is the mystery of God among us.

And our experience of the Mystery of God is continually outstripping what we are able to say about that experience. Speaking about God is like lighting candles in order to see the sun. Our efforts to express our experience of God, our words, are like small lighted matches that are blown out by the tremendous reality of God bearing down on us like a storm.

It is very much like the experience of a lover who, though she or he may be the finest artist with words, must always lament that her words are far too feeble to express the love that is in her heart. This comparison is an appropriate one. For our experience of God is not primarily an intellectual insight. It is above all an encounter in love. And for a lover what happens is her or his heart is always much deeper than words can convey.

At this point we need to personalize this experience of God manifested to us in Jesus, the Word made flesh. These moments of progressive experiencing of the identity of Jesus are not confined to the community of the Church. They occur in the lives of each one of us, as we move from hearing about Jesus to experiencing him in our daily existence, from reading about him in books or hearing about him in talks to feeling his presence and activity in our lives. And there is not just one such moment. There are many, as we move toward an ever-deepening understanding of the meaning of Jesus in our lives. All that is required of us is an openness to his presence.

Thus we can say that there is a Church-Christology, the understanding of Jesus' identity that exists and grows in the Christian community. And there is a personal Christology, which is made up of the many ways in which the Lord Jesus has manifested himself to each of us. This personal Christology is unique to each one of us. For no one knows another person in exactly the same way. This is not to say that each of us has a different Jesus, but rather that different elements of his many-faceted reality have left their imprint on each of us in its own special way.

Nor can it be said that a Church Christology and a Personal Christology are at odds with one another. Rather they enrich one another. Yet we need to keep emphasizing that neither will be adequate to express the depths of who Jesus really is. We need not be distressed by the inadequacy of language. The important task is not to find words to express our experience –as Church or as individual persons – but rather to respond to the experience in faith and love offered to us.

The people of Jerusalem are a sober reminder to us that it is possible to miss the meaning of the experiences of Jesus offered to us. The magi, on the other hand, symbolize that openness to God's presence in Jesus that so changes our lives that we move in new and uncharted directions. Like the magi we find ourselves traveling by an entirely new route.

Baptism of the Lord

Isaiah 42:1-4, 6,7
Psalm 29: 1-2, 3-4, 8, 9-10
Acts 10:34-38
Matthew 3:13-17

The way we name things affects the way we think about them. If we put a wrong label on something, we may misunderstand what it is that we are talking about. We call today's feast: "The Baptism of the Lord." Yet if we read the text closely we shall see that the central focus of the story is not so much the baptism or even the conversation between Jesus and John; rather the main focus is on what happened after Jesus was baptized, namely, the theophany, in which the Spirit of God comes and rests upon Jesus and the Voice of God speaks from heaven. The Voice of God reveals who Jesus is and what his mission is to be. The Voice proclaims: (1) Jesus is God's Son; (2) He is God's Chosen One; (3) He is the One on whom God's favor rests.

This proclamation introduces us to two themes foreign to our thinking, but prominent in the Old Testament. The first theme is the description of the King of Israel at his enthronement being called "God's Son." The other theme is that of the "Suffering Servant," described by Isaiah in our first reading: the one whom God has chosen and with whom God is pleased, the one who will bring forth justice to the nations, the one who will bring

49

light to a darkened world, the one who will bring sight to the blind.

To grasp the underlying meaning of these two themes, we need to understand an OT notion that, at first hearing at least, is quite alien to our thinking. The notion I am referring to is the notion of corporate personality. Let me explain. When the king is called "Son of God" at his enthronement, this is said to him, not primarily as an individual, but as the embodiment of the people. He was not only king of Israel. In a most important sense he is Israel.

That is why, when the king does evil the whole people is punished. Remember the time when King David took up a census of the people, God is displeased with him? What happens? The whole people are punished, not just David. This episode expresses the understanding of corporate personality. The king is the people.

What we must realize, in order to understand today's Gospel, is that these terms the "Son of God" and "Suffering Servant," when applied to Jesus, take on this corporate meaning. Jesus is the Son, God's Beloved One, the One on whom God's favor rests. He is all this in his own person, but mysteriously also as the representative of a new humanity. What the baptism story tells us is that in Jesus a new humanity comes into being. Gregory Nazianzen in the reading for today from the Liturgy of Hours puts it this way: "Jesus rises from the waters, the world rises with him."

This was an important notion for Paul. For him Jesus Christ is surely an individual; but he is also much more: he is the New Adam, the beginning of a new creation. Just as the Spirit of God hovered over the waters at the first creation, so at the baptismal event, God's Spirit hovers over the waters, in which a new human race comes into being in Jesus.

What I am saying is that the whole point of this long liturgical time of Advent-Christmas- Epiphany is that Jesus not only became one of us: but in a very true – and mysterious – sense *he became us.* He became us in that collective meaning. He is all of us because he is humanity in its corporate reality. He is at the same time the One and the Many. Our task as Christian disciples is to grow into him. We exist as individuals in separateness – or so it seems. Our vocation is to overcome separateness – or rather to see that it really isn't there – and experience our oneness with Christ and in him with all our sisters and brothers.

Overcoming separateness does not mean losing our uniqueness or our personal identity; it does mean discovering where that uniqueness and identity are rooted.

Jesus is the New Humanity. We are in him. Our task is to find ourselves in him. For *he became us that we, all of us, might become him.* This is the *admirabile commercium,* the admirable exchange, that this season's liturgy speaks of so often. It is an exchange which involves that rather slippery, elusive concept of "corporate personality."

We are very much individuals and we must grow as individuals. Yet the paradox of Christian spirituality is that this growth can take place only in the context of that complicated network of relationships that make us all one corporate Person in Christ Jesus our Lord.

I wonder if the name Artaban means anything to you? Does it strike a bell in your memory? Perhaps it would take on meaning for you if I told you that he was the hero of Henry Van Dyke's wonderful Christmas story, "The Other Wise Man." He and his three friends who were astrologers saw a strange star in the sky and concluded that it heralded the birth of a great King. They decided to follow the star and find the great King. They had planned to meet at a designated place from which they would journey together. Artaban had three precious jewels to offer to the great King: a sapphire, a ruby and a pearl. On the way to the place of rendezvous, he comes upon a man who is sick and dying. He stops, nurses him back to life. The delay caused him to miss his friends. So he must sell his sapphire to buy the necessary equipment to make the journey alone. He arrives late. On the road to Bethlehem he stops at a cottage. A young mother is singing her baby to rest. She tells him that three strangers following a star had passed that way three days earlier. As she speaks to him there is noise and confusion in the street. Women are weeping. Soldiers at Herod's orders are killing the little children in the village.

The young mother is white with terror. Artaban goes quickly and stands at the doorway of the cottage. The soldiers approach. Artaban speaks: "I am alone here and I am waiting to give this beautiful ruby to the prudent captain who will leave me in peace." The captain is amazed at the jewel's beauty. He takes it and orders his soldiers to move on.

Artaban goes to Egypt looking for the great king. He finds traces, but they vanish like footprints in the sand. After more than 30 years of wandering, he returns to Jerusalem. It was Passover time. He hears that a crucifixion is to take place: two thieves and a man who gave himself out to be Son of God and King of the Jews. Artaban thinks: the ways of God are strange. Perhaps I have been brought here at this time, so that I may ransom him with my one remaining jewel, the precious pearl.

Meanwhile a young woman is being dragged by soldiers. She spies Artaban, begs him to save her from slavery. Once again conflict rises in his heart. Is this his last temptation or his last opportunity? He takes the pearl from his robe and gives it to her to win her freedom. All of a sudden the sky darkens, stones are loosened, dust clouds fill the air. Artaban and the girl crouch behind a wall. Suddenly a tile shaken from a roof falls and strikes the old man on the temple. The girl bends over him and hears a voice ever so faintly. She hears him answer: "Not so, my Lord. When did I see you hungry and feed you or thirsty and give you to drink? Or naked and clothe you? For thirty years I have searched for you and never seen your face or ministered to you." And the voice came to him: "In as much as you ministered to the least of my sisters and brothers, you ministered to me." Wonder and joy filled his aged face. His journey has ended. His treasures are accepted. The other wise man has found the king.

I tell this story for three reasons. First, it's a great story. Second, it is another way of saying that Jesus became not just one of us but, in a sense we cannot fully understand, Jesus became us. Third, I tell this story because it helps us to deal with the inexplicable reality of the hurricanes, the floods, the fires, the tsunamis that make tragedy of so many lives. *Jesus not only became us; he became them.* Whatever help we give for the survivors of such tragedies reminds us of that haunting scriptural refrain: "Since you did it to the least of my brothers and sisters, you did it to me." I guess there can be no higher motive than that to get us to open our hearts and our purses in offering the help so desperately needed by so many – and needed now.

SECOND SUNDAY IN ORDINARY TIME

Isaiah 49: 3, 5-6
Psalm 40: 2, 4, 7-8, 8-9, 10
1 Corinthians 1:1-3
John 1: 29-34

There is a strange statement in today's Gospel. And it's no mistake. For it is said twice. It's those strange words of John, spoken by the way, to no particular audience that we can identify. When he sees Jesus, he says: "I do not know him." Our immediate instinct is to want to say: "But John, of course, you knew him. Leonardo da Vinci and ever so many other Renaissance artists painted pictures of you and Jesus playing together when you were little boys. How can you say: "I do not know him."

Fortunately, Renaissance painters are not theological sources. True, there are some plausible reasons for thinking that John and Jesus may have had some contact – not at their mothers' feet, but in the Judean desert – but we simply don't know. And in reality, it is of secondary importance whether or not they ever had contact with one another before Jesus came to the place where John was baptizing. For the knowing of Jesus which John is talking about had nothing to do with physical features; it concerned the inner identity of Jesus.

What John wants to tell us is that Jesus was the Lamb whose death (accepted by God in resurrection) brings about the remission of the sin of the whole world; that he was the preexistent One and the One in whom God's Spirit dwells permanently.

What I am suggesting is that this scene from the very beginning of the 4th Gospel is already proclaiming the Christology which it is the intent of the 4th Gospel to proclaim.

I would especially like to reflect on one element of that Christology: the fact that John saw the Spirit of God descend like a dove on Jesus. Now someone might be inclined to say: "Well, that certainly is something special (the Spirit of God descending on someone), but it isn't really unique. God's Spirit came to rest on others: prophets, kings, etc. But the text goes further: it says descended on Jesus and remained there. The word which is translated "remained there" is the Greek word "menein." This is a key word in the 4th Gospel. It means "to abide", "to remain permanently." This word "menein," in fact, is not only a key word in the 4th Gospel; it is a frequent word. Time and again Jesus uses it to describe his own relation to God and also to his disciples. He abides in the Father; the disciples abide in him. What John came to recognize, which he had not known before, was that Jesus was not simply moved by the Spirit of God (as other great people in the past had been); but that God's Spirit was permanently in him. Jesus has full and continuous presence of the Spirit. God's Spirit and Jesus' Spirit are one Spirit.

What happened to this "man named John" was that God blew his brains, expanded his horizons. This revelation enables him to step out of the Jewish mold in which he had been reared, so that he could see Jesus' relationship not just to Jews, but to all the world. There is a tremendous leap forward of the understanding of salvation history, when John speaks those remarkable words: "Behold the Lamb of God who takes away the sin of the world." This is a new vision: God acting in Jesus to remove sin and alienation, not just from a chosen people, but from all peoples of the world. It surely blew his mind to recognize that Jesus was not just the Messiah of Israel; He was Saviour of the world.

It is as if he understood, as no one had ever before, what Isaiah meant when (in our first reading) he said of God's Servant: "It is too little for you to be my servant / [just] to raise up the tribes of Jacob.., / I will make you a light to the nations / That my salvation may reach to the end of the earth."

If I may put it this way, John had what we would call a transcultural experience: the kind of experience that we Christians are called to today. It is an experience that calls us to deal with the same difficulty John had to face. It is hard for us to think of Jesus as belonging to anyone but ourselves. Yet there is this puzzling statement of John telling us: "He takes away the sin of the world." We want to think of him as taking away our sins or at most-taking away the sins of others when they become one of us. We want to keep Jesus to ourselves. We don't want him to be universal Saviour – at least not outside the parameters of salvation we have set up.

Yet we have to recognize (as John had to) what it means to say that Jesus had the fullness of God's Spirit permanently. This means that he is able to touch the life of every person born into this world. We can't fence him in. We cannot think, for instance, that he acts only in the Church. We cannot restrict his action to the sacraments.

We have to acclimate ourselves to thinking that Jesus can save through other religions. Not just through other Christian religions, but likewise through those that are not Christian. Even though there may be imperfections and errors in these religions (and we can't forget we have our own share of imperfections and errors, too), we must come to see that there can be much good in them and God can act through them to bring people to salvation. This means that when we pray for the conversion of people, our essential prayer must be for their conversion to God. This is not to minimize the value and importance of the Church and the precious gift that it is to us. What it means is that we cannot absolutize the Church. God alone is absolute.

During the week of prayer for Christian unity, soon to come, we shall beg God to send the Spirit to remove the scandal of disunity among those who believe in Jesus Christ. We must work and pray for Christian unity, but not with the smugness of our Catholic past that claimed we had the whole truth and that Protestants had better "come back" to us if they want to achieve Christian unity. Since Vatican II, we have come a long way in appreciating the Christian heritage of other Christian Churches and in our realization of the importance of dialogue and the need really to listen to one another. Hans Kung has expressed it this way: we need to have optimal loyalty to our own religious faith and maximal openness to the faith of others.

But we must not forget that, even if we were to achieve perfect Christian unity tomorrow, there would be millions of people in the world – all loved by God – who would be completely unaffected. As we pray for our sister and brother Christians, we pray also for all these others who have never known Christian Faith, yet are dear to God's heart. We must know too that we can learn much from them, especially about spirituality and prayer.

This is what grows out of the vision of Christ that began to dawn on John when he came to know Jesus as the one who takes away sin: not just Jewish sin, not just Christian sin, but the *sin of the whole world.* It is that vision that we must translate from John's time to our own.

And never in history has the need been greater. Hans Kung has written: There will "be no peace between the nations of the world without peace between the religions [of the world]." I remember reading an article in the *London Tablet* by William Johnston, an Irish Jesuit who has spent most of his life in Japan. In his article he speaks, among other things, of the Japanese novelist, Shasaku Endo. Endo is a deeply committed Catholic, yet he has concerns regarding the way Christianity appears in the East. Endo felt that Christianity was too much of a Western religion. As such it was dogmatic, uncompromising, patriarchal. It saw reality in terms of black-and-white. Its history was full of "I am right and you are wrong," bringing inquisitions, intolerance, punishment of dissidents, and lacking in compassion.

Asian thought, on the other hand was "grey," flexible, tolerant. It stressed both-and rather than either-or. Above all, Asian thought was feminine, grounded in a predominantly *yin* culture. Endo said that his faith came through his mother. He was delighted when Father Johnston gave him a book about Julian of Norwich and "the motherly love" of Jesus.

As we progress into the third millennium there are wonderful possibilities for dialogue between religious faiths of the West and those of the East. And this kind of dialogue, as well as dialogue among the religions of the West with one another, must not be looked upon as simply worthwhile projects for the future of religion. They are necessary projects for the future of the world. Hans Kung, as I mentioned, sees the peace of the world depending on peace among religions. William Johnston expresses it even more strongly. He puts it this way: "Now we can say that dialogue between religions is necessary for world survival. What a responsibility we have!" *(The Tablet,* 5 January 2002)

THIRD SUNDAY IN ORDINARY TIME

Isaiah 8:23-9:3
Psalm 27: 1, 4, 13-14
1 Corinthians 1: 10 - 13
Matthew 4: 12-23

More than 25 years ago I was at the very spot that is the setting for today's Gospel. Very early in the morning I had arisen and left the hotel which was on a hill overlooking the sea of Galilee. I climbed down the very steep hill, sometimes walking, other times just sliding and slipping and finally made it to the shore of the sea of Galilee. Just as I arrived there (it was about 5:00 o'clock in the morning), a boat was coming into shore. I had my camera with me and took a photo. I felt as if I had been transported back to today's Gospel story.

As I reflected on this wonderful experience, it occurred to me that today's Gospel could make a great video. First, the video would sketch a wide-spread landscape showing hills, fertile land and also a lake (the waters of Galilee are about as large as Conesus Lake. Matthew calls it "the sea" of Galilee. Once you have seen it it's hard to call it any more than a lake). Against this panoramic background, the principal actor appears on the scene. He utters one sentence – a sentence that does not seem to be addressed to any particular audience.

Following this, the video zooms in on that bit of the landscape that I saw that morning. And there are fishermen casting their nets. The principal actor speaks once again. Again only a single sentence, but this time to a very definite audience: four fishermen. His words are a simple invitation to follow him. Then, we would need a wide-angle lens, as the landscape expands: one sees huge stretches of land and the principal actor walking through the countryside, proclaiming his message to great multitudes of people. Though it would take only a short time to see such a video, each element is so ripe with meaning that one would want to stop the video at each point and let each scene sink into one's heart for reflection. Perhaps we could do this – pause on each element of the video, not through pictures, but through the words.

First, there is the landscape into which the principal actor walks. It is not Jerusalem, the center of Jewish faith. Rather it is what Matthew calls "Galilee of the Gentiles." The term would not have been Matthew's invention. It was the common way of referring to this people of rather dubious origin. They were a mixed breed: foreigners who had come in from the north, had adopted Judaism, but with quite a different flavor from that of the rigid orthodoxy of Jerusalem.

One can't help but wonder: why would a religious leader start here rather than in the obviously more pious area of Jerusalem? Why is the landscape not the holy city and the Jerusalem temple? Matthew doesn't answer this question. He simply introduces the principal actor into this Galilean landscape.

Matthew indicates the time of his appearance. Surely not a propitious time. Another man who had had a message to proclaim had just been arrested and awaited almost certain death. That man's name was John. Jesus makes his appearance on the scene very soon after John's arrest. In telling us this Matthew is not just offering an historical note. He is suggesting something more ominous: namely, that Jesus could very well expect to end up the same way as the Baptist.

This is emphasized, as Matthew makes the first words of Jesus' proclamation the self-same words that earlier Matthew had put on the lips of the Baptist: "Reform your lives. The kingdom of heaven is at hand." He does not even bother to add what he will state later: "Believe in the Good News."

In the first scene of our video, then, Jesus appears as a lone figure addressing seemingly no one in particular, but actually all women and men without restriction; and what he says is a message of reform in view of the coming of the kingdom. Next we see the zoom-picture: a very particular scene: fishermen casting their nets into the sea. Jesus, we are told, watched them as they did their fishing. Perhaps he sat down on a rock. One of these men he would one day name: "Rock."

Then (perhaps when they had completed their fishing) he gets up from the place from which he was watching and moves toward them. They see him approach. He looks upon them, then, in a tone of quiet invitation that was at the same time a command, he simply says: "Come, follow me."

This picture we are looking at in our video shows no struggle or hesitation on their part. The four to whom he spoke simply left everything – their nets, their boats and their father. It is a very simple picture: he calls and they are at his side – and for good.

Then the landscape changes once again. It's the same landscape: Galilee, but this time our camera gives us a wide-angle view. We see a panorama of Galilee: various towns, a number of synagogues and our video closes with Jesus, seen at a distance, in one of these towns doing what he did in all of them: proclaiming the good news of the kingdom and healing people with all sorts of illnesses. As we look at this landscape and these quick views which sum up the whole of Jesus' Galilean ministry, we may ask ourselves: where do we fit into the video? Surely our place is with Peter, Andrew, James, and John: at the side of Jesus. Though many centuries separate us from them, the call to discipleship is the same now as it was then.

Jesus said to them: "Follow me." It's not an ideology we are invited to accept and give our allegiance to. Nor is it a system or a religion or a creed or even a church. It is a person. A disciple is one who, in company with others, follows Jesus. Period. That is it. Whatever else is added in the course of time is important precisely insofar as it helps us to true discipleship. Did the four who joined Jesus help with the nets and the boats before they left? There is no indication that they did – which doesn't necessarily mean that they didn't.

But clearly the emphasis is on the urgency of Jesus' call. Repentance has to be preached – now. The Good News has to be announced – now. Our part in this video also helps us to realize that the call to discipleship is one. There are no second-class citizens in the Kingdom. In due time Zebedee and the others would get their call. There are no grades of discipleship. But there surely are stages: some may be farther along the way to true conversion than the rest of us.

The word Jesus uses for "repent" is the Greek word metanoia, which is in turn the equivalent of the Hebrew word Shuvh. Shuvh means a 180-degree turn toward God. This is an interesting way of looking at the experience of conversion: turning so completely from self that we are face to face with God. To move from "self as center" to "God as center" is indeed a 180 degree turn. It is what discipleship calls us to. And it takes time to make that complete turn. Actually, a life-time.

We need to realize, too, that discipleship is not a call to DO some specific thing, but to BE something. In a sense discipleship is devoid of content. We are called to a that, not to a what. Discipleship tells us that we must always be and act as Jesus. It does not tell us in the concrete situation what that means. We have Jesus' example and his call to love. We have to translate this example and love into specific actions in the concrete situations we face situations that continually change.

There are those who say: make this decision by asking the question: "What would Jesus do in this situation?" That's an emotional trap. All too easily it gets translated into: "This is what I would do. Therefore, it must be what Jesus would do." Jesus, remember, lived in different age and culture from ours. We can't really tell what he would do in some particular situation we face in our time.

The proper question to ask is: "Given the example of Jesus and his command to love one another, what would Jesus want ME to do in this situation?" This question is not an easy one to answer. Our ability to answer it adequately depends on how much we have absorbed the spirit of Jesus — by reflecting on the scriptures, by listening to the words of people whom we trust as true disciples of Jesus, by sharing with one another how we understand the mind of Christ. We have to listen to the magisterium of the church, but we also have to tap into the corporate wisdom of the Christian community — the ordinary Tom, Dick and Mary who strive to live as disciples of Jesus. That's all of us. That's you and me. We teach one another how to be disciples. We are, each one of us, both teachers and listeners.

FOURTH SUNDAY IN ORDINARY TIME

Zephaniah 2:3, 3:12-13
Psalm 146:6-10
I Corinthians 1:26-31
Matthew 5: 1-12

The Gospel of Mark, which we are presently reading on the weekdays, emphasizes the actions of Jesus: his mighty works saving people. Matthew, whom we are now reading on Sundays, emphasizes the sayings of Jesus. Matthew's Gospel, between the Infancy Narratives and to the Passion narrative, is made up of 5 fairly long discourses of Jesus, with certain actions in between.

These five discourses suggest Matthew's desire to present Jesus as the new Moses, with the five discourses paralleling the 5 books of Moses. Traditionally we have called the first of these discourses "The Sermon on the Mount." This further extends the parallel: just as Moses went up the mountain to receive the law from God, so Jesus ascends a mountain to present the New Law to his people. He is the New Moses giving the New Law.

Today we hear the Sermon on the Mount which begins with the beatitudes. When you read the Sermon on the Mount, it is immediately clear that Jesus is making strong and severe demands on us. How are we to understand these demands? Through the centuries there have been a number of ways of viewing them. One way is fundamentalism. Fundamentalists simply say: "we must take Jesus at his word quite literally. That is difficult. But since he asked it, we have no course but to obey – if we really wish to be his followers."

Martin Luther offered a quite different approach. He maintained that what Jesus asks for in this sermon is not just difficult; it's impossible. Why, he asks, does Jesus make impossible demands of us? Jesus' purpose, Luther says, is to drive us to a state of despair, in which we would see our own helplessness to do what he asks. This, Luther believed, would move us simply to throw ourselves on the mercy of God which, in turn, would enable us to realize Luther's central teaching: we are saved, not by our good works, but solely by faith in the redemptive act of Jesus.

Albert Schweitzer, the noted humanitarian, also a biblical scholar, suggests yet another approach. The Sermon on the Mount, he claims, is proposing "an interim ethic." What he means by that is that Jesus believed that the end of the world was coming very soon. Hence he made demands on his disciples that surely would be too much to ask for a long period of time, but could be demanded for the short time that would elapse before the end of the world. It was a kind of martial law imposed for a short time.

If you examine these approaches carefully, what you will note is that each of them assumes that the Sermon on the Mount presents law: a difficult law (but you have to obey it – the fundamentalist stand); an impossible law that you can't obey (and which therefore leads you to despair – so Luther); or Schweitzer's view: a difficult law, but intended only for the short haul. Each of these views assumes that in the sermon you have the proclamation of law.

Many scripture scholars today reject this way of looking at the Sermon on the Mount. They would maintain that its intent is to present, not law, but Gospel. In understanding this approach, it is important to realize that this sermon is not a discourse that Jesus gave all at one time. Rather it was a putting together by the early Church of a number of sayings of Jesus. The purpose for putting them together was to create a summary instruction that could be given to newly baptized Christians. It was in other words a baptismal catechesis.

Hence it is not a new Mosaic Law, but a call addressed to the newly baptized, setting forth goals and deals they were to work for, if they were to live to the fullest the new life into which they had been initiated by Baptism. It is a call to growth, to live the Gospel fully and completely. Obviously this takes time; and in the process of growing into those ideals, people would sometimes fall short. The sermon was there, not to accuse them when they failed, but to cheer them on to keep working for the ideals set forth.

Yet these ideals and goals are not abstractions. They are presented in the form of vivid pictures: a person striking you on the cheek, someone taking your coat from you, or someone forcing you to walk an extra mile. These pictures are vivid examples, not of laws that we must obey, but rather of goals we must strive to achieve.

These vivid pictures tell us the qualities our actions should exhibit and the direction in which we ought to be moving if we are to live the new life that Jesus brought to us.

In other words, what the Sermon on the Mount presents is a very concrete picture of what it means to be children of God and disciples of Jesus. But what this means can never be spelled out in a code of laws. It can only be expressed in a call to reach for the heights, to strive to become perfect as God is perfect.

It makes a great deal of difference how we view the Sermon on the Mount: is it law or Gospel? Law always prescribes the minimum. The Gospel is a call to give all – at least to the best of our ability; and hopefully that ability grows throughout our lifetime.

Law looks to certain segments of our lives, leaving much of life untouched. The Gospel impinges on every aspect of our lives: nothing escapes its call. Law is restrictive; the Gospel is freeing. Law is definite and precise: you can know exactly what the law requires. The call of the Gospel is often open-ended and unclear. For the Gospel shows the goals we must strive to achieve, but leaves us to search, sometimes in darkness and anguish, for the appropriate means to reach our goals. Law is static: its requirements remain always the same. The call of the Gospel is oftentimes a call to the unexpected and the unforeseen. Law can be dull; the call of the Gospel exciting.

This is not to deny that laws have a part to play in our living of the Christian life. But we need to be clear that law exists solely to help us respond to the call of the Gospel. Laws do not have value in their own right. The fault of the kind of blind obedience which was once a favorite device in novitiates and seminaries was that it made the law an end in itself. We cannot tell people, at least adult people: "Do what you are told simply because you are told." This is servility, not obedience. True obedience is responding to the call of the Gospel and obeying the law because and when it helps me in that response. Even when I have done all I can to observe the law, there will still be much left undone that I am called to do. Law touches my life only lightly. The Gospel is all-encompassing.

Jesus who gave us the Gospel realizes that there are times when we fall short of the ideals and goals of Gospel discipleship. In a few weeks we will enter upon Lent. Each year we are given the season of Lent to invite us to look more closely at the goals and ideals to which we are called by the Gospel. Lent is not a time to punish ourselves by doing things we don't want to do. There is no reason to believe that we please God when we make ourselves miserable. These little practices are OK, but they are not what Lent is all about. Lent is rather a time to grow, a time to look at those areas in my life where I need to grow if I am to respond ever more fully to what the Gospel calls me at this time in my life. The beatitudes might well be a good place to start. It will be a different call for each of us. Maybe if we dared to do so, we might ask someone who

knows us well to help us discover what a Gospel-centered
Lent might be for us.

FIFTH SUNDAY IN ORDINARY TIME

Isaiah 58: 7-10
Psalm 112: 4-5, 6-7, 8-9
1 Corinthians 2: 1-5
Matthew 5:13-16

I am unhappy – with the first reading. I am unhappy with it not because of what it says, but because of what it omits. It begins with verse 7 of chapter 58 of Isaiah and – sad to say – it omits the first six verses of that chapter. These first six verses are important if we are to understand what the prophet is telling us. The full challenge of the prophet's words become clear only if you read those earlier verses. So I extend an invitation to you: as soon as you leave chapel, go immediately and read the full chapter 58 of Isaiah.

When you read the whole chapter you will notice what God is demanding of us in this chapter. What will become clear is that God asks not for religious ritual, but for human responsibility. God is decrying religious festivals and fasts if they are separated from the rest of life and life's responsibilities. "Look," God says, "you're only serving your own interest on your fast days... You fast and then proceed to quarrel and fight. You forget about the needy and the poor among you. Let me assure you: the kind of fasting you are doing will never be heard on high."

What Isaiah is saying is that God doesn't give a hoot for our liturgical celebrations, if we are not doing our best to love and serve one another, to love and serve all who are in need.

This is not to say that our liturgies are unimportant. Clearly we must do everything we can to make our liturgies good celebrations (good music, good homily, good participation). But in the long run, it is what happens before and after liturgy that counts. Not only Isaiah, but practically all the prophets of Israel makes clear that God loathes our religious rituals, if they do not move us to go out to our neighbors in love and concern, especially to our neighbors who are poor, oppressed, helpless.

Once upon a time we looked upon the Mass as a kind of spiritual filling station, to which we returned week after week to load up on grace so that we could manage to get through the next week relatively unscathed by temptation and sin. By the time that supply of grace was used up, next Sunday came around and we went off to church again for a grace-refill.

This was an impoverished, even inaccurate way of viewing liturgy. But there is another – and much more authentic – approach to understanding what we do when we gather here in chapel. This perspective views God's relationship to us in a very different way. It refuses to confine God's actions in us simply to sacred places and sacred moments. The grace of God –which is God's self-communication to us – is always and everywhere present in the world. God's grace is not an intervention "from the outside," from a God who is "out there."

For our God is not only transcendent (above and beyond all created reality); our God is at the same time immanent: a God whose presence and grace are everywhere in creation, everywhere in the world. God is in our midst, continually calling us to conversion, to heartfelt communion with our sisters and brothers, to compassionate concern for the needy, the oppressed, the victims of injustice and prejudice. And God does this in our everyday lives. This means we do not have a relationship with God in addition to the relationships we have with others or apart from our relationships with God. Our relationship with God is inseparable from every relationship we have. We experience God most completely when we experience God in ourselves and in other people.

This means that God acts, not just in this Chapel or even primarily in this Chapel (or any church). God acts in the world. Hence if the experience of God is to be found at all, it will be found, first of all, in the joys and struggles of "real" life, not just or even primarily in religious ritual. Or to put it the other way around: we will experience God's grace in the ritual of our liturgies only if we are already experiencing it (or at least beginning to) in daily life. This is to say that the acts of worship which we call liturgy must not be seen as isolated, special interventions of grace into otherwise profane and graceless lives. Rather these acts of worship are symbolic expressions of what Rahner calls "the liturgy of the world." It is this experience of God occurring in our daily lives that we have to bring to liturgy. And if we are not experiencing God (or at least seeking to experience God) in the everydayness of our lives, there really isn't much we have to bring to liturgy.

What does this view of liturgy have to tell us about the way we ought to proceed during Lent? How about this? During Lent this year: don't try to be more "religious." Try to be more human. Try to be more loving. Then bring all that to worship.

Isn't this what Isaiah is calling for? Share your food with the hungry, he says, shelter the oppressed and the homeless, give clothing to those whose clothes are so tattered that they are falling off their backs. We are also told to speak kindly of other people: no false accusations, no malicious speech. Are these not simply challenges to be more human, more humanly responsible, more loving? Isaiah tells us that, if we do deeds that make for true justice and true peace, then our light "shall break forth like the dawn." He goes on to add: "and (then) your wound will be healed." Reflect on these words.

We have to ask ourselves during this Lent: What is the wound we have as individuals and as a nation that needs healing during this Lent?

Must we not say that our national "wound" is a gigantic hubris: our feeling of superiority, our insistence that we are first and that our ways of doing things are best and must prevail. This wound will be healed only when we acquire a national humility, only when we begin to do the things that express our understanding that, precisely because we are looked to as leaders of the free world, we have the responsibility to live by the rule of law. We have a responsibility to deal with poverty and violence and racism and discrimination. We have the responsibility to respect the integrity and the wisdom that other nations bring to the global table of world discourse. Then and only then will we be looked upon as co-equal partners among the community of nations. Only then will be seen as friends by the peoples of the world. Only then will our wound begin to be healed. Only then will our light shine like the dawn that brings light to us and to the nations of the world. Only then will Jesus' words be fulfilled, that our light will shine forth in the world and give glory to God.

SIXTH SUNDAY IN ORDINARY TIME

Sirach 15: 15 – 20
Psalm 119:1-2, 4-5, 17-18, 33-34
1 Corinthians 2: 6-10
Matthew 5:17-37

Fittingly, our responsorial psalm today is the antiphon: "Happy are they who follow the law of the Lord." One of the themes of the book of Sirach, from which our first reading is taken, is a reverential love for the law, the Torah. By the time this book was written (the second century before Christ), the rabbis had come to believe that both the written law and the oral law had been given by God to Moses. The written law was given to Joshua and eventually passed into the custody of the priests. The oral law Moses handed over to the prophets, who in turn handed it over to the rabbis. The rabbis of Jesus' time made two claims about the law.   (1) that the law meant both the written law and the oral law and (2) that the whole will of God is contained in the Law. Hence the mentality: obey the law and you will live. Following the law means choosing life; disobeying the law is to choose death.

The Gospel presents Jesus' understanding of the law. What is clear is that he rejects both these claims made by the rabbis. First, he steadfastly refused to put the oral law on the same footing with the written law. Secondly, he refused to make the simple equation which the rabbis made, and which Sirach makes, namely, the equation that the Law = the Will of God.

This is why Jesus is careful, on the one hand, to say that he has not come to abolish the law; on the other hand, he carefully avoids saying that he came merely to obey the law. He rejects the words "abolish" explicitly and the word "obey" implicitly. The word he chooses to express his attitude toward the law is "fulfill."

It is important to discuss the difference between these two verbs: "obey" and "fulfill." Many do not understand the difference. Yet it is what Christian faith is all about. The rabbis were the first to misunderstand Jesus. Zealous protectors of the law as they were, they viewed Jesus as an out-and-out lawbreaker. He disregarded the hand-washing prescribed by the Law. He healed the sick on the sabbath – which the Law said was a day of rest from any work; and their interpretation was that even healing was work. Jesus was condemned to the cross because he was a lawbreaker.

Yet the paradox of his life is that while he seems to break certain laws without any qualms, he showed the utmost respect and reverence for the Law. The reason for this is that he saw beyond the external prescriptions of the law to the spirit that motivated a proper obedience to the law. Jesus reinterprets the law. This is what he means by fulfilling the law. He moved people to look beyond what the Law says to what it means. One way of putting it is to say he turned the law outside-in.

He was quite willing to admit, with the rabbis and with Sirach, that the law is an expression of God's will and that God's will calls us to make a choice of life over death. But for Jesus – and here he is miles apart from the rabbis and from Sirach – no external law could ever be anything more than a partial expression of God's will.

Jesus' understanding of God's will differed radically from that of Sirach and the rabbis. For them the will of God was wholly contained in the written law and the oral traditions. For Jesus, on the other hand, the will of God is not a force pressing down on us from the outside. Rather the law is nothing other than the personal presence of God's Spirit, dwelling in our hearts and activating our inner power to choose life over death.

To put it quite simply: Jesus fulfilled the law by transcending it. He transcended it by returning to a very important tradition in Israel that somehow seems to have got lost after the return from the exile.The tradition I mean is the tradition of the heart, expressed so eloquently by Jeremiah and Ezekiel.

Five centuries before Christ, these two great prophets had spoken of the new covenant that God would give to his people: a covenant in which the Law would be written, not on tablets of stone, but on the fleshly tablets of the human heart. To Jeremiah, the Lord had said: "I will give them a new spirit. I will place my law within them and write it on their hearts."

In stressing the inner meaning of the law, therefore, Jesus was not being an innovator, but very much of a traditionalist: returning to an important perception of the law that had been there, but unhappily had, for all practical purposes, been lost.

But Jesus was doing more than simply returning to a past tradition. He was, as I said, turning the law outside-in. He was probing the meaning of that tradition of the heart. He was exposing a narrow-minded and false perfectionism which kept the outward prescriptions of the law in all its details and with the most scrupulous care, but missed the heart of the law – which is Love. The important truth that Jesus is teaching is this: the law does not exist just to get something done. Its deeper goal and purpose is to make us grow. Legal perfectionists – in Jesus' time and in our own – miss the heart of the law, because they miss the Law of the Heart.

A Christian legalism which sees only what the law prescribes, and not what the law is meant to achieve, can easily become a minimalist Christianity in which we are satisfied if we do what the law says. But minimalism misses the point: that the Law is not just a call to do something; it is a call to become something: to grow in love and Christian commitment to God and in concern for our sisters and brothers. A mere external law is, by its very nature, static, whereas the inner law of the Spirit is a dynamic law calling us to reach for the heights of Christian perfection.

We must not see the law as a ceiling, namely a point beyond which we need not go. Rather the law is a floor on which we stand: a support from which we can reach out to do more and to become more for God.

The Christian inner law of love must never be reduced to its least common demand. For it is a call to strive for the highest reaches of holiness. It is a call to more, not less. This is what Jesus means when he says:

"Your righteousness must exceed that of the Scribes and Pharisees."

SEVENTH SUNDAY IN ORDINARY TIME

Leviticus 19: 1-2.17-18
Psalm 103:1-2, 3-4, 8, 10, 12-13
1 Corinthians 3:16-23
Matthew 5: 38-48

The first reading and the Gospel contrast two ways of thinking about God. Both the readings announce a lofty principle: God's people must be like their God. In Leviticus the principle is stated in this way: "You shall be holy for I, the Lord your God, am holy." This is said no less than eleven times in Leviticus. In Matthew Jesus puts the principle in these words: "Be perfect as your heavenly father is perfect." This principle has deeply biblical roots. It flows from the creation narrative, in which we are told that God made the man and the woman in his own image and likeness. If human beings are in God's likeness, they must act like God.

What does it mean to act "like God?" Leviticus applies the principle in very concrete ways: You must not hate in your heart anyone of your kin. You must not take revenge on them or bear grudges. Leviticus sums up its application of the principle in a very lofty rule of action, a love commandment: "you must love your neighbor *as* yourself."

If you look at the Gospel, you will see that it does much the same thing as Leviticus. It applies the principle – that we must be like our God – in very concrete ways: "Do not resist an evil-doer. Turn the other cheek. If someone takes your coat, give that person your cloak also." Then, again like Leviticus, it sums up its application of the principle in a love commandment: "You must love your enemies."

Note the significant fact that in the love-command Jesus has altered one word. And that one word radically changes our understanding of who God is, what is meant by God's holiness and how we must relate to others. It is hard to see how there could be any more drastic change than to substitute "enemy" for "neighbor." At first hearing, one wants to say: "This reading can't be right. Someone must have tampered with the text. Perhaps a copyist made a mistake or Matthew pushed the wrong keys on his computer." But there is no textual escape, no way of mitigating the fact that Jesus has indeed substituted "enemy" for "neighbor."

How do we explain this almost outrageous change? The principle has not changed: we must still be and act like our God. What has changed is the notion of "what God is like." For Leviticus "what God is like" is fashioned in terms of what a good human person would be like. Such a person would surely love those who are lovable, but could hardly be expected to love someone unlovable. The Old Testament God was a God who loved, but – in the long run at least – God's continued love was conditioned on people somehow proving themselves lovable. God loved, but there were conditions. That is what God was like to the author of Leviticus.

You don't have to go far into the New Testament to realize that Jesus had a different idea of "what God was like." For Jesus God is "perfect." The word is the Greek "teleios." When we use the word "perfect," we tend to think of "moral perfection." But the fundamental perfection of God is perfection of being. God is perfectly Herself /Himself, always true to God's Very Self. This means that God is totally aware – which, in turn, means that God is supremely contemplative. For that is what contemplation involves: a total awareness of reality, especially of one's own reality.

When we talk about God's perfection in relation to us, we must say that God is always true to what God has made. God cooperates with what God has made, sustaining all things in existence. God sustains them, never doing violence to them. What God made, God made out of love. God's perfection demands that God not cease to love what God has made. *They may deny their being* and act in a way that is unlovable toward another. But *God cannot deny their being.* God cannot act in a way that is unlovable toward them. God, therefore, is supremely the Non-Violent One. The one thing we can do which God cannot is: not to love. God cannot look out at us and say: "Oh, Yes, there is a person who is obviously unlovable. I shall withhold my love from that one." I can say that about someone. You can say that. But God cannot say that.

The point of the Gospel is that, while we can say that, we are called not to. We are called to be perfect as God is perfect. We must love others, not just when we see

85

something lovable in them, but even when we don't. And the reason is that because of the grace of Jesus Christ, we have become loving human beings: God's love has been poured into us. We must, therefore, strive to move - slowly, gradually and painfully – toward that Unconditional Love that describes for us "what God is like."

If we follow the Leviticus application of the principle (Be like your God), we end up loving those who are lovable. If we follow Jesus' application of this principle, we end up being – or trying to be – non-violent. What does this mean?

First of all, it doesn't mean being a doormat letting people walk all over you. Non-violent persons must always resist evil, but such resistance must be done in a. context of love. Non-violent persons must always confront an evildoer with the truth, but they must do so in a loving way.

Jesus has said: Those who are faithful in little things will be faithful in the bigger things. We might transpose that into another key and say: those who are non-violent in little things will be non-violent in greater things. That is why for those who choose the way of nonviolence, the most important area of nonviolence is our daily living, our daily interaction with the people with whom we live. There will be times in our relationships with one another where we shall be in disagreement. We can express that disagreement in a strident, antagonistic way that widens the rift between ourselves and the other. Or we can express our disagreement in a considerate, loving way that can heal any rift that may be between us. The words we use, the tone of voice we adopt, the body language we use are decisive in making what we say either violent or non-violent.

If before we expressed our words of disagreement, we paused and expressed words of love in our own heart, if we said silently to the other: "I love you because God does and I am supposed to be like my God," such an inner preface could change my outward speech: words that might have been violent could turn into into considerate loving words.

Will such a way of acting succeed in really healing the disharmony that exists? We don't know beforehand. It may work or it may not. But that is not the primary issue. What really matters is that, when I act non-violently, I put a little more love into a world starved for love. If all of us did that consistently, changes would eventually take place. The destiny of our world is not ultimately in the hands of politicians, but in the hands of those who choose to follow the scriptural call: "Be like your God": our God is who is at once contemplative and non-violent in dealing with us, as we must be in dealing with our sisters and brothers.

EIGHTH SUNDAY IN ORDINARY TIME

Isaiah 49: 14-15
Psalm 62: 2-3, 6-7, 8-9
1 Corinthians 4:1-5
Matthew 6: 24- 34

It would be difficult to bring together two more beautiful texts to express the loving providence of God than today's first reading (from Isaiah) and the Gospel. The text from Isaiah 49 sees that providence imaged in the deepest, the closest and the most instinctual of all bonds of human love: the love of a mother for the child she carries in her womb. A mother can never forget the child of her womb. Yet even if one thinks of a very exceptional case in which a mother's love might grow cold, the love of God – which mother love only faintly mirrors – can never grow cold.

If the Isaiah reading describes God's loving providence as the love of a mother, the Gospel depicts that same love through the image of a father's concern to supply the needs of his children. God is Mother. God is Father. His relationship to us is one of indescribable intimacy, care, compassion, concern for all our needs, whatever they may be. How absurd really that we have ever thought of our God as a God of vengeance and wrath. He is ever the caring Father, the tender, loving Mother.

It is in the light of this understanding of divine providence and care for us that we need to reflect on what I think is the challenge offered in today's Gospel. The challenge is forcefully expressed in the very first line of the gospel: "No one can serve two masters." If we want to grasp the full import of Jesus' challenge, it is helpful to pause a moment on the exact meaning of the words that Jesus uses.

The word "serve" does not quite convey the meaning Jesus intended. The Greek verb used by Matthew is "douleuein." The verb "douleuein" derives from the Greek noun "doulos" which means "slave." In ancient times the slave was totally the property of another. His time, his energies were not his own; they belonged to his master.

Which brings me to the other word in Jesus' statement: the word "master." The word that is used in the Greek text of Matthew is the word "kurios," a word whose vocative case we are familiar with from the Latin liturgy, namely, "Kyrie." The Greek "Kurios" is used in the Greek Old Testament to translate the holy Name of God — the name given to Moses and that is sometimes rendered as Yahweh. In the text of Matthew, therefore, "Kurios" has a stronger meaning than "master;" it has taken on the connotations of the divine Lord, toward whom we must all be "doulos": slaves, servants, completely subject to his control and to his will.

Against this etymological background, one can perhaps understand more clearly the question Jesus is posing in the Gospel. Who is the "Kurios," the master, the Lord, to whom I will be "doulos," slave, servant, devoted follower? And the point is: there will be a "kurios" in our lives. We have to make the choice: who will that "Kurios" be? This is what the Gospel is continually doing – calling us to make a choice. And the call of today's Gospel is the most fundamental challenge: to whom or to what shall we give supreme control of our lives? Who, what, will be "Kurios?"

We know that the Christians of the first four centuries faced that choice in very concrete terms. Oftentimes the Roman Empire demanded of them that they say: "Caesar is kurios." This they refused to say – even though it meant their lives. The confession they insisted on making was: "Jesus is Kurios." These three words "Jesus is Lord" constituted the earliest of all Christian creeds. It meant Christians accepting Jesus' challenge: "you cannot serve two masters." They chose Him over Caesar – and often at great cost.

We are no longer forced, at least in the same unambiguous way, to choose whether we will be slaves of Caesar or of Jesus. But what Jesus is telling us in the Gospel is that there is a rival to Him that seeks to claim the role of "Kurios" in our lives. Interestingly, Jesus sees as a rival to him, not one of the capital sins, not a pride on our part that would seek to be one's own servant, not worldly interests that would strive to claim our total allegiance. No, what Jesus sees as the rival to his claims over our lives is: Worry. As far as I know, there was never a god in the Greek or Roman pantheon called "Worry." Nonetheless, Jesus is telling us that we can make "Worry" a kind of god. For we can become slaves of our

90

worries and fears, rather than the slaves of Jesus that we profess ourselves to be.

Most of us probably don't have to identify with the worries Jesus speaks of in the Gospel. We have food, clothing, shelter: our physical needs are reasonably well provided for. But we do have our own sets of worries and concerns and fears that can take up our time and sap our energies.

We have our fears about getting along with others and our concern lest we be misunderstood. We may have worries about our families, about our health, maybe at times about the inevitability of death. We worry sometimes, especially as we get older, about the things we have to let go of now or may have to let go of in the future. This is a kind of generic description of the worries that can plague us. Each of us can make the picture concrete for herself or himself.

What Jesus is telling us in the Gospel is very simply: stop worrying. All your worrying is needless: your heavenly Father does care for you. It's useless in any case: for most of what we worry about we probably cannot change. What is worse is that worrying is harmful to us, for it distorts reality: it prevents us from seeing things as they really are.

But worst of all, Jesus warns us, Worry is actually a failure in faith. It is a failure to believe that God is our Father and our Mother and that He does care for us, more deeply even than we can care for ourselves.

Jesus calls us to make an exchange. Give up our concerns, our worries, our fears and receive in exchange God's care, His serenity, His peace. The exchange is a real bargain for us!

To put this in other words: Jesus is calling us to bring perspective into our lives: Seek first God's Lordship in your life; then He will take care of the rest. It should be obvious that Jesus is not advocating a shiftless, thoughtless, improvident attitude toward life. What He is challenging is a careworn, worried, fearful attitude that takes all the joy out of life. He does not deny the need of a proper prudence in our lives. What He is questioning is an over-cautious attitude that makes us anxious and overly fearful. We need to be prudent, yes; but we also need to be serene with the kind of peace that God wants to give us.

In ultimate terms, Jesus' question to us is: Who will be Kurios, Lord, in your life? Will the Kurios that will own our time and energies be our surface fears and anxieties? Or will we accept as Kurios, Lord, in our lives the One who wills to be both Mother and Father to us?

We are on the brink of Lent. Lent is a time of conversion: a time therefore for discovering a proper perspective and for setting right priorities. It is a time to face, honestly and explicitly, what our answer is to the question: Who really is Kurios in my life? Or maybe, better: how am I growing in my realization that I have chosen Jesus as Kurios? How can I manifest this realization in my Life ever more fully?

NINTH SUNDAY IN ORDINARY TIME

Deuteronomy 11:18, 26- 28, 32
Psalm 31: 2-3, 3-4, 17, 25
Romans 3: 21- 25, 28
Matthew 7: 21-27

It's so good to see you here. I am delighted to be able to celebrate liturgy with you. I am delighted also to be able to speak with you. And as I speak I wonder if you will hear me or if you will listen to me. There is, you know, a big difference between hearing and listening. Hearing is *something that simply happens.* It simply means that a sound has been received by your ear. But the sound by itself carries no real meaning with it.

Listening, on the other hand, is *something you do.* When you listen you concentrate on the words and sentences you hear so that they yield meaning for you. Listening to me is the way that my thoughts or ideas are conveyed to you. If what I say is meaningful, if it makes sense to you, then your listening can be a way of learning.

Some people are described as "hard of hearing." Quite a lot of people can be called "hard of listening." There was the man who said: "When I get into a difficult situation, I wish I had listened to my mother." He was asked: "What did you mother say?" His answer: "I don't know. I didn't listen." Hearing and really listening, I want to insist, are as different as night and day. To be a good listener, one has to want to listen, no matter what is said, whether it is pleasant or unpleasant. Dick Cavett once said: "It's a rare person who wants to hear what he does not want to hear."

Now tell me: do I sound like I am in a classroom, giving a lecture on audiology? Not really. Because I don't know anything about audiology. The reason I speak about "hearing" and "listening" is because I believe that that is what Jesus is talking about in the Gospel. Jesus calls us to be good listeners. He assures us that if we want to build our lives on a solid foundation, we must listen to his Word.

What does it mean to listen to the Word of God? Where do we find the Word of God so that we may listen to It? Let us count the places. The obvious place to look for God's Word would of course be the scriptures. Less obviously but perhaps more frequently, the voice of God speaks to us in the everyday experiences of our lives: in the people we live and work with. We interact with them and through this interaction we come to a realization of what God is calling us to do and to be.

Still another privileged place where we meet God is prayer. For many people prayer simply means *talking to God.* And when we talk to God we are generally in request mode, trying to reach a God who seems to be very distant from us.

When I went to grade school, I majored in the Baltimore Catechism. The Baltimore Catechism is one of the greatest books produced by the American Church. It has some absolutely marvelous questions. Unfortunately, it also has a lot of bad answers. One of the truly great questions was a three-word question: "Where is God?" You can hardly think of a question more important than this: "Where is God?" The question calls forth a splendid answer: "God is everywhere!" The composers of the Catechism ought to have left ten blank pages to enable people to recover from this marvelous statement: "God is everywhere!"

But instead – sad to say – the catechism writers blew it. They followed this stupendous statement with the wrong question. They asked: "If God is everywhere, why can't we see him?" when they should have asked was this: "If God is everywhere, how can we experience God's presence?" How can we enjoy the intimacy with God that this statement so obviously implies?

Now, there's a question that really gets you somewhere. It takes us readily to contemplative prayer, to contemplation. Contemplation rests on two pillars. The first is the fact that God is the Source of all reality and the Ground in which they exist. The second pillar is my conscious *awareness* that God is the Source and Ground of all. This means that if we were to take God out of the picture, everything would cease to be. Apart from God nothing can be.

The contemplative learns that prayer especially involves learning to listen to God speaking to us from within, as it were. Speaking not necessarily in words, but in events, in other people, and particularly in silence. The measure of our spiritual growth is the earnestness of our efforts to find time for silence in our lives that we may continue the interior journey. Thomas Merton expressed it well: "Our real journey in life is interior, it is a matter of growth, deepening and an ever greater surrender to the creative action of love and grace in our hearts." (*Road to Joy*, 118)

We need continually to remind ourselves that a true unity, a true communion, is really there. For all too often we don't see it: we see separateness and division among people. We need to reach a deeper level of perception to see our communion with one another, to see what is truest about us.

It is the failure to reach this level of perception that can cause the violence, the terrorism, the unhealthy relationships that can cloud family life, community life, the life of nations and of the whole global community.

Contemplative prayer helps us to achieve this perception. For prayer means moving from where we are: namely, in God, -- to an *awareness* of where we are, namely, in God. It is this kind of awareness that can change lives and communities and cultures. *It is a life lived on the inside and not just on the outside.* True prayer is moving from a life that is purely exterior to a true interior life. Prayer calls us to the inner experience that ultimately dominates our whole lives. The German poet Rainer Maria Rilke warns us of the shallowness of a life that is "always looking out, never looking in."

Some time ago I was on my way to visit friends in Canada. At Hamilton, the QEW becomes a bridge that is quite high to allow good sized boats to come in from Lake Ontario into Hamilton's harbor. They often have blinking signs up at the entrance to the bridge warning you of the weather. On this occasion the sign said: "Strong Winds." Then in very large blinking letters: "BE AWARE! BE AWARE!" I was so intrigued by the sign, because it was using the language of the contemplative that I decided to stop at the road maintenance building to inquire. I said to them: "I wondered about that sign on the bridge. 'Be Aware. Be Aware.' By any chance, were those signs put there by a contemplative? I ask because the words are part of the contemplative vocabulary." They were so surprised. They said: "How did you know? Yes, that sign was actually put up there by two contemplatives. In fact, the only two that we have in our work force."

How about that? Would you believe it? Now, of course, this visit to the maintenance building is what we call in scripture studies *midrash*. *Midrash* is a literary form, a technique that creates a story around a word or a series of words. I built my story around the words "Be Aware." I didn't really stop at the road maintenance building. But it could have happened. For there was a sign and that said "Be Aware." And "Be Aware" is indeed the language of the contemplative.

For the contemplative is one who knows that the Lord Jesus is always there. Our problem is to "Be Aware."

ASH WEDNESDAY

Joel 2:12-18
Psalm 51: 3-4.5-6.12-13.14.17
2 Corinthians 5:20 – 6:2
Matthew 6: 1-6, 16-18

Martin Luther King Jr. concluded a talk in Los Angeles in 1963 with these words: "I say good night to you by quoting the words of an old negro slave: 'We ain't what we ought to be, and we ain't what we want to be, and we ain't what we're going to be. But, thank God, we ain't what we was." This may serve as a kind of motto for Lent. As we begin Lent, we realize "we ain't what we ought to be," and we hope to change that. We hope that when Lent comes to an end, we can say, at the very least, "Thank God, we ain't what we was."

Interestingly the two readings for today are about blowing horns. The Gospel calls us not to blow our own horns, not to take pride in all we try to do to live Gospel values. So during Lent we are not to brag about the good things we are doing.

But the first reading tells us that we must blow horns, trumpets, to announce the merciful love and compassion of God. The reading from Joel calls us to rend our hearts, not our garments. Joel is referring to an ancient custom among the Jewish people: the tearing of one's garments. This custom, referred to in the Talmud, is explained by Moses Maimonides, the greatest Jewish scholar in the

Middle Ages. One should rend one's garments in approaching the site where the Jewish temple once stood. One should also rend one's garments at the death of a family member. For a distant relative you would make only a slight tear – which could be sewn up again after 30 days. But for a father or mother, it was necessary to tear, not just the outer garments, but all one's garments so as to reveal the heart. This tearing had to be done in public and the garment may never be sewed up.

Joel had this customary practice in mind, but he was thinking of a different kind of rending or tearing– one far more important than the rending of a person's garments. He calls us to a rending that is truly interior. Rending garments is an exterior action with no necessary resonance within. Joel wants us to get inside ourselves. His concern is with what happens in the human heart. He tells us to rend our hearts, not our garments.

As I was preparing this homily, I thought of the many metaphorical ways in which we use the term "heart." We speak of a person wearing her heart on her sleeve. What we mean is that her feelings are always on the surface: you always know how she will act. Or we speak of someone being "soft-hearted," (generous and outgoing almost to a fault). Or "hard-hearted" (difficult to reach, unsympathetic). Or we might describe a person: "She has a big heart' (clearly we are not talking anatomy). Sometimes we say "Have a heart." (we aren't really asserting that the person has a missing piece of anatomy). When we say "My heart is heavy," we are not talking about extra weight.

Yesterday I was doing this reflection on the various meaning we give to the word "Heart," then this morning, when I read morning prayer, I discovered that the very first antiphon was "My heart is ready, O God, my heart is ready." What a great sentence with which to begin Lent!

Note how all these usages of the word "heart" that I mentioned are concerned with the inner self, our own identity Thomas Merton once wrote that rending our garments only lets in the cold; rending our hearts lets in the grace and the merciful love of God. Rending our hearts is a kind of open-heart surgery that makes our inner self aware of God and of others.

Jesus has the same lesson for us in the Gospel. Jesus is always reaching for the human heart. He speaks about the three traditional works of piety honored among his people: almsgiving, prayer and fasting. He invites us to do all these things, but to do them from the inside. Jesus calls us to live on the inside, not just on the outside. The poet Rilke pointed out the deadliness of the lives of people who "are always looking out, never looking in."

It's that looking in that Lent is all about. It's not the amount of the alms we give that matters, but the bit of our heart that accompanies the giving. Fasting makes sense only if it an action that softens our hearts and opens them to others. When we prayer it's not the amount of prayers we say, it's where they come from that counts and the way it flows from our heart and helps to unify our lives.

It is not just what we do that matters, but the concern and love and compassion that they attempt to embody. During Lent don't try so much to be more religious. Try to be more genuinely human and loving and compassionate. This brings us another "heart expression." Let's put our whole heart into whatever we want lent to mean for us. This involves tearing open our hearts so that God can do the necessary surgery to make us whole again. "My heart is ready, O God, my heart is ready."

One more reflection from the Gospel. Three times Jesus tells us: 'Don't be hypocrites." The Greek word "hypocrites" has as its first meaning: an actor, one who plays a role on the stage. As you know, the players in a Greek play wore masks. Lent, Jesus says, it a time to get off the stage, to tear off the mask, so that we can find our true identity. That identity is not located in what we do, or in the roles we play, but in who we are at the depths of our being, where we meet God, the source of our identity. It's rending our hearts that enables us to get within and find the diving presence there. "Yes, my heart is ready, O God, my heart is ready."

This kind of readiness will make us better persons. It will make it possible for us to say with the old negro slave whom Martin Luther King Jr. quoted in his talk in Los Angeles: ""We ain't what we ought to be and we ain't yet what we want to be, but at least, thank God, we ain't what we used to be."

THE FIRST SUNDAY OF LENT

Genesis 2:7-9; 3:1-7
Ps. 51: 3-4, 5-6, 12-13, 17
Romans 5:12-19
Matthew 4: 1-11

Fittingly we begin Lent at the beginning – with the creation story. In reading the Genesis story of creation, we need to remember that these stories were written for unlettered, unsophisticated people who could never have understood creation as we do, namely, *creation ex nihilo,* creation from nothing. To these simple people it seemed clear that if God was going to make something, God needed some materials to start with.

For them what existed in the beginning was water, earth, sky, air – all mixed up. It was a kind of formless mass of undifferentiated material. In a word it was Chaos. What did creation mean? It meant God bringing Order out of Chaos.

This is the background that enables us to understand the sin of Adam and Eve. Their sin was a confrontation of the creature with the Creator: a vain attempt on the part of the creature to destroy the Order God had put into the universe. They were unable to destroy that Order: they could not return it to its primitive Chaos. What they could do, though, was to disturb that Order. They introduced into God's good creation an element of disharmony and alienation. They are so alienated from God that they try to hide. They are alienated from one another: they hurl accusations at one another. They are alienated from the rest of creation that had been placed in their care.

The purpose of this Genesis account is not to tell us of some primal sin, but rather to help us understand what sin really is. Sin is an act of the creature vainly trying to return the Order of the universe back into Chaos. Sin upsets the Order of God's good creation. It brings disharmony, disorder into my life and my relationships. It makes for guilt, unhappiness, sorrow.

But don't go away yet; stay with me. There is more and wonderful stuff to come. It's in the second reading – from Romans. Paul speaks of a whole new dimension of the human reality. It is a joyful announcement of Grace. God's Grace revealed in Jesus Christ. And the wonderful point that is made is that Grace is greater and more powerful than human sinfulness. While Paul refers to the sin-narrative in Genesis, his primary intent is not to tell us about some primal sin, but to affirm, in the most resounding way possible, that whatever the evil and chaos wrought by sin, all is MORE THAN put right by the victory of Jesus.

The key words in Paul's text are the Greek words *polio mallon* which in translation means "HOW MUCH MORE." It's a phrase that burst the bonds of translation. Paul lines up, as it were, all the disasters that sin and disobedience bring in their wake: condemnation, loss of grace, spiritual death. In other words, all the chaos that sin seeks to bring into God's good world. Paul fairly shouts at us: OK. Line them all up, then place them side by side with Christ's victory and see how marvelously the Victory of Christ reverses them. No matter what evils sin has produced, Paul continues to shout at us: HOW MUCH MORE has not the grace of Christ done for us and set things right again.

The Gospel is the traditional one for the first Sunday of Lent: the Gospel of the temptations of Jesus. In a way it offers a balance to joyful exuberance of Paul. We must keep in mind that the Jesus Paul speaks about in *Romans* is the Risen Jesus, the Easter Jesus who, because of His obedience, was raised by God to new, immortal life in which there is no sin, no temptation, no disharmony. The Gospel brings us back – almost jerks us back – to the days of Jesus' mortality, during which he took on the human condition – fully and completely.

The saving message of this Gospel is that living the human condition meant for Jesus the same thing it means for us. We are tempted to sin. He was tempted to sin. We are tested about the way we use our gifts. So was He.

Reading the temptation narrative as if it were the history of actual events simply distracts us from the meaning Matthew is trying to convey. The story is an effort "to get inside the mind of Jesus" as it were, as he ponders the courses of action he may follow in His ministry. He is Messiah. How will He use His gifts as Messiah: for his own personal advantage (the first temptation), to gain popularity and acclaim (the second temptation), to achieve political power for himself (the third temptation)?

And we would be missing the point of Matthew's narrative, if we were to think that he is suggesting that Jesus faced all these temptations in the beginning and then was free from temptation ever after. On the contrary, what he is telling us is that all through his ministry Jesus had to face and overcome the very human possibilities of self-seeking and of failing to trust totally in God.

We must not miss the point, either, that in each of the temptations Jesus answers the tempter with words from Deuteronomy. Deuteronomy is one of the most moving books in the Hebrew Scriptures. It's a meditation on Israel's forty years retreat in the desert, during which their fidelity to God is continually being put to the test. It's a book that speaks movingly about God's love for Her people. It is no mere fancy to think that Jesus must have pondered this book deeply and keenly. It was perhaps in this book about God's goodness and love that He found the master-key to His whole life, which is summed up in His words: "Not my will, Father, but Thine."

We have to think about the sinful situations in our lives that tempt us to turn our lives into chaos (or, to put it more bluntly, to make a mess of our lives). We have to think too of the sinful global situations that we face as a country. I can think of nothing that seems more calculated to plunge our world into chaos than modern warfare. Unlike what was true in times past, when war meant armed men on one side fighting armed men on the other side, the victims of modern warfare are mostly innocent civilians. All too often today the term "collateral damage" has become a sanitized way of describing mass murder. As a country we face a fierce testing of our fundamental commitment to life and goodness and peace. We can yield to the temptation to escalate the spiral of violence that continues to bring more and more chaos into God's good creation. Or we can choose to work with other nations of the world. We can become their friends, and together seek ways far better than war to deal with violence and its perpetrators.

We need to realize that for us this must be something we do for and with Jesus. We need to remind ourselves of His solidarity with us: first his solidarity in the human condition (that solidarity that must always surprise us, but never shock us) which means that He had to struggle to remain faithful to God's will. Then, secondly, there is His solidarity with us as the Risen One, which makes available to us the polio mallon, the Much More, the strength of a victory we have not won, but whose power belongs to us, because He has won it for us.

The seeming paradox of Lent – which is really the paradox of the Christian life – is that we move toward Easter, yet the Risen One is already at our side and His power is already within our grasp.

THE SECOND SUNDAY OF LENT

Genesis 12:1-4a
Ps. 33: 4-5, 18-19, 20, 23
2 Timothy 1:8b-10
Matthew 17:1-9

Two questions to keep you alert: (1) From what book of the
Bible was the first reading taken? (No fair peeking into the
Missalette!). Genesis? OK. Second question (harder one):
What chapter of Genesis was read? Chapter 12? Yes. Why
is chapter 12 of Genesis of special importance? For at least
two reasons. The first is that with this twelfth chapter of
Genesis we enter into historical times. Abraham and Sara
belong to human history. The eleven chapters which
precede are about pre-history: times we know nothing
about, except for a few stories preserved in oral memory.
Cain, Abel and Noah are not historical figures: they belong
to the folklore and myth of the ancient Near East. Abraham
and Sarah, on the other hand, are part of recorded history.

The second reason this chapter is important is the
significant fact that it gives the first description of an
historical person who has faith in God. This is not to say
that there may not have been people before Abraham who
had faith in God. But this is the first record we have of
someone who has faith in God.

More than that, this reading also offers the first articulation
of what faith means. Faith, as revealed in the Abraham
story, is *a call to give up all that one has hitherto*

experienced as security so as to trust solely in God.
Abraham is called to give up the security of family and
country and set out for an unknown destination. As the
Epistle to the Hebrews expresses it: "Abraham went out,
not knowing where he was going."

Faith, this story is telling us, is a journey in which we have
no clear idea of the destination or the way to get there.
But we have something greater: the consciousness that
God is with us on the journey and that we make the
journey at God's behest.

We may wonder why this story about the journey of faith is
used on this Second Sunday of Lent, when traditionally we
retell the story of the Transfiguration. The reason is that
the Transfiguration story also marks the beginning of a
journey. The Gospel-writers place it at the beginning of
Jesus' journey from the north-most part of Galilee to the
south: a journey that will bring him to Jerusalem and will
conclude with crucifixion and death.

In the Transfiguration story faith in God takes on a new
dimension. It becomes Easter-Faith. Our faith is no longer
simply faith in God. It is faith in the God who raised Jesus
from the dead. When the writers of the Gospel pen the
story of the journey to Jerusalem, they already know its
ending: that the story concludes not with disaster, but with
victory. In order that we, the readers, may know the
victorious outcome from the very beginning, they prefix to
the journey narrative, this wondrous picture of Jesus in
glory. They are saying that they were in on the divine

mystery (when they wrote) in a way that the disciples at the time were not. And they want to share the secret with us too: that the journey ended not at a cross, but at an open grave: the open grave of the Risen One.

The Gospel writers knew it after the event. The disciples did not know before how the story of Jesus would end. The question that inevitably forces itself on us is the question: How much did Jesus know? Did he know at the beginning of the journey what the journey's end would be? Did he know that God would raise him from the dead? This question is at the very center of our understanding of Jesus. We believe Jesus is both divine and human. That is not the heart of the question. The heart of the question is what do we mean when we say he is human? Was he a divine actor playing out a drama in which he knew the whole script from the beginning? The Christology that I was taught many years ago affirmed that he did know the whole story beforehand. In fact, that theology said that he possessed infused knowledge and the beatific vision from the moment of his existence in this world: not bad equipment with which to start out the human venture. If by Jesus' being "human" means this very hyped up human nature, then it is difficult to understand how the Epistle to the Hebrews can say: "He became like us in all things except sin." Having infused knowledge and the beatific vision is not exactly what we are like.

Must we not say that it is a necessary part of being human to have to walk in the darkness of faith? If this is true, then must we not say that Jesus took this journey to Jerusalem without knowing how it was going to come out? Jesus had a keen mind. He knew that his teaching (especially what he said about God) had incited opposition. He could very well have seen the very real possibility that his journey to Jerusalem might well mean his death. He went, believing it was God's will that he go, trusting in God, yet not foreseeing the future. How else can we understand those piercing words in the Epistle to the Hebrews:

> *In the days when he was in the flesh, he offered prayers and supplications with loud cries and tears to God, who was able to save him from death, and he was heard because of his reverence.*

"Loud cries and tears" do not suggest an all-knowing Jesus who had no need for faith. Rather it suggests one very much like us. Nor was his prayer heard in the way we might have expected.

As we make our Lenten journey, we know – what Jesus did not know when he was in the flesh – that at the journey's end we shall experience the Easter-Mystery and participate in Jesus' victory. But first we have to die as Jesus did. We have to die and be reborn as new persons. For there is in each one of us a new person hidden in the depths of our being, waiting to be born. There is a Seed of God straining to burst the shell of our surface self in order to actualize our capacity to be transformed into God. But for that person to emerge, we have to die – to selfishness and self-centeredness. We have to slough off the surface, superficial self that lives in separation, in alienation, in isolation, in competition – and find our true selves in God. We have to be transformed. We have to be transfigured.

Interestingly the Greek word that is used for the transfiguration of Jesus is the word *metamorphosis,* which means "transformation."

St. Paul writes that Jesus Christ is the first born of many sisters and brothers. He is the archetype and the prototype of all humanity. What happened to him (namely entering in his humanness into the life of God), this is what is destined to happen to us. But before it can happen we have to die to all that is false in us, to all that is phony, to all that is illusory. That means ridding ourselves of everything in us that cannot be transformed into God. It is that transformation that is at the heart of our Lenten faith-journey toward the fullness of the Easter mystery.

THE THIRD SUNDAY OF LENT

Exodus 17: 3-7
Ps. 95: 1-2, 6-7, 8-9
Romans 5: 1-2, 5-8
John 4: 5-42

She is quite a lady — this Samaritan woman. We just heard the story of a day in her life. And what a momentous day it was. She had come to the well as was her daily custom. To her surprise, she encounters a stranger there. The stranger was a man and a Jew. She is not embarrassed to be there — alone and with a man. In fact, she seems rather to enjoy it.

He asks her for a drink. She does not immediately acquiesce. Instead, in a sort of amused way, she points out the cultural inhibitions that ought to make her hesitate in responding to his request. "How come," she asks, "that you, a Jew, ask a drink from me a Samaritan and a woman?" It's hard to avoid the impression that she is flirting with him.

At the same time, though, if we look more deeply at her question, we may perhaps come to realize that, contrary to the bad press she has had from male commentators on this text, she proves herself to be a deeply religious woman.

Her response to his request for a drink is to pose a theological issue: why is he breaking with Jewish tradition

113

by speaking in public to a woman and by sharing a drinking cup with a Samaritan? Is she perhaps asking why this kind of tradition is allowed to exist in the first place? Why should not men and women be able to converse with one another in public? What should religious differences between Jews and Samaritans engender enmity between them?

When the stranger speaks of living water, again she poses a theological question: "Are you," she asks, "claiming to be greater than our patriarch, Jacob?" When he speaks about water welling up to eternal life, she is impressed and asks for it, even though she as yet has no understanding of what he means.

At this point the issue of her five husbands comes up as well as the fact that she has no husband now. Most commentators have taken this in a literal sense and seen it a reference to her shady past. Some have even suggested that her remark "I have no husband" is her attempt to seduce this stranger, as if she is saying, "Since I have no husband now, I am a free woman."

Yet it seems clear that it is hardly possible to give a literal meaning to the "five husbands." It is highly improbable that any Jew or Samaritan man would marry a woman several times divorced.

Perhaps a better way to read the story is to say that at this point this woman is not just an individual. She represents Samaria, the northern kingdom that broke away after the death of Solomon and was taken into captivity. When the people of Samaria eventually returned home they were often unfaithful to God and turned to the worship of the five gods of Samaria. (Josephus, the Jewish historian mentions these five gods.) Hence the reference to the woman's five husbands may well be read as a reference to Samaria and its worship of the five gods of the surrounding peoples.

Her reply to Jesus after he speaks of her "husbands" and of the fact that she has no husband now leads her to see the Stranger as a prophet. The prophets often described the relationship of God with God's people as a spousal relation. The worship of false gods meant going after false husbands. Time and again the prophets would say to the people something similar to what Jesus said to the woman: "You have no husband. You have forsaken your spouse."

This, therefore, is very much a part of the theological conversation between Jesus and the woman. Having come to see him as a prophet, she asks another question that was of serious concern for the Samaritans, namely, what is the proper place to worship God: Mt. Gerizim in Samaria or Jerusalem?

What Jesus makes clear is that with him the messianic age has arrived and, in consequence, the question of where to worship becomes irrelevant. The true worship of God will be in spirit and in truth.

The woman is impressed. She speaks of the Messiah who is coming who will tell us everything. She wonders: "Could this Stranger be the Messiah? Jesus confirms her partially drawn conclusion with the simple, profound revelation: "I am he, the one speaking with you."

At this point of Jesus' self-revelation, the disciples, who had gone into the town to get food, return and they are amazed — not that he was talking to a Samaritan, but to a woman. Nor would that have been able to understand that a deep and genuine theological dialogue had taken place between them.

"Nowhere in the Fourth Gospel is there a dialogue of such theological depth and intensity," writes Sandra Schneiders. "Jesus is presented as legitimizing female participation in male- appropriated roles."

We are told: "Then the woman left her water jar and went off to the town." Like the apostles in the synoptic Gospels who left boat and nets and family and tax booth to follow Jesus, she leaves her water jar behind. She abandons her daily concerns and goes off to evangelize the whole town.

Another proof, if proof be needed, that she was not a woman of ill-fame, but someone highly respected by the townspeople, is the fact that they hear her word and come themselves to believe in Jesus. Sandra Schneiders has written: "This woman is the first and only person (presented) in the public life of Jesus through whose word of witness a group of people is brought to 'come and see' and 'to believe in Jesus.'"

She is the apostle who brings the Good News to the Samaritans, as Mary Magdalene will become the apostle to the apostles, as she proclaims that she has seen the Lord.

This story of the Samaritan woman can be read at another level. It can be seen as everyone's story. Your story. My story. We too need someone to interpret for us the ambiguities of life, someone to lead us to a deeper understanding of life's meaning. Only then can we come to know ourselves.

And in the final analysis, it is the Stranger who does this for us: the Stranger who comes at unexpected moments, often walking untrodden paths, making odd and unusual requests, offering new and unforeseen challenges, awakening in us a new sense of our personal worth and dignity.

And the place where we experience that Stranger is not really outside us. The well is not really a well. It is a symbol of what is deepest in us, our own hearts. Thus, as we reread this Gospel, we begin to see that it is not just about a Samaritan woman or a well.

It's about the human heart silently letting in the Stranger. It's about the contemplative depth of our being where in silence we discover the Stranger.

In the poet's words:

> *Closer and clearer*
> *Than any wordy master*
> *Thou inward stranger*
> *Whom I have never seen.*
> *Deeper and cleaner*
> *Than the clamorous ocean*
> *Seize up my silence*
> *Hold me in Thy Hand!*
>   Thomas Merton: *Stranger*
>   Collected Poems pg. 289

THE FOURTH SUNDAY OF LENT

1 Samuel 16: 1b, 6-7, 10-13a
Ps. 23: 1-3a, 3b-4, 5, 6
Ephesians 5:8-14
John 9: 1-41

Someone has said: "Ask an impertinent question and you may get a pertinent answer." That may well apply to some of the questions in today's Gospel. Actually it is full of questions (18 in all): some factual, some theological, some very critical and some that might be classed as impertinent.

People take different approaches to questions. I think it can be said that all people (or at least most people) belong to one of two classes. There are question-askers and question-dodgers. Both of these classes exist in the Church today and the sad truth is that there is very little communication between the question-askers and the question-dodgers.

People who prefer to dodge questions do so for one of two reasons: Either they are convinced beforehand that they already have all they need to answer any question. Or they may dodge the question, because – either overtly or covertly – they are afraid that they may not be able to discover any satisfactory answers. Such people are even ready to sacrifice honesty on the altar of security.

If I were asked to identify myself in terms of these two categories, I guess I could say that a fairly neat summary of my life-story would read something like this: I moved from being a question-dodger (and I was one of the "I have all the answers" kind of question-dodger, not the fearful dodger variety) to becoming a question-asker, even, occasionally at least, asking the impertinent question.

Perhaps now we could look at the many questions that are raised in today's Gospel (eighteen in all, as I mentioned). There is the theological question about God's dealings with us and what the causes are of physical blindness. This is the disciples' question: "Was this man born blind, because of a sin of his own or of his parents?" Jesus answers their question in the negative and then cures the man of his blindness.

There is the factual question raised by the Pharisees: What actually happened? It is quite obvious that they don't want to accept the answer given them. They ask the man who had been blind, "Where is the one who you say cured you?" And he says: "I have no idea where he is." At this point they deny what appears to have happened and they do so for a theological reason. Such a thing, they say, could not be from God, for it was done on the Sabbath. Interestingly, others who were there are puzzled. They ask the Pharisees: "How can a sinful man do such signs?"

The Pharisees try another tack: they ask another theological question directed to the man who has now become the center of attention: "What do you have to say about this man who, you say, cured you of your blindness?" Our hero answers: "I think he is a prophet."

The Pharisees find him too much for them and give up on him for the moment. So they make inquiries about him from his parents, perhaps hoping to learn that he wasn't born blind at all. The parents confirm the facts: he is their son and he was indeed born blind. But because of fear they refuse to be drawn into the argument about whether or not he was cured.

The Pharisees decide to call the man back. They tell him that they know that Jesus is a sinner (though they don't divulge how they knew this.) [It comes of course out of the system they live by]. Again our hero's response is right from the heart and right on the mark: "I don't know whether he is a sinner or not, but I sure do know that I was blind and now I see. I am grateful to him, sinner or no sinner."

The Pharisees are really frustrated. They ask him to tell all over again what happened. Again our hero answers – and you can't help detecting a sly bit of irony in his words – "Oh, you want to hear the story all over again? Are you thinking of becoming his disciples too?" They see his question as impertinent and rebuke him for even daring to think such a thing. Hereupon he gives them quite a good homily with some very good theology about how God chooses the instruments God will use. His homily ends with the punch line: "If this man were not from God, he would never have been able to do such a thing." They are scornful of his message: "You were born totally in sin, and are you trying to preach to us." Note here a typical tactic of

121

question-dodgers; "You can't possibly have the right answers, because you are out of the system." So they expel him from the synagogue. Once he is out of the synagogue, Jesus comes to him and puts the climactic and deeply theological question to him: "Do you believe in the One sent by God – the One Daniel called 'Son of Man'"? Full of faith and joy, the man responds eagerly: "I sure would like to. Just show me who He is." Jesus replies: "You have seen him, and the one speaking with you is He." The man's profession of faith is immediate: "I do believe Lord." He falls on his knees and does homage to Jesus.

Notice how this man has maneuvered himself, through a whole series of questions, and moved from seeing his healer as "a man named Jesus" to a profession of deep faith in the one whom God has sent to bring light into the world.

The passage ends with a typical Johannine conclusion: Jesus divides the world. Because of him the blind see and sometimes those who had vision lose their sight. A lot depends on the honesty with which they face the questions Jesus raises.

And just as the questions and answers the man in the Gospel went through rose out of his experience, so questions and answers about the fact of Jesus have little meaning for us, until in some way they touch our own experience.

We know all the speculative answers: those answers that come from our question-dodging days. These were answers given to us, answers we received from past generations. They tell us that Jesus is the Risen One. Jesus is the human one in whom the fullness of the Godhead dwells. Jesus is Lord of our lives, Lord of all creation.

These answers we receive from the past constitute a precious heritage for which we must always be grateful. But we need to realize that we have to make these answers our own. To do this we have to question these answers: not with the thought of rejecting them, but of learning what they mean for us today, here and now in our lives. Each of us has to continue to ask the question: "Who is Jesus Christ for me?" We can never stop asking that question. We may have to formulate the question in new ways, ways that may never have occurred to people in the past. That is why catechisms are of very limited value. They tell us where we once were, not necessarily where we are now. More than that no one answer to the question of Jesus is ever adequate. We should take joy in that part of the answer that God has already given us and that we have experienced. But we cannot rest there. We need to look forward in hope to the INEXHAUSTIBLE MORE that awaits us all, if we face, rather than dodge, the question: "Who is Jesus Christ for me?" To say to God's Holy One: "Who are you for me, anyway?" may seem like an impertinent question. But let's be assured that asking it will yield wonderfully pertinent answers.

THE FIFTH SUNDAY OF LENT

Exodus 37: 12-14
Ps. 130: 1-2, 3-4, 5-6, 7-8
Romans 8:8-11
John 11: 1-45

What sort of person was this man Lazarus whose story appears so central to today's liturgy? His two sisters, in a message to Jesus, describe him as "the one whom you love." They inform Jesus that Lazarus is ill. Jesus waits two days and comes to Bethany on the third day and raises Lazarus from the dead. Is there a message for us, as we looked toward Easter, in Lazarus being raised from the dead on the third day?

Lazarus appears once more in the Gospel narrative: at the meal where his sister Mary anoints Jesus' feet with precious ointments. He was just there. He never speaks; at least we are not told that he did. How would a man raised from the dead look? What might he have to say? Where would his thoughts be? Robert Browning tried to deal with these intriguing questions in a wonderful poem in which Karshish, a traveling Arab physician, writes to his friend Abib about this man who people claim was raised from the dead. Karshish tells his friend that there is strangeness about this man. It's as if he is living in two worlds:
Heaven opened to a soul while yet on earth,
Earth forced on a soul's use while seeing heaven.
(Robert Browning: *An Epistle*)

Why is this story given to us on this last Sunday of Lent? Perhaps one reason is to confront us with the reality and the inevitability of death: the death of loved ones and, finally, our own death. St. Anselm once expressed a truism: "The farther you are from the time of your birth the closer you are to the time of your death." So many young people think that death is not for them. It is for older people. When we become older people, death's inevitability becomes more real to us. And we are much more earnest about discovering the meaning of death.

Death puts faith to the supreme test. Experience teaches us that there is finality about death: it ends something: something beautiful, something we prize something we want to reflect on, as we have reflected on the wonderful lives of our sisters who have died this year. All that was ended by death. When a loved one dies, death's finality is a fact — an almost brutal fact — that we are forced to face.

Sometimes, when a loved one dies, we accept because we must, but maybe we wish that we could have them with us for a few more years. In the second book of Kings (Chapter 20) we read of good king Hezekiah. He was mortally ill; he prays for more time. God answers his prayers and adds 15 years to his life. But, in the long run of course, it didn't matter that much. After the 15 years, the finality of death claimed Hezekiah, as it claims all the children of Adam. Remember the solemn words in Gray's "Elegy in a Country Churchyard"?

The boast of heraldry, the pomp of pow'r,
And all that beauty, all that wealth e'er gave,
Awaits alike the inevitable hour,
The paths of glory lead but to the grave.

The important question that faith had to deal with is *not the finality of death,* but whether that finality is also *ultimate.* For, as Sandra Schneiders has written, "the finality of death lies not in what it terminates, but in what it inaugurates." *(Written That You May Believe,* 155)

This question: Does death inaugurate something? is answered in today's Gospel, though not in the raising of Lazarus, but in the conversation of Jesus with Martha. Let me explain. Consider Lazarus. In one sense being raised from the dead was for him a wonderful reprieve. He was given a few more years. Yet in another sense, it was no big deal. His life presumably took up where he had left off. Thus if he were forty when he died, he would have returned as a man of forty. If he had died of a heart attack, then he returned to mortal life with a bad heart. He perhaps lived a few more years. Then he had to die again. We might ask the question: "Did he really want to be raised from the dead? Would he have chosen it, had the choice been his?" The answer depends on the answer to another question: does death terminate everything; or does death inaugurate something? Does it inaugurate immortal life? If it does, then we can presume that, had he been given the choice, Lazarus would have said: "No thank you" to being raised from the dead a second time. He might have said to Martha: "Dying twice is enough." Please put a DNR sign at

126

my tomb. And, for heaven's sake, keep Jesus away from my tomb."

The raising of Lazarus, then, does not answer the question about the ultimacy of death. It does not answer the question: does death inaugurate something new and wonderful? It is in Jesus' conversation with Martha that these questions find the faith-answer we seek. Martha says to Jesus: "Lord, if you had been here, my brother would not have died. But even now I know that whatever you ask of God, God will give you." Jesus tells her: "Your brother will rise." "I know he will rise in the resurrection on the last day," she responds. Her response indicates that she is thinking about a future a long way off.

Jesus' reply makes clear that he is talking about a future that is present now. For he tells her: "I am the resurrection and the life: whoever believes in me, even if he dies, will live, and everyone who lives and believes in me will never die." Faith in Jesus adds a whole new dimension to our present life. Union with the risen Jesus in this life constitutes the possession, here and now, of eternal life. If we believe in Jesus our present life itself is redolent with eternal life.

As we reflect on this Gospel narrative, suddenly the stage changes. It is no longer Jesus speaking to Martha, but to each of us. Each of us has to hear Jesus' question: "Do *you* believe this?" At this point believing becomes not theological assent, but a spiritual transformation that is deeply personal. It is not something that we can prove (indeed we have no desire even to think at that level). Believing in Jesus is experiencing Jesus as the Risen One. It's accepting Him. It's saying "Yes" to him as the one who gives us life, immortal, unending life.

Faith in this respect is like love. Love can't be proved either. (You wouldn't even want to think of love at that level). It's like living in a family or a community and discovering that love is there. You receive it. You experience it. You return it. And it makes life worthwhile.

It is living faith in Jesus, living faith in his resurrection, living faith in his incorporating us into his risen life that assures us that, no matter how real and no matter how depriving it may seem, death is temporary and passing, for it has been overcome by Jesus' resurrection.

This is the faith we share. It is this faith that makes it so important that we belong to community, that we belong to the Church. For belonging to the Church means, in ultimate terms, being united in a community of Easter people, who believe that Jesus was raised from the dead, who believe that he lives eternally and, therefore, believe him when he says that he gives us eternal life. Stripped down to its basic essentials, that is what Church is: a community of Easter people. Recently Dr. Rowan Williams, archbishop of Canterbury, defined Church as "what happens when people encounter the risen Christ" and commit themselves to "sustaining and deepening that encounter" with others.

We face death unflinchingly, for we have the assurance of faith that it inaugurates something most wonderful: immortal life in God.

PALM (PASSION) SUNDAY

Isaiah 50: 4-7
Ps. 22: 8-9, 17-18, 19-20, 23-24
Philippians 2: 6-11
Matthew: 26:14-27:66

There is so much one could say about Matthew's passion story. Let's look at the prayer of Jesus. Twice we are told of his prayer: first in the garden, then on the cross. The prayer in the garden is a scene of struggle. Jesus is confronted with the reality of suffering and, like all of us, he shrinks from it. What he foresees will happen, he does not want to happen; and he prays God that it may not happen. We are told that he prayed three times, but we are told what he said only the first and second time. The two prayers are slightly, but significantly different.

The first time he prays: "Father, if it is possible, let this chalice pass me by. Still, let it be as you would have it, not as I." There is the temptation in this prayer to think: "maybe, somehow, I can avoid what seems to be the unavoidable." Yet this is followed by total obedient submission.

The second prayer seems to flow from this obedient submission. For the second prayer seems to imply that the Father's answer had been that what he prayed for was not possible. In this second prayer, the petition has almost entirely disappeared. There is only that total obedience of which Paul writes in our second reading.

The second time Matthew describes Jesus as praying is when he hangs on the cross. The context of this prayer from the cross is utter darkness. "From noon onward darkness came over the whole land until three in the afternoon." It is out of this mysterious darkness in the middle of the day that Jesus' prayer emerges. At first hearing, it sounds like a prayer of desperation, of despair, emerging from an inner darkness that corresponds to the darkness outside. "My God, my God," Jesus prays, "why have you forsaken me?"

We miss the point of this prayer, if we do not realize that these words are but the beginning of a prayer and that the prayer Jesus was saying on the cross was a prayer he had said often during his life – in the liturgy of Israel and in his own personal prayer. For these words are the beginning of the 22nd psalm: the great psalm of Israel's salvation. It is a psalm in which desperation struggles with hope and confidence in God; and the hope of God's help and the confidence of God's salvation win out.

It is important to note that Matthew tells us that a few minutes later Jesus cried out again. This time he does not tell us what Jesus cried out. But it makes a great deal of sense to envision the following scenario: Jesus begins the psalm aloud, crying out the first verse.

Then He prays quietly. Finally, he once again cried out. Presumably he cried out loud the last part of the psalm. Which is to say that he cries out aloud the triumphant note of salvation on which the psalm ends and in that cry gives up his life.

It is a moving picture for us to reflect upon. Jesus came among us to be our Saviour. But we must never forget that he came as one fully human as we are. Therefore, he who became like us in all things save sin, had to experience what we experience.

He who saves had to experience himself the *saving love* of God. "In the darkness of his death struggle the saving love of his father seemed distant, even denied; and so Jesus cries out with Israel's prayer of deliverance, a prayer that in the paradox of faith both laments God's absence and draws upon his living presence." (D. Senior, *Passion in Matthew*, 139).

In the wake of this dying prayer, a whole new world is born. The temple curtain, which separated God's presence from God's people is torn apart. The earth trembles and quakes. Rocks are split apart and people come forth from their tombs (though Matthew is careful to point out that this coming to life of the dead actually took place after Jesus' resurrection).

It is not just important Christian events we celebrate this week. It is the coming to birth of a whole new world. What is happening in nature symbolizes it. But most of all it is something that is happening in our own hearts. We are being made over. We are being made new.

But we must not forget today that we live in a world that needs to be made over, that needs to be made new. Many years ago Caryll Houselander wrote a book which she called *This War Is the Passion*. She was referring to World War II that was raging at the time. But today the passion continues to live on in Iraq, in Afghanistan, in Libya, in the Holy Land, in Lebanon. We must identify in nonviolent love with all those who are suffering the ravages of war and terror and hunger.

We must also say that the passion is being enacted in the Church, not just in the liturgy, but in the priesthood. This is a difficult time to be a priest. There was a time when priests were looked up to as wonderful examples of living the Gospel. Things have changed.

The priesthood needs to be born anew out of the passion of Christ. There needs to be a resurrection. The clerical culture of privilege and special honor and generous favors has died. And perhaps good riddance, as priests embrace new reality in the Church, as now they can take their place among the other faithful, not as superior to them or more privileged, but as part of a community of equal sisters and brothers who are eager to love and serve one another. And this must apply to bishops too.

The passion is today – a passion that (like Jesus') – will lead to new life. A whole new Church is being born in our very midst.

HOLY THURSDAY

Exodus 12:1-8, 11-14
Ps. 116:12-13, 15-16bc, 17-18
1 Corinthians 11:23-26
John 13: 1-15

If you were to choose one word to sum up today's liturgy, it would be, I think, the word Love. I am reminded of the oft-quoted words of Fr. Pedro Arrupe:

Nothing is more practical than finding God, that is, than falling in love in a quite absolute, final way. What you are in love with, what seizes your imagination will affect everything. It will decide what will get you out of bed in the mornings, what you will do   with your evenings, how you spend your weekends, what you read, who you know, what breaks your heart, and what amazes you with joy and gratitude. Fall in love, stay in love, and it will decide everything.

Today's readings are about the spontaneity of love.

Over the years the readings for these days of the Triduum have become so much a part of us that we tend almost to think of them as predetermined, as if the script was already written way ahead of time and Jesus is simply acting it out. It is as if he cannot speak or act in any other way. Such a way of looking at these readings leaves no room for spontaneity on Jesus' part, no possibility of his acting on the impulse of the moment.

Yet it seems to me that is exactly what we have in tonight's Gospel: a sudden, spontaneous action on Jesus' part. It is wrong, I believe, to feel that Jesus had it all planned out beforehand: that at a certain point in the supper, he would dramatically arise from his place and perform the most menial of tasks: wash the feet of his disciples. The text doesn't say he did it when they arrived, which would be the logical time to do it, if all were planned ahead of time.

Rather we are told, after having taken his place at the table for the supper, he rose from the supper and suddenly began washing the feet of the disciples. A strange thing to do in the middle of a meal. And yet the text suggests that, far from being planned, this was a spontaneous action on his part. He experienced a sudden impulse to do it. The disciples were astounded. Peter expressed their reaction when he blurted out: "Lord, you can't do that. You are our Master. You can't act as a slave." In general, Peter does not come off very well in the Passion narrative, but here he is right on target. Jesus simply should not be doing this.

And we might ask: "Why did he do it? What prompted him to do it?" Perhaps the answer to this spontaneous show of love on Jesus' part may be found in the words with which the supper story begins: "Having loved his own who were in the world, he loved them to the end."

This act of humility on Jesus' part can have a number of meanings: it can point for instance to Jesus' humiliating acceptance of death on the cross and this could be the meaning of his loving them to the end. It is also clearly, as he tells them, an example of what they should do for one another. But perhaps tonight we could think of it, first and foremost, as an act of extravagant love, telling us how we are loved by him and how we must love one another in return.

It is worth pointing out that, as we heard in our second reading, it was at the supper that Jesus gave the command: "Do this in remembrance of me." Again the word *this* may mean a number of things: sharing a meal to remember his presence among them. But also it may mean: "Love one another to the extreme. Wash the feet of one another."

This surely brings us to the central theme, not just of Holy Thursday but of the whole of the Holy Triduum. It is all about love. Love expressed in washing feet. Love expressed in sharing a meal. Love expressed in laying down one's life for one's friends.

Unfortunately, the word "love" has become a common, generic, "over-the-counter" word. It is used so frequently and so casually about so many things that any real content gets lost. Tonight – the night of Great Love, we need to take it out of the category of clichés and unwrap its true meaning: we must see it for the total self-giving that it means in Jesus' life and that same self-giving he calls us to in our lives with one another and with all our sisters and brothers. He calls us to see him in ourselves and in one another. We are the Body of Christ. Each of you is the body of Christ. All of us are the body of Christ. The Eucharist is not just about Jesus and his wonderful gift of himself. The Eucharist is also about us, about who we are and how we relate to one another.

Thomas Merton has a moving piece in which he says that if we could see each other as we really are, we would want to get down on our knees and adore one another. Think of that for a moment. It does indeed make sense. For if we saw one another as we really are, we would be seeing Christ. For it is in us, in one another, that Jesus is present among us.

What does this mean? Something pretty revolutionary. It means that when we receive the Eucharist, when we come to this altar to share the Body and Blood of Christ, it is the Risen Christ who comes to us. But the Risen Christ is united with all his sisters and brothers. We cannot separate Christ from his Body. We cannot receive Christ without at the same time receiving one another, without receiving all those who are united to Christ as His Body. Which is the same as to say that if we are not receiving them, we are not in truth receiving him. St. John Chrysostom in one of his homilies said: "You have tasted the Lord's blood, yet you do not recognize your brother, your sister. You dishonor this table." Those are pretty strong words.

When we receive the Eucharist, we receive one another. We can't get away from this truth: that each one of us is truly the body of Christ. St. Paul says: "All we who are many are one body, for we all partake of the one bread." (1Cor 10:16-17) When the Eucharistic minister says to us: "the Body of Christ," we respond "Amen." We must recognize that we are saying "Amen," not to Christ alone separated from his members. Rather we say "Amen" also to one another and to all Christ's members. It is so easy for us to forget this. So easy to come to this altar and think of a Jesus separated from his members, separated from our sisters and brothers. We need to realize that such a Jesus does not exist.

There is yet another aspect of Jesus' symbolic action at the supper that we need to note. We are told that he *"laid aside* his garments."* This action is a symbolic description of his *laying down* his very life. He lets go of everything, even life itself. He gives all to God and for us.

As Jesus laid aside his garments, we must *lay aside* our self-centeredness, our desire to have others serve our needs. We have to *let go* of all the things that prevent us from being for God and for others. He tells us quite simply and clearly: "I have given you a model to follow, so that, as I have done for you, you should also do [for one another]."

The passion of Jesus which we celebrate tomorrow cannot be separated from what Jesus lived and what he taught. We must never forget that the supper action of Jesus, in washing the feet of his disciples, makes clear to us that he came not to dominate us, but to serve us; not to condemn us but to save us; not to place limits on us but to make us free. He acted to enable us to see that He is not apart from us but one with us. We must never allow ourselves to forget all this when we come to this Eucharistic table.

I want to offer a suggestion to help us experience Jesus' presence in one another. When the time comes to exchange a sign of peace, I'd like to suggest – to those who are willing to do so – that of saying "peace" to one another, we look at the person and say: "You are the Body of Christ."

GOOD FRIDAY

Isaiah 52: 13-53:12
Ps. 31: 2, 6, 12-13, 15-16, 17, 25
Hebrews 4:14-16, 5:7-9
John 18: 1-19, 42

In reading morning prayer this morning, I was struck by one of the antiphons. It spoke of "Joy to the World." "The wood of the cross has brought joy to the world." The phrase clearly recalls the Christmas hymn: "Joy to the world. The Lord has come." The Christmas joy was about the descent of the Lord Jesus into the world. This Easter "Joy to the World" is about his ascent from the world and his return to God. For the Fourth Gospel the raising up of Jesus on the cross is not a symbol of suffering. It is rather the first stage of his being raised up into God, from whom he came and to whom he goes.

John's passion narrative is not about suffering, but about Joy to the World, because Jesus has accomplished the world's salvation. If you notice, there is in John's narrative no agony in the garden. Indeed, throughout the whole passion narrative Jesus is shown as completely in control of the situation at every turn. In the garden, for instance, Jesus' very admission of his identity so overpowers his enemies that they fall to the ground, lying there before him entirely still, like a movie suddenly stopped at one frame.

It's a passion narrative without a passion. It is the most dramatic of all the Gospel passion narratives. There is dialogue, movement. There are two stages in the story. Pilate is seen moving back and forth from the outer stage to the inner one. As you read the story you soon realize there is only one character in the drama who is truly real. With the possible exception of Pilate, John shows little interest in the other characters in the drama. The Jewish authorities are mere shadows. Judas disappears without our knowing anything of his fate. Peter leaves the stage without our knowing of his repentance.

John seems to get the minor characters off center stage as soon as possible. During the entire drama, the spotlight is always on Jesus. John's reason for this concentration is that Jesus is the only one in the whole story who is in touch with what is truly real. The others are mere shadow figures, because they are out of touch with reality.

Pilate is perhaps an exception to the shadowy character of the other personae in the drama. There is a fairly extensive dialogue between Jesus and Pilate that almost takes on the nature of a theological discussion – about Truth, about the meaning of Kingdom. But, in fact, Pilate is only a foil used by John to express the theological truths he wants to present to his readers. Jesus is the one Real Person.

A key moment occurs in the drama about midway through the story. Pilate, wanting to release Jesus and hoping to play on the sympathies of the crowd, has Jesus scourged. After scourging him the soldiers in mockery put on him the trappings of a king: a garment of kingly purple and a crown, but it is a crown not of gold but of thorns.

Pilate presents Jesus, thus garbed and crowned, to the people. His words are: "*Idou ho anthropos.*" In Greek there are two words for man: *aner*, which means "man" as male and *anthropos* which, though often translated as "man," has an inclusive sense. More properly, therefore, it simply means "a human being." (like *ecce homo* in Latin).

Some might take Pilate's words as words of derision: "Look at this wreck of a human being." But if we remember that John often writes at two different levels of meaning we can see that in giving this line to Pilate, John wants to enunciate a most essential truth about Jesus. For John Pilate's words involve a whole theology of the Incarnation. What Pilate is saying is: "Here is *the human being*. Here is the one who is all that God wills a human being to be."

For John, Jesus is the representative human being and he is that in every possible way. The head bleeding from the thorns, the body lacerated by the scourges portray a Jesus who stands for all the oppressed in society: the poor, the homeless, the undocumented immigrants. He stands as the victim of terrorism and injustice and war. Jesus in John's Gospel is not just *aner*, man as male. He is *anthropos*, the human being. He is everyman and everywoman. He stands as a witness to human nobility in the face of suffering.

But if he is the archetype of all of suffering humanity, he is at the same time "the firstborn from the dead," the prototype of a humanity destined to journey, as he was journeying, toward the fullness of life in God. The Jesus of John's passion narrative is not a Jesus who is about to die. Rather he is the one who is to experience dying and rising not as separate events, but as one single undivided reality. Already on the cross he is the Risen One. For he does what only God can do: he sends the Spirit upon his disciples. This is the way John describes Jesus death: that he gives the Spirit. The other Gospels are content to describe Jesus' death in traditional terms, namely, they say: "He expired." John says so strikingly that his death was really the gift of his Spirit to the disciples and to us. John says: "He handed over his Spirit."

Idou ho anthropos, Ecce Homo. Today we are called to look and see *the human being*, the one who stands in for every man and every woman, the one in whom there is no falseness or illusion, the one who is fully and truly and forever himself. One of us, sharing fully our human condition, showing us what God wills us to be. Yes, *Here is the human being. Ecce Homo.*

EASTER SUNDAY

Acts 10: 34a, 37-43
Ps. 118: 1-2, 16-17, 22-23
Colossians 3: 1-4
John 20: 1-9

I want to greet you on this Easter Sunday. It is a feast that is all about life, new life, never-ending life. We need to revel in this feast especially at this time in our history. In a world where everywhere there is the smell of death — death by arms, by cold and starvation, by bombs and tanks, we desperately need this feast of hope: this feast that tells us in the sequence: *mors et vita duello* — life and death engaged in mortal combat. And life wins out. As the sequence continues, speaking for all of us: "Yes, Christ my hope is risen, risen from death, bringing us new life."

This is the promise of our hope: life in the end will win out. Because Christ is risen death has no ultimate power over life. Easter says to us: death is swallowed up in the victory of life. This is our hope. Our joy. Our faith.

Easter calls us to a stupendous act of faith. Let's reflect a bit on that. Several years ago, I wrote a St. Anthony Update article which I entitled: "Easter: The Story that Lives Forever." The editor at St. Anthony Messenger changed the title (without consulting me, an unfortunate practice that publishers often exercise). He changed it to "The Resurrection: How We Know It's True."

I must say I like my title better: "Easter: The Story that Lives Forever." For the resurrection of Jesus is the Event that is for all ages of history: ages past, present and to come. It is an event that is unlike any event that happened since the first creation. Every other event that has happened in the human story takes place, and then is swallowed up in a cavernous past. Things happen and then pass into history. They happen just once, never "once and for all." Even if the effects of an event continue for a long time, the event does not. It is lost in the past of history.

But this is not true of the Event we celebrate on Easter. The Resurrection of Jesus is a "Once and for all" event. A story that lives forever. It belongs not to the past, but is an ever present Reality. It is the one Event that is contemporary with every age of history. The Easter Event is, not so much something that happens in history, but something that takes leave of history. As Karl Rahner has written: "The Way of the Cross has a fifteenth station, at which we take leave of the march of time to be received into the inconceivable wonder of the love of God." (T.1., 7, 168)

Rahner makes the interesting point that, when the Risen Jesus entered into glory with God, he was not entering into a preexisting place called heaven. Rather the resurrection "established heaven" in its most radical sense. For resurrection established the human possibility of union with God. It means entering into an entirely new kind of human existence in the timelessness of God's love which is eternity. It is entering fully into the life of God.

The Jesus of history was mortal. He could die — and he did die. The Risen One, on the other hand, can never die. He is totally in God who is all life. This says to us that Jesus, the Risen One, is freed from the limitation of particularities. In his mortal life he was limited by the particularities of time, geography, culture and gender. In Risen life the limitations of particularity are removed. Jesus is no longer confined by our world of time and space, yet he is at the same time very much with us. The Risen One is everywhere. He belongs to all history and to all peoples. He is the contemporary of every age. He is our contemporary. He *is* ever in our midst.

His everywhereness is the core reality of our spirituality. That is what contemplation is all about: being aware that He is there. For He is indeed everywhere. He comes to us in hidden, sometimes subversive ways. He breaks through into our lives and our history in surprising and unsuspected ways. We are never really prepared for Him.

Look around this chapel. Please do look. See Christ present in the person next to you, in the person over there, and over here. For in the Eucharist He is present not only on the altar; He is also present around the altar. He is in the person to whom you gave a helping hand today. He is in the harried person at the cash register of Wegmans who takes your money, in the nurse who takes your blood pressure, in the pharmacist who dispenses the many pills we take.

And he is in Iraq with our courageous service men and women and with the suffering people in the cities of all war-torn nations. He is with the countless number of the poor and homeless in so many of our own cities and in the rural areas of our country: people who often have to make a choice between food and medicine. He dwells amidst the thousands of people in the Sudan who die because they have no food or medicine. He is in those people in our world and in our midst who are homeless, sick, dying, discriminated against. The forgotten people of the world. He is in them reproaching us when we ignore their plight.

Indeed, he is everywhere – and the world is never quite ready for him. Sadly, so often it doesn't realize his presence, maybe doesn't even want it. But any effort to confine the Christ, to limit His Presence, is doomed to failure. There is no escaping him. He is beyond our control.

He energizes His Church, leading it and always going on before it, even into areas where, for the moment at least, the Church is afraid to venture. Always a step ahead of us. Always beckoning us to new horizons we have not yet reached. Especially today — as we face conflict and even panic in the Church such as we have never experienced before — we need to see him so far ahead of us, beckoning us onward. He is the lover of the Song of Songs, springing across the mountains, leaping across the hills. He gazes through the windows, peering through the lattices. A lover, He calls us to love: to love Him and to love the believing and the unbelieving world He came to save and in which he dwells.

HE IS RISEN! HE IS RISEN! ALLELUIA! ALLELUIA!!!

THE SECOND SUNDAY OF EASTER

Acts 2: 42-47
Psalm 118: 2-4, 13-15, 22 -24
1 Peter 1: 3-9
John 20: 19-31

The reading from Acts describes the first Christian community as it existed after Pentecost. There was a deep sense of unity: a unity that flowed from four elements of their life: (I) They were united in hearing the teachings of the Apostles; (2) They were united in the celebration of the Eucharist and; (3) united in the prayers they said together. Finally, (4) united in a common ownership of what they possessed which included a special concern for the needs of the poor.

So remarkable was this community that, Luke tells us, they won favor with God and added new members every day. As we read this account we are filled with a sense of admiration for these early Christians. Maybe even a bit of envy: why can't we be like that?

As we read further into the Acts our admiration gives way to a healthy skepticism. For as we read on, we find quarreling going on among different factions in the Church. Which suggests that probably they were not notably different from us, in fact from Christian communities that have existed through the centuries and even to today. The sad but honest truth is that the Church has always been made up of the fervent and the slothful, the saints and the sinners. There always seems to have been factions quarreling over what was essential and what was not.

What dawns on us, if we read this passage of Acts with a sense of history, is that Luke's intent was not to tell us exactly what the early Church was like, but what it ought to be like. He is presenting an ideal of what the Church community ought to be, but – regrettably – often is not. What we are given is not an historical record, but a goal that Christian community should be striving for. Let's look at the different elements of that goal.

First, there is faith sharing: we share the faith that comes from the apostles. This does not mean a faith that has been encapsulated in ageless formulas, but a faith that has to be struggled with in every age.

For faith is not simply assent to certain formulas; it is a commitment of fallible persons who share not just formulas, but lived experiences. We do not believe in formulas but in the realities which they express. Community, then, is first of all people who share a lived experience of God and of God's involvement in our lives.

Secondly, community means sharing a vibrant life of prayer and worship which recognize God as the source and center of Christian life. The highest expression of this life of prayer is the Sunday Eucharist. I say "Sunday Eucharist" rather than simply Eucharist. For the Sunday Eucharist is qualitatively superior to the daily Eucharist. For Sunday is the Lord's Day: the day par excellence on which Christian people gather to articulate and celebrate their experience of faith.

Faith-sharing and prayer as elements of Christian community are closely related. For when we truly believe, we experience the need to articulate what we believe and to do so in communion with those who share that faith.

Another element of community described in Acts is possession-sharing. What does this mean in today's Church? Probably not exactly what Luke describes in his idyllic picture of community. Translated into our day, possession-sharing means striving to eliminate, in Church and society, the sharp dichotomy between those who have and those who have not.

Which means that one of the great tasks of the Church is to work for justice and equity in our society. It means working to change the structures of a society that tends simultaneously to create great wealth and great poverty. This means working within those structures to see that there is equity and fairness. This sometimes calls for difficult decisions. At times it may mean working with people or groups with which we may have differences of opinion on some issues. A situation we have to live with if we are to accomplish something together.

If we are going to be faithful to the Gospel and make a preferential option for the poor, we also have to be concerned about what government does with tax money.

The unspeakably enormous amount of money spent on war is crushing us as a nation. If we spent more money for people throughout the world who are starving in great numbers, we would be seen as a compassionate nation. We would have more friends. We could even eliminate poverty and hunger from our country and from the world, if we had the will to do it.

In the early sixties remember how, after the Russian Sputnik launched into space, President Kennedy vowed that before the end of the decade we would put a man on the moon; and, despite the funds and research it required, it happened in July of 1969. What if we were to say that by the end of the next decade of this century, we shall eliminate poverty and hunger from the face of the earth? We could do it, if we were not squandering our tremendous resources making war.

Thus community, as described in Acts, has a theological element: a shared faith that is reflected upon, spoken about with an ever deepening perception of its meaning for people's lives. It has also a cultic or liturgical element: a shared participation in prayer and worship. And finally there is a social element: sharing what we possess. We have to come to grips with what all this means for us as community.

Is it possible to read the two stories in the Gospel in terms of community? In the first story Thomas is absent from community and he is unable to believe in Jesus Risen. In the second story he is in the midst of community and he is able to believe.

In the first story Thomas feels very much as the outsider since he wasn't there when the community experienced the Lord's presence. In an act of bravado calculated to cover up his sense of being on the outside, he imposes all sorts of conditions that must be fulfilled before he will believe.

I am reminded of the story of Pope John XXIII. He was receiving Jacqueline Kennedy in audience. He was wondering what he should call her: Mrs. Kennedy? Madame Kennedy. She was ushered into the room. He forgot all his reflecting, opened his arms and welcomed her: "Jackie." So in the Gospel Jesus suddenly appears and Thomas forgets all about the conditions he had laid down. He rushes to the Lord and brings the 4th Gospel to a rousing conclusion with the strongest profession of faith in the Gospel: "My Lord and My God!"

Thomas, the outsider, was unable to share the faith of the community. But once he is in the midst of community he recognizes the Risen Jesus. We need to reflect how important the faith of each of us in community is to the faith of one another. Our faith leans on that of others; and their faith is strengthened by our faith.

While Jesus appeared to individuals, it was his appearances to the community that were crucial. For it was Jesus' appearances to the gathered community that gave the early Church the substance of the message it was to bear witness to in the world.

It is in community that we receive faith and are nurtured in faith. Yet community, we must remember, is not of our making. It is the gift of God. The God who raised Jesus from the dead is the God who gives us Christian community. In this Easter season we thank God for raising Jesus from the dead. We must not forget to thank God for what is in its own way a huge miracle: the gift of Christian community.

Today we are experiencing in the Church a crisis of authority. We need to remember that the faith of the Christian community is our faith. It is our right and our duty to weigh in on the way in which that faith is expressed and lived in the world. It is getting late. We need to act quickly to work our way toward the ideal of community presented to us in today's liturgy.

THE THIRD SUNDAY OF EASTER

Acts 2: 14, 22-33
Psalm 16: 1-2, 5, 7-8, 9-10, 11
1 Peter 1: 17-21
Luke 24: 13-35

Of all the stories of the resurrection appearances, the Emmaus narrative is surely the most exquisitely beautiful. Luke tells it with wondrous artistry. He writes at two levels: the historical and the liturgical and it is the liturgical level that is primary.

He wrote, we must remember, many years after the event. By the time he wrote, the disciples of Jesus had become a community whose central experience as community was the Eucharist or, as they first called it, "the Breaking of the Bread."

When these early followers of Jesus gathered for this central experience of their community life, they did a simple and very human thing. They told the stories that gave meaning to their lives and they shared a common meal. Each Sunday, over and over again, they told their stories about Jesus whom they now accepted as Lord of their lives; and they shared a meal in which they remembered him and in the remembrance experienced his presence among them.

It is this common Christian experience that Luke wants to write about. To tell it, he uses the story of two disciples on the way to Emmaus. The historical kernel behind this very polished narrative of Luke is the story of two disillusioned disciples of Jesus. One of them is named: he is Cleopas. The other is unnamed, but very likely Cleopas' wife, who stood beneath the cross of Jesus. The couple are returning to their home in Emmaus.

Emmaus is west of Jerusalem — which means that, as they journey home, they were walking toward the setting sun: an apt image of their dejection and loss of hope. Suddenly on this road toward the setting sun, they encounter the Dawn — the One in whom a new kind of existence was about to dawn for them — but they have no awareness of it, as this Stranger joins them and walks along in their company. The Stranger interprets the Hebrew Scriptures for them, and their hearts burn within them as he does so. But still they have no inkling as to who he is.

They arrive at their Emmaus home and invite the Stranger to accept their hospitality for the night. After they had settled themselves in the couple's little home, he joins them at their evening meal. All at once the roles are reversed: suddenly he is the host and they are the guests. He says the customary Jewish prayer over the bread. Then he breaks the simple fare of bread to share it with them. Suddenly, miraculously, their hopes are restored: they recognize the One who had died and who was now alive. Then he disappears.

Immediately, without waiting for the dawn (for now the dawn is in their hearts), they retrace their steps: this time walking toward the east: the place of the rising sun. When they arrive, breathless, at Jerusalem, they find that the others have had the same experience as they. And they became, all of them, a community, because — however diverse they may have been in other ways — they have shared a common experience.

When Luke comes, many years later, to write the story of the couple on the Emmaus road, the story is transformed for him and by him into a Eucharistic experience. The Emmaus road becomes the lectern, where scriptures are proclaimed and hearts burn, as Jesus opens the meaning of God's word. The simple table in a humble home in Emmaus becomes the Eucharistic table, where the Risen Jesus shares himself, and continues to share himself, with those who believe in him and love him.

How beautiful and how simple this description of the liturgy of the early church – and of what liturgy should have remained through the centuries and ought to be today. Just this: Christian hearts burning with love and joy as they listen again and again to the stories they share about Jesus; then the continually repeated miracle of recognizing his Presence in the simple sharing of a meal.

Over the centuries we have tended to overlay this simple, beautiful experience with elements which have sometimes obscured what we are really doing. Or – worse still – we have turned this experience into an obligation: and that obligation reduced simply to the duty of being present, without the need for burning hearts: for deep sharing with the Lord Jesus and with one another.

The intent of the liturgical renewal of Vatican II has been simply to restore the liturgy to what the *Constitution on the Liturgy* calls "a noble simplicity:" - the simplicity and deep humanness of the Emmaus liturgy described in today's Gospel. We have been called to take the Emmaus road: to come in worship more deeply and more consciously as a community.

We are a community only when we have a common memory. And our common memory is not just our remembrance of what has been handed down to us in the scriptures and in the traditions of the past. We have a common memory of the many stories of how the Risen Jesus is present and acting in our lives here and now. I know that "telling one's story" and "discovering where you are on the journey" are in-words today and can be used in a superficial way.

Yet the fact remains that the Good News of the Gospel is first and foremost "News," and news is narrative. It is story. We have to insert ourselves in our present existence into the "Jesus story" that is at the heart of the Good News. I remember years ago, when I was in Brazil, talking to a catechist and asking her if the Second Vatican Council has made any difference in her life.

"Oh, yes," she said: "I used to think that the Gospels were the story of Jesus. Now I have come to realize that they are my story too." Yes, we all have to insert ourselves into the "Jesus" story.

And it is the totality of our lives, not just a part of them, that we must insert into his story. But there is a special time at which we embed our life-story into the wondrous news of God acting in Jesus to bring us to salvation. And that is the time of liturgy, the time when we celebrate Eucharist.

Words are a powerful expression of our thinking and our attitudes. A change in thinking and in attitudes must necessarily be mirrored in the language we use. It is no longer an apt description of who we are and what we are doing on Sunday to talk about "going to Mass," as if it were a casual thing that we can do anywhere or in any place. Being community and becoming community ever more deeply, experiencing in Jesus our oneness with God and with one another, becoming more and more aware of that oneness, seeing that oneness expressed in the stories we share and in the eating and drinking we do together – all of these are involved in our Emmaus experience.

It's all about hearts burning. It's about eyes being opened to a presence. It's all about recognizing that Jesus is in our midst as we break bread together.

Community is not just a collection of isolated individuals who happen to live in the same place. True community is people who know and love one another and who keep struggling to know and love more profoundly. This kind of community is beyond our capabilities. It is always God's gift to us. It is in the context of such a divine gift of community and our recognition of its source that we are able to experience burning hearts and a shared meal. This is what liturgy is all about. It is that simple.

THE FOURTH SUNDAY OF EASTER

Acts 2:14a, 36-41
Psalm 23: 1-3a, 3b-4, 5, 6
1 Peter 2:20b-25
John 10: 1-10

Each year the 4th Sunday of Easter is Good Shepherd Sunday and we read a different portion of chapter 10 of John's Gospel. Today's reading is the first part of that chapter and, I dare say, the most difficult to understand and to speak about. It is about the Good Shepherd; yet the Good Shepherd is not mentioned.

One approach to today's Gospel is to reflect on the two terrains that are mentioned: one is the *sheepfold* in which the sheep are enclosed. This is the place of safety, of salvation, of rest and refreshment. Then, secondly, there is the *grazing land,* which is the place of danger, of risk, of seeking.

The sheepfold is an enclosure, often built alongside of a house. It has stout walls and only one door guarded by a gatekeeper. The enclosure has no cover, but the walls keep the sheep secure against the worst elements of the cold and also against attacks by robbers or animals.

In an ideal situation the sheep would graze near their sheepfold during the day and then be led into the sheepfold each night. But this ideal situation does not exist in Palestine, at least for much of the year. In

Israel during the dry season – from mid-April to mid-September – no rain falls.

The land near the sheepfold, on which the sheep graze, gets burnt by the hot sun and the pickings for food are sparse. Hence during the dry season, the sheep tend to wander far from their sheepfold in search of food. During this time the shepherd is constantly with his sheep: leading them to better pastures, sleeping with them, protecting them from predatory animals and from thieves. The life of the shepherd, especially at this time of the year, is one of great intimacy with his sheep.

Reflecting on these two kinds of terrain (the sheepfold and the grazing land) may help us to understand the two images John uses in today's Gospel to describe Jesus. First, there is the image of the door and, then, the image of the one who leads the sheep out to the grazing land and whose voice the sheep recognize.

Insofar as the sheep are thought of as being in the sheepfold, Jesus is the gate or the door. It is through him that the sheep enter into the safety and security of the sheepfold. But insofar as they are wandering in search of greener pastures over grazing land that is so often dry and brown, he is the one who leads the way.

As the door (or the gate), Jesus stands for the security and the safety and the salvation that we can find only in him. As he is the one who leads us, he helps us to see and to deal with the risks and dangers that beset us, as we wander through what is often a vale of tears and darkness, seeking God's green pastures, seeking His presence.

The sheepfold is the place of safety; the grazing land the place of danger. As the Door, he leads us into the one; as the Shepherd, he leads us through the other.

Thus, he is the Door we must go through to find our inner self. He is the Door to prayer, to contemplation, to being at ease in the presence of God. Through him we go to God. There is no other way. He is the Door.

But our lives are spent not only in the sheepfold. Indeed, most of the time we are in the grazing land of our world and our culture. So often it can be grazing land that is dry and barren. We look for love and we find that it is power that is prized. We seek peace through justice and fruitful dialogue and we find so many vainly committed to seeking peace through war and violence.

In a society that seems to care only for the strong and the powerful, Jesus leads us and teaches us the value of lowliness and poverty. In a world that seems to know only one way of dealing with violence, Jesus teaches us the efficacy of a nonviolent way of life.

He leads us as we seek for the good that is in our society. He invites us to learn the values of the gospel and to incarnate them into the structures and social systems that so deeply affect the lives of people. He calls us to build a new society in holiness and truth and justice.

It is only in John's Gospel that Jesus is called the Good Shepherd. But John's image has been so powerful that it has become normative for our understanding of the shepherd images in the other Gospels.

Thus the Synoptic Gospels have a parable that tells about a shepherd who leaves ninety-nine sheep to seek the one stray; and then calls all to rejoice that he has saved this one stray sheep. This parable was not intended to apply to Jesus, but to God. It was intended to describe what has been movingly called the "soteriological joy of God"— which means his love which takes such infinite joy in saving us.

In our thinking about Jesus, this "soteriological joy" of God has been assumed into John's image of the Good Shepherd. The Good Shepherd is the one who leaves the ninety-nine to seek the lost sheep. The Good Shepherd shares in the "soteriological joy" of God.

If the Synoptic parable emphasizes the joy of being brought safely back into the sheepfold, the Johannine Shepherd has an intimacy with His sheep that simply is not a part of the Synoptic parable.

We might put it this way. In the Synoptic parable there is a one-way relationship: the shepherd reaching out in love to His sheep; and it is a beautiful and moving picture. But the sheep of the Synoptics seem to be sheep such as we might think of sheep today, as rather stupid beings, unable to do much of anything for themselves. In the Johannine image, however, the picture is very different.

The sheep of John's Gospel are not stupid. Between them and the Good Shepherd, there is a relationship of reciprocity, and mutuality, an experience of intimacy. They know their Shepherd's voice. They listen and by choice they follow him. This relationship of intimacy and reciprocity means that the shepherd respects the freedom of the sheep. They go in and out. They are allowed to go where they choose and as they choose. For the shepherd gives abundant life to his sheep. Indeed, as we reflect on this gospel, we cease to see them simply as sheep. Instead they become all of us. Free human beings enabled and empowered by our Good Shepherd.

More and more authority in the Church must model their relationship with the laity in terms of the shepherd image found in John's Gospel rather than in the Synoptics. They must see the members of the church not as submissive people always wanting to be told what to think and what to do, but rather as free people of God, whom they must call to mutuality and cooperative sharing in the life of the Church.

Bishop Pedro Casaldaliga, a retired Brazilian bishop much loved by our sisters in Brazil, once wrote a pastoral letter to his diocese entitled "The Wind Continues." In it he calls for a new model for the ministry: one shaped by the heart of Christ and sensitive to the cries of the poor, the suffering, the helpless. It must be divested of the trappings of power. It must be collegial and decentralized in its functioning. It must be truly catholic and that means dedicated to ecumenism, inter-religious dialogue, as well as cultural and ministerial pluralism. And all must be at the service of peace, justice and life.

He concluded his pastoral letter with words of a letter Van Gogh wrote to his brother Theo: "We have seen many windmills fall, both in society and in the Church, yet we continue to proclaim, in hope and commitment, that 'The wind continues.'" The Wind. The Holy Wind. The Holy Spirit.

THE FIFTH SUNDAY OF EASTER

Acts 6:1-7
Psalm 33: 1-2, 4-5, 18-19
1 Peter 2: 4-9
John 14: 1-12

We might say that the readings for today reveal the early Church, struggling with a perennial problem, namely: what does it mean to be Church? In age after age issues arise that have never been faced before: at least never been faced in the form they take at a particular time. The reading from Acts raises a problem that very much concerns us today: namely, the problem of inequalities in the Church. The particular instance of that problem which emerges in our first reading was this: the Greek speaking Christians were upset because they felt that their widows were not receiving the same treatment as the widows of those who spoke Hebrew. A kind of Social Security problem, we might describe it today.

Strange, isn't it that there should be discrimination in an institution dedicated to overcoming discrimination? But honesty forces us to say that it was there from the very beginning.

There was a second problem that surfaced at the same time: a problem that has strikingly contemporary overtones. The problem was a shortage of ministers. The Apostles took bold and hitherto unchartered steps to resolve both these problems.

This reading from Acts witnesses to the human imperfections we must never be surprised to find in the Church. But it also witnesses to the fact that the Church operates at her best when she solves the problems that arise by a process of growth. In this instance the growth that takes place is a development in the structure of the Church. A new ministry is born: the deaconate.

History also makes clear that this growth element is evident, not only in the coming into being of the deaconate, but also in the rapid evolution of that ministry. Initially deacons were appointed to meet a particular need: taking care of the proper food distribution for the widows in the community. But very soon we see them going way beyond the limits of their original appointment. They become not just minister to the widows. It soon happens that they are out preaching the Gospel.

This episode is a good example —and there are many throughout history — of how solutions to particular problems can set in motion developments that move the Church in new and unexpected directions, as the Church tries to respond to the human needs of the community — in the light of the Gospel.

This principle of growth and evolution, existentially described in our first reading is given a theological articulation in the second reading — in which the Epistle of Peter offers a superb description of what it means to be the church community. There is a rich ecclesiology in his words: You are "living stones" to be built into a "spiritual house."

At first hearing the image may strike one as curious. Stones by their very nature are inert, lifeless. How is it possible to speak of living stones? The text is not intended to evoke an image of stones suddenly becoming alive, as singing, dancing, speaking stones. Rather "living stones" point to a mystery at the very heart of the reality we call "church." The mystery is the paradox of an unchanging reality that is continually undergoing change.

The Church must have the fluidity we associate with life. This means that it has to be open to change — and at times drastic, painful change. At the same time, it must have stability, such as we would associate with stone. The Church has to be in touch with the Word of God that is Jesus Christ, who is the way, the truth and the life. If it were unfaithful to God's holy Word, it would cease to be Christian. At the same time, it must be in intimate touch with the living experience of the people of God. Were it to lose touch with the lives of people, it would cease to be relevant.

What I am suggesting is that there must be in the Church a creative tension between the Word of God as it has come down to us from past generations and that same Word of God as it comes in touch with what is going on in the lives of people in the here and now. The Word of God is inexhaustible. No one age ever understands fully the Word of God. New events, changes in circumstances, may move us to see the Word of God in a new light. Seeing the Church's teaching from a new viewpoint may give us a new and deeper understanding of what God wills for us here and now.

It is my conviction that today we are in a position where we need to reflect anew that the Church is made up of LIVING stones. What is happening in the life of the Church today calls for drastic change. The terrible pedophilia problems have been a frightful scourge for the Church. It has been a time of betrayal. At a time when lives have been irrevocably hurt, we as Church need to do all we can to alleviate or lessen that hurt. It has been a time of unpardonable secrecy and cover-up. The slogan "The Good of the Church" has been evoked to hide actions that were sinful and criminal. All this has finally forced a new openness on the part of Church authority.

What is more significant than the openness on the part of church leaders is the opening up of new roles for the laity in the Church. It is not so much that authority is giving new roles to the laity; rather, that they are assuming them. As someone has said: "The laity are no longer traumatized, they are galvanized." They know that the clerical culture of privilege and deference — that goes way back to Constantine and the 4th century — is dead. For the future priests will have to achieve respect the old fashioned way: they will have to earn it.

Some of the questions that remain unanswered: Will people be energized enough to "take back the Church"?

Will they demand a much greater role in decision-making? Will they insist on their right — a right guaranteed in canon law — to have the Eucharist? Will they demand that there be a much wider pool of candidates eligible for priesthood? Will they insist on being heard because of the "bill of rights" that comes to them with their baptism?

The hierarchy of the Church has responded with significant — though belated — action on the problem of sexual abuse. Their belated response to this issue highlighted — to a great extent-their lack of connection between the bishops and the people of the Church. We can only hope for a greater connectedness on these and other pressing issues that divide the Church. And it is going to be a new Church — a Church in which the silent laity of the past will find their voice.

How can we get the voice of God's people heard in the church? One of the things I think needs to happen is a change in attitude on the part of the magisterium, most particularly the Roman Magisterium. They must move away from the position that they are expected to have all the answers to an attitude of listening to public opinion in the church.

In 1959 (before the Council was convened) Karl Rahner wrote that church leaders need human help as well as divine. In his book *Free Speech in the Church* he says:

> *Public opinion is one of the means whereby
> the Church's official leaders, who need*

human help as well as divine, get to know something about the actual situation within which and taking account of which, they are to lead and guide the people. They need to know how people are thinking and feeling...what their problems are, what they find difficult...where they find the traditional answers or rulings insufficient, what they would like to see changed...and so on.

This of course will make unaccustomed demands on church leaders, in the way of patience and a greater openness to dialogue. It will also call them to an admission of a certain degree of uncertainty on some issues and a willingness to wait for time and dialogue to bring greater clarity.

It will mean that church teaching and policy will be less assured that it always has the right position. This will call for a greater flexibility and a more hospitable openness to change than has been true in the past. This will enable God's people to become "living stones."

THE SIXTH SUNDAY OF EASTER

Acts 8: 5-8, 14-17
Psalm 66:1-3, 4-5, 6-7, 16, 20
1 Peter 3:15-18
John 14: 15-21

The Church has surely fallen on unhappy times. The media frenzy about the terrible scourge of sexual abuse in the Church makes one hesitant to pick up the morning paper, fearful of what new allegations will be revealed. We grieve especially for the victims, people who have suffered from abuse by priests — people whose lives have been damaged irreparably. They must be our chief concern. Also we have to grieve with the communities that have suddenly discovered that the unquestioning trust they once placed in priests has been shattered. But we — or at least I – can't help grieving about the priests too. Many of them did many good and wonderful things as priests, though the evil they did make it impossible for them to continue functioning as priests. But they were colleagues and it still hurts.

But the Church has fallen on evil times in other ways too. Excitement has gone out of the life of the Church: the excitement we experienced with Vatican II, the excitement of our diocesan synod in the 1980s. The steps being taken to recentralize the Church have taken a lot of the joy out of the Church for those who really love the Church and believe it is their Church. And it feels almost as if it is being taken away from them.

It is against this rather bleak picture that I want to reflect on today's readings. Both the reading from Acts and the Gospel tell us about the reality we call Church. The first reading — from Acts—presents a model of Church that is all too familiar to us: a Church hierarchically structured from the top. Notice how the work of Philip the deacon has to be authenticated by the mother church in Jerusalem. True, the Jerusalem church is not upset when it hears of the wonders worked by Philip in Samaria. Yet they feel the need to investigate. Note how the reading seems to imply that the Spirit came to Samaria only with the coming of Peter and John. We are told that the people in Samaria had only been baptized. They had not yet received the Holy Spirit.

Now, theologically to say that they were baptized but had not yet received the Holy Spirit makes no sense whatsoever. From the earliest days of the church even till now, Baptism has always meant the receiving of the Holy Spirit. So what in the world is the author of Acts trying to tell us? Certainly not about another sacrament distinct from Baptism, called Confirmation. This distinction came only centuries later. Nor is the author talking about a second Baptism beyond Baptism with water.

The author's intent is quite simple. He wants to make clear that the spread of Christian Faith is ordered, not haphazard. For this reason, at every new stage of growth – and the spread of the faith to Samaria was indeed a new stage – what happens must be authenticated by an official representative of the church. Hence the author of Acts presents Peter and John going to Samaria for this purpose and he presents it as if the action of the Holy Spirit were held up, till they arrive though clearly that action had already occurred as a result of the preaching of Philip.

This model of the church – the institutional model, if you will, wherein the action of the Spirit is recognized through the action of Church leaders – has been with us a long time, indeed from the very beginning. People, therefore, who want to accept the Church, but not the "institutional Church," are opting for an impossibility. There is no Church other than the institutional Church.

But, when we say this we have to hasten to add that this is by no means the whole story. We cannot rest content with the "institutional model" only. We cannot restrict the action of the Holy Spirit to what its leaders do or say. There are other insights into the reality of church that equally existed from the very beginning. One of these insights is in today's Gospel. It may be called the "Paraclete model" of the Church.

The Greek word "Paraclete" means literally "being called to the side of someone." And generally called to their side to help them, to intercede for them, to plead their case. Jesus was, for his followers, the first Paraclete: he was at the side of all to lead, to feed, to plead, to comfort, to save. Now Jesus tells his disciples that he will send another "Paraclete," another helper who will be at the side of all Jesus' followers as the One through whom Jesus will remain with his own. Jesus is with all of us, not just with our leaders. He is with us through the Spirit, the Paraclete who, he assures us, will be with all of us always.

These two models of the Church — (1) the one in which the Spirit operates in the Church's leadership and (2) the other in which the Spirit operates in all the disciples of Jesus – are certainly different ways of understanding Church. But they are not mutually exclusive. They are meant to be complementary. The leadership model assures us that there is someone, first in the local Church (the bishop), then among all the local bishops (the bishop of Rome) who, after all the dialogue has taken place, is able finally to say in the name of all: "This is the faith of the Church. This is what we believe." Unless we are content to see the church as a kind of endless debating society, where nothing is ever definite, we very much need this kind of leadership.

On the other hand, the "Paraclete" model, in which the Spirit operates in all the members, helps to insure a vitality, a creativity, a flexibility, as the Spirit operates among many people to deepen our understanding of who Jesus is and who we are as his disciples.

For the good of the Church we need both models. The complementarity of the two models works most smoothly, when there is deep mutual respect between leaders and members, when one is not seen as a threat to the other.

Such mutuality is not easy to achieve and we seem to be living at a time when the marriage of the two appears almost as if on the verge of divorce. A true mutuality can only be reached, when there is willingness on both sides to listen. This means a listening, not just to human voices, but also for the intimations of the presence of the Holy Spirit, the Paraclete.

The Church can move out of its troubled waters today only if a context of mutual respect and sincere and willing dialogue is allowed to prevail. The laity of the Church must find their voice and demand that dialogue. Then we will understand the statement in the book of Revelation, where we read this admonition: "Let those who can hear, listen to what the Spirit is saying to the churches."

THE ASCENSION OF THE LORD

Acts 1:1-22
Psalm 47: 2-3, 6-7, 8-9
Ephesians 1: 17-23
Matthew 28: 16-20

Karl Rahner calls this the feast of "Holy Pain."

If we are to understand this feast, we have to demythologize the language we use to describe the mystery it celebrates. When we profess our faith that Jesus "ascended into heaven and sits at the right hand of God," we have to understand that we are in the realm of imagery, not literal description. Thus, the Ascension does not mean that Jesus made a space trip or that he accomplished a geographical feat of "going up" or "going out" from planet earth. Nor are we to think quite literally of an actual chair being placed next to God for Jesus to sit on.

The intent of all this imagery is to make clear that the earthly life of Jesus which he lived in mortal fashion (as we all do) had come to an end. That earthly, mortal life – in which he was limited by time and space – was over – forever.

The Ascension is Easter revisited. It is part of the fullness of the Easter event. For it means, in a more positive sense, that Jesus has been glorified in his humanity. It is worth remembering that for the author of the Fourth Gospel,

Ascension took place on Easter. Recall Jesus' words to Mary Magdalene on Easter: "Go and tell my disciples that I am ascending to my Father and your Father, to my God and your God." For the Fourth Gospel, therefore, the glorification of Jesus' humanity – which is the Ascension – happened on Easter. It is part of the one Paschal Mystery.

Luke in his writings spreads the Paschal Mystery over a period of time. Thus, he has the Ascension occurring 40 days after Easter. Spreading out the mystery in this fashion is a way of helping us to let the mystery sink in and penetrate us. It enables us to experience the mystery more fully. But we must never forget that the justification for thus spreading out the mystery is our inability to grasp it in its entirety. But Ascension does indeed belong to the one indivisible Paschal Mystery.

What does the feast mean? What does it mean to say that the humanity of Jesus is glorified? For starters, *the glorification of Jesus means that for the first time humanity realized fully what humanity can become.* For the first time a humanity realized the capacity for divinity that belongs to every human being.

Karl Rahner has defined the human being as an openness to the Transcendent. The Ascension means that, since the humanity of Jesus was fully taken into God, that openness to the Transcendent, that capacity for divinity which defines the human being, has been fully actualized in Jesus.

Thus, Jesus becomes the prototype of what is to happen to us. This is what St. Paul is talking about when he says that "Christ is the first-born of many brothers [and sisters]."

Yes, the glorification of Jesus' humanity reveals in all their glory the divine possibilities that belong to our humanness. What happened to Jesus' humanity is a *paradigm* of what will happen to ours. Jesus was glorified in his total humanity. So shall we be. We are not Platonists. We believe that we shall be glorified, not as just souls, but as bodily persons. We shall be lifted up to God as bodily persons. That is why Karl Rahner called the Ascension "the festival of the future of the world." (*Theological Invest.*#7, p, 182) We Christians, he says, are the most sublime of materialists. For we believe that as Jesus was taken bodily into God, so shall we be. *Jesus exalted, therefore, is our Future, present in the world.* The Ascension is thus the feast of our hope. It is our firm belief that we share in a wondrous victory, which we did not win, but which was won for us. Through the Spirit of Jesus we are one with Him. This means we already possess, if only inchoatively, eternal life. This is our joy: that we have already begun to share his glory.

Karl Rahner has also called Ascension Day *the feast of holy pain*. For the immediate disciples of Jesus it was a painful experience, yet it was holy pain, for they came to realize that Jesus was leaving them only to be present to them in another way. This of course prepares us for the feast of Pentecost – the feast that tells the new way in which Jesus is present to us, namely, through the Holy Spirit.

THE SEVENTH SUNDAY OF EASTER

Acts 1:12-14
Psalm 27:1, 4, 7-8
1 Peter 4: 13-16
John 17:1-11

This is the Advent Sunday of the Easter season. For the readings call us to prepare for a coming. The coming of course is the coming of the Holy Spirit whom Jesus had promised to send. The sense of waiting and expectation so evident in today's readings mirrors the same paradox we experience during the time of Advent. In Advent we look forward to the coming of the Lord who yet is already present among us. On this Sunday we await the coming of the Holy Spirit who is already among us.

This is a paradox, but not a contradiction. For to await the coming of the Spirit who is already with us is to look forward to such a deep experience of his presence that it will seem as if the Spirit were coming for the first time. I suppose we might say that our feelings today are somewhat like the feelings of an expectant mother waiting for her child to be born. She experiences the child before it is born; but it is a whole new experience of that child's presence when the child comes to birth. We are continually being born again of the Holy Spirit, as the Spirit takes possession of more and more of our lives.

The Spirit of God is always present and acting in our lives. Our deepest spiritual problem is that we are so often unaware of that Presence and Activity within us. Liturgically then, this Sunday may be perceived as a day of awakening to a more profound realization of the presence of Jesus' Spirit in our lives.

The readings are most appropriate to this way of understanding today's liturgy. They are all about prayer. The first reading, from Acts, is about the prayer of the disciples with Mary in the upper room; the Gospel is about the prayer of Jesus to His Father. We are not told, in the reading from Acts, how the disciples prayed. We are simply informed that they devoted themselves to constant prayer. We can assume that they chanted the psalms. And probably they spent time in quiet and silence. But whatever we may surmise their prayer to be, it surely must have been suffused with an air of expectancy. For Jesus had told them to wait for a number of things: the coming of another Paraclete (how they must have wondered what He meant by that); and also the doing of things even greater than he had done. They surely did not understand what all this meant. Their very sense of bewildered wonderment only heightened the atmosphere of expectant waiting that hung over the upper room.

We are told more explicitly about Jesus' prayer. For the Gospel presents us with Jesus' words to the Father. And if we say that the disciples' prayer was one of expectation, this prayer of Jesus before he went to his death was one of total awareness. He was aware of the mission he had carried out. He was aware of the glory that waited Him. He was aware of the disciples and their needs. He was aware of our needs. He prayed for them and for us. So, we may well think of this Sunday as "Prayer Sunday" – and this could well move us to reflect on our own prayer experience.

Our prayer needs to be touched with a sense of expectation. God calls us, but so often we do not know what it may be that he will call us to. Our prayer must, therefore, include a readiness to be surprised by God, an openness and a willingness to walk untrodden paths. This is especially necessary in a period of tension and transition in the life of the Church, such as we are experiencing today in an unprecedented way.

Above all else I believe, our prayer should mean awareness: awareness of who God is and who we are, an awareness of people and of the needs of the world in which we live. This kind of awareness points to unity, communion. For the whole point of striving to seek awareness in prayer is to overcome the illusion of separateness and division which is part of our fallen state and which distorts reality.

We tend to be victims of what I have called "spiritual apartheid" that sees God and His creation in separateness instead of in unity and communion. Thus we see things in fragmentation and division. But this is only the way things appear on the surface. At the deepest level of reality all things are united in God who is the Hidden Ground of Love of all reality. The point of prayer (especially wordless prayer) is to make us aware of all this: to enable us to experience this Ground of Love in whom we exist and in whom all things find their identity, uniqueness and interrelatedness.

Prayer gives me a vision of reality that cannot be grasped when I live only on the surface of life.

Once I experience God as the ground of my being, I also experience in God my sisters and brothers. And this experience gives a whole new meaning to Jesus' words that we must love our neighbor as ourselves. I come to realize what this commandment means. It is not an "as if" command. It does not mean love your neighbor as if your neighbor were yourself; rather it means love your neighbor because your neighbor is in very truth your other self. We are all one in God. Yet it is not enough to say this. We have to experience it. We have to become aware.

When we do achieve such awareness, we begin to understand the meaning of the eternal life which the Fourth Gospel speaks of so often. It is not "after-life," but a brand new quality in the life we live now. It is the kind of life we live when we come to realize that God is the Ground of Love in whom we are. This is what the Fourth Gospel means when it says that "eternal life is to know God." It is also, it says, to "know Jesus Christ whom God has sent." To know God and to know Jesus whom God has sent is to know all human beings in their unity: not in separateness, but in communion. To know God and Jesus is to know that here and now and at every moment we all belong to God and we all belong to Jesus. Jesus is in the

Father and the Father is in Jesus. Jesus is in us and in him we are in God.

Both of the readings talk of unity: the reading from Acts of the union of the disciples with one another and with Mary; the Gospel, the unity of God and Jesus and the disciples. We need continually to remind ourselves that this unity, this communion, is really there. For all too often we don't see it: we see separateness and division among people. We need to reach a deeper level of perception to see our communion with one another, to see what is truest about us. It is the failure to reach this level of perception that can cause the violence, the terrorism, the unhealthy relationships that can cloud family life, community life, the life of nations and of the whole global community.

Prayer helps us to achieve this perception. For prayer means moving from where we are: namely, in God – to an *awareness* of where we are, namely, in God. It is this kind of awareness that can change lives and communities and cultures. *It is a life lived on the inside and not just on the outside.* True prayer is moving from a life that is purely exterior to a true interior life. Prayer calls us to the inner experience that ultimately dominates our whole lives. The German poet Rainer Maria Rilke warns us of the shallowness of a life that is "always looking out, never looking in."

PENTECOST SUNDAY

Acts 2:1-11
Psalm 104: 1, 24, 29-30, 31, 34
1 Corinthians 12: 3b-7, 12-13
John 20:19-23

Today's wonderful feast, Pentecost, celebrates God's gift to us of God's oneness with humanity. Let me put it this way: At Christmas God became human. At Pentecost, which is the climax of the Easter event, God became humanity. At Christmas God took a body from Mary. At Easter- Pentecost God took a body from humanity, from us. That is what Paul is telling us in our second reading, when he says: "We who are many are one body." Or, as he writes even more explicitly later in the same epistle: "Now you are the body of Christ."

The readings of today's liturgy celebrate the breaking down of the barriers that prevent us from being true community. To grow in community means removing the *language barrier* that prevents people from communicating with one another. To grow in community means to break down the *time barrier* that prevents one generation from speaking meaningfully with another. To grow in community means to remove the barriers of our own emotional insecurities: our self-centeredness; our fear of ourselves (being afraid to be ourselves before others); our fear of other people (afraid to let them be themselves before us): all those things in us that make us want community to serve us instead of placing ourselves at the service of community.

In a word: building community means breaking down the threefold barrier: of language, of time, of sinfulness.

The first reading describes the Pentecost event and sees it *as the removal of the language barrier* that prevents people from understanding one another. That is the meaning of many different people from different places hearing the Gospel and hearing it proclaimed in a language they can understand. Pentecost is thus a reversal of the story of the tower of Babel in Genesis. People try to build a tower that will reach heaven; instead they actually construct walls that prevent them from communicating with one another.

From Pentecost on, the story of human community has been the story of men and women vacillating between Babel and Pentecost; between erecting barriers and building bridges. The Pentecost liturgy reminds us that our great task today is to build bridges of dialogue, bridges of shared reflection on what it means to be disciples of Jesus in today's world, bridges that encourage the expression of differences as a way to come to a common vision that we can all accept and live.

In the second reading Paul tells us that "No one can say 'Jesus is Lord' except in the Holy Spirit." In other words, you and I, some twenty centuries removed from Jesus' earthly life, can say today that "Jesus is Lord" because we have the Holy Spirit given to us. What this means is that *Pentecost removes not only the language barrier, but also the time barrier that would otherwise separate us from the Lord Jesus.* For Pentecost means that Christ who seems to have left this world, actually returned. He returned to live in our midst, to be with us. He is with us in a different way, but just as truly with us – through His Spirit given to us.

We need to be clear as to what this means. We must not think of the Spirit as a substitute for Jesus, as if to make up for Jesus' no longer being with us. On the contrary, Jesus sends his Spirit, not to compensate for his absence, but to ensure his presence. Pentecost, therefore, breaks the time barrier that would seem to separate us from the Jesus of his time. The Resurrection, which marks the end of Jesus' mortal life, is the beginning of Jesus' being with us in a new way: namely, through the Spirit whom he will send upon us. In the days of his mortality, Jesus was present in limited time and space; now through the Spirit, Jesus is with us always and everywhere.

It is, therefore, theologically incorrect to see the Eucharist as the way in which the Risen Jesus remains present among us. No, he is with us always through the Spirit whom he has sent.

The Spirit is Jesus' alter-ego. He is, so to speak, Jesus *redivivus*, Jesus reborn. Indeed, as the Eucharistic prayers of the Mass say, we call on God to send the Spirit for two purposes: (1) to overshadow the gifts and transform them

189

into the sacramental presence of Jesus. But (2) we also ask God to send the Spirit on us that we may be transformed into the living Body of Christ on earth. It's all the work of the Spirit.

The Gospel reading tells us that the Spirit of Jesus comes to us as the peacemaker. He brings peace because he brings forgiveness for the sins that divide us. For, let's face it, at the deepest level, the greatest obstacle to community is sinfulness, our own sinfulness that we must acknowledge, but also the systemic sinfulness that can infect an institution.

On this feast of the breaking down of barriers, our Eucharistic celebration should be a thoughtful act of repentance for any barriers we have allowed in our lives to separate us from God or from one another. It should also be a thoughtful act of gratitude for the many ways in which we have been able to grow in our openness to God and to one another. It should be a happy rejoicing in the barriers we have seen others break down and the barriers we have succeeded in breaking down ourselves.

The most obvious obstacle preventing us from achieving the peace God wants us to achieve is — it seems to me — a sense of arrogance: an arrogance that refuses to be wrong, an arrogance that insists that there is only one way of seeing the truth, an arrogance that is unwilling to learn from those who disagree, and – even worse – an arrogance that forbids the right to disagree. Such a mentality existed in the Church over a hundred years ago. In 1907,

Modernism was condemned. Modernism was an attempt to come to terms with the secular and scientific culture of the Western world. The modernists were not always right, nor were they always wrong. But there was no room for them in the Church. The Modernist test effectively destroyed careers and ended any serious consideration of new ideas for more than a generation. George Tyrrell was excommunicated in 1907. His friend, Maude Petrie, said: "Rome lauds those who agree with her because they don't care; she punishes those who disagree with her because they care." Modernism remained a scare in the Church for more than a generation. Every one of us priests was obliged to take an oath against modernism before we could be ordained. That oath was abolished only in 1967 after the Second Vatican Council.

Above all, on this glorious feast of Pentecost I want to be hopeful. At the same time, I want to point out that Pentecost is about the Holy Spirit descending, not just on the twelve apostles, but upon all the 120 people who comprised the earliest community of disciples of Jesus. The feast of Pentecost is, therefore, a reminder to us that the Holy Spirit speaks not only to church leaders, but also to all the faithful. This is the true meaning of Pentecost. It is also the clear teaching of the Second Vatican Council. The Holy Spirit works in the Church, not to separate bishops and people, but to unite them in true, humble Christian community.

Yet we cannot ignore the fact that there are issues that we must face as a Church. And that some of them have been taken off the table without adequate discussion in the whole Church. There is danger of retreating into an intellectual ghetto. We must be concerned about a hierarchy that is in danger of losing contact with ordinary people. Honest dialogue is a necessary element of a true sense of community in the Church. We have every right to ask for it; even demand it.

Dare to be Church for the Church and the world.

TRINITY SUNDAY

Exodus 34:4b-6, 8-9
Daniel 3:52, 53, 54, 55
2 Corinthians 13: 11-13
John 3: 16-18

This is an odd day liturgically. It's a feast that should not be. Liturgy is supposed to be about events in salvation history, about ways in which God intervened in human history to bring us to salvation. But today's feast is not about events. It's about God. More than that, it is about the inner life of God: something that is totally beyond our comprehension. Can't you see how very discouraging a day this is for a homilist? Then there is that warning of Meister Eckhart: "One who speaks about the Trinity lies." So I am asking you not to expect too much from me today.

One thing I can do is look at the history of the feast. It was celebrated for the first time in France at the beginning of the second millennium. Alexander II who was pope at the time refused to celebrate it in Rome. He reasoned there should be no particular day devoted to a feast of the Blessed Trinity, any more than there should be a feast of the Blessed Unity, and actually if we were to follow the religious roots out of which the doctrine emerged, it would make more sense to celebrate a feast of the Blessed Unity. Pope Alexander II went on to say that every liturgy celebrates the Unity and Trinity of God. Hence there should be no special feast. Still, the feast continued to spread and finally it was put into the universal calendar in 1334. Thus the feast has been a part of the church calendar for only about the last third of the Church's history.

We must remember too that it took four centuries of the Church's history before the Church arrived at what it considered an adequate statement of the doctrine of the Trinity. When we read the Gospel and hear Jesus refer to the Father and to himself as Son and to the Holy Spirit, we are inclined to say: "Oh, yes, Jesus is talking about the Trinity." To say this, however, is to project onto Jesus' words a development in Christian thought. We must remember that Jesus spoke out of a background of Judaism which professed a strong and uncompromising monotheism. When Christian Faith first encountered the Gentile world, it came in contact with the polytheistic religions of the Greco-Roman world. The earliest Christian writers, therefore, were intent on defending the oneness of God, the Holy Unity, against the plurality of gods that existed in the pagan world.

In this defense of the belief that God is One, Christian Faith was conscious of its indebtedness to Judaism. At the same time the followers of Jesus were conscious of a distinctively Christian affirmation of some kind of pluralism in the One God. The problem the Church grappled with in the first four centuries of her existence was: How can there be otherness in God (namely, Father, Son, Spirit) without there being plurality in God, namely, three Gods? The result of the Church's reflection came in the doctrine of the Trinity developed in the 4th century Councils of Nicea and Constantinople (the first two ecumenical councils).

What can we say about the doctrine? The first thing we have to say is that when we speak about the Trinity, we are not talking about the inner life of God. The inner life of God is something we simply cannot comprehend. When we talk about the Trinity, we are talking about the ways in which God relates to us, about the ways in which God is present in the world.

There is in the Hebrew scriptures some sense of "otherness" in God. The book of Proverbs speaks eloquently about God's Wisdom and how she is involved in the creation of the world. Wisdom is described as an extension of God in the world, a power that is other than God, yet not other, at God's side as God's craftsman, delighting in God, playing before God, yet delighting also in people.

Perhaps we can kind of back into a discussion of what the Trinity means by reflecting on the exaggerated sense of individualism and personal autonomy that seems to define our society today. The ACLU, for instance, stridently condemns practically anything that puts a curb on personal freedom. In our society our precious individuality must be defended at all costs. My rights, my needs, my possessions, my fulfillment, my interests -- these seem to be the paramount values.

So in our society of consumerism and hi-tech, it's always "others" who are the problem. They impinge on our rights, on our desires, on our needs. They want their way. Their freedom intrudes on mine. This nagging interference of others constantly challenges our autonomy. In fact, it was this intrusion of others into our lives that led Jean Paul Sartre to conclude that today, to understand hell, we don't need to think of fire and fiendish devils with pitch-forks. No, he says: "Hell is simply other people." Otherness is the enemy.

The message of Trinity Sunday is just the opposite: "Heaven is other people." Eternal life thrives on otherness. Otherness is in God. Otherness brought the universe into being. Sophia-Wisdom expresses the "otherness" in God. Holy Wisdom is with God as the world is created. "When the Lord established the heavens, I was there." What the book of Proverbs is saying to us is that in the beginning there was otherness of persons. In the beginning, before the world came to exist, there was community, divine community. There was divine delight in the other. In the beginning there was the relation of three persons: Father, Son, Holy Spirit. Otherness belongs to the very being of God. There is otherness in God's oneness. There is community, mutuality in God. Heaven is sharing in that mutuality. Heaven, therefore, is others. It's community. It's entering into the otherness of God.

Heaven is the place of perfect contemplation. But there is something incomplete about contemplation if it is not shared. That is why heaven, where the ultimate perfection of contemplation will be achieved, will not be a place of separate individuals each with his or her private vision of God; rather it will be a sea of love flowing through the Oneness of all the saints: a Oneness that guarantees the uniqueness of each. The sea of love, in which we find our oneness with all, is the life of the three persons of God, totally one in what they are, wonderfully unique in who they are. In God there is no selfishness or isolation, only a selflessness overflowing and super-abounding in joy in the perfection of their gift, --their gift of their One life to One Another.

I must conclude this homily, as I began it, by repeating the warning that Meister Eckhart gives to any congregation of the faithful who listen to a homilist who has the presumption to give a homily on the Trinity. His warning was: "One who speaks about the Trinity lies."

THE BODY AND BLOOD OF CHRIST

Deuteronomy 8:2-3, 14b-16a
Psalm 147: 12-13, 14-15, 19-20
1 Corinthians 10:16-17
John 6: 51-58

One of the liturgical hymns in the mid-sixties was the song called "Sons of God." Ignoring the exclusive language, even its bad music, we have to say that its real problem was its theology. "Gather round the table of the Lord. Eat his Body. Drink His Blood and we'll sing a song of love."

Suppose you were to meet someone who had never heard a thing about Christianity and she asked you: what is the central act of our religion? Suppose you said, as that song did: "The central act of our faith is our gathering round a table where we eat the body and drink the blood of our founder." Her mildest reaction might be: "You really do that? You really eat somebody's body? How can you do that? Frankly it sounds so gross."

How would you react? Well, I suppose you might say: "Look, it isn't what you think it is. It isn't even what it sounds like. We eat Christ's Body and drink His Blood sacramentally." I'm not sure the person would understand. You might have to give them a quick course in sacramental theology. Maybe in the course of your explanation you might point out that "sacrament" is the English equivalent of the Greek "mysterion" or "mystery."

That is really where we ought to begin our reflection on the Eucharist: with the realization that it is mystery: the mystery of the continuous presence of the Lord Jesus among us as the source of life for us, as the One whose Spirit sustains us on our pilgrimage through life, as the One who draws us into the very life of God.

What I have just said expresses something of what the mystery is. But the very statements I have made are simply part of the mystery. A mystery is a reality about which we can say a lot of things, but we can never say all of it. In fact, it would probably be better to say: we can never say most of it. After we have said all we can about mystery, we have to be honest and admit that by comparison with the depth of the mystery, we have said practically nothing. In the long run we have to live with mystery with the realization that we do not really grasp mystery; rather we are grasped by mystery.

The seventh volume of Merton's journals has an intriguing title: "The Other Side of the Mountain." The title comes from Merton's words describing his view of Mt. Kanchenjunga in Nepal. He writes: "There is another side of Kanchenjunga and of every mountain -- the side that has never been photographed and turned into postcards. This is the only side worth seeing." The Eucharist is mystery. The deepest elements of it simply escape our words.

A mystery is like a huge many-sided diamond. You have to keep turning the diamond around to see its full beauty. When we speak about mystery of the Eucharist, we see different aspects and we use different sets of words to express these different aspects. But no matter how many different sets of words we use, they can never embrace the mystery in its totality. There is still the other side of the mountain. Let me speak of three different ways of talking about the Eucharist: (I) as meal, (2) as sacrifice, and (3) as Reserved Sacrament.

The primary way of thinking of the Eucharist is to see it as a meal. Our second reading and the Gospel stress this aspect of the Eucharist. The reading from Corinthians is about the supper Jesus shared with his chosen ones, as his earthly life was drawing to a close. The Gospel is about another meal that Jesus shares with everybody. In both cases Jesus shares food, life, sustenance with those he loved. He presides at a community meal.

Since Jesus has returned to God, it is the Spirit that makes him present in the midst of the community. That is why in the Eucharistic Prayer the Spirit is invoked twice: once to change the bread and wine into Christ; the other to transform people into the Body of Christ. The Spirit makes Christ present on the altar and around the altar. He is made present on the altar to feed, to strengthen, to sustain, to give life to his Body that is around the altar. This is the meaning of the words of our second reading wherein Jesus says: "This is my Body which is for you."

This I believe is the primary way of thinking about the mystery of the Eucharist. But there are other aspects. The Eucharist is also a sacrifice. Just as today the meal aspect of the Eucharist is being emphasized, so there was a time when the sacrificial aspect of the mystery seemed most important. And it is an element of the mystery that we must never overlook. It is important to see the Eucharist as a sacrifice. It is equally important to understand what that means. The Eucharist does indeed make present for us the sacrifice that Jesus made on Calvary.

But when we speak of the Eucharist as sacrifice, we must be careful not to get caught up in any effort to link Jesus' sacrifice too closely with the bloody sacrifices that are so prominent in the Hebrew scriptures. Jesus' true sacrifice was his total and unconditional submission of himself to the will of God. As Paul says in Philippians: "He became obedient unto death, even death on a cross." His sacrifice was in his obedience. It is that total obedience to God that the Eucharistic Jesus calls us to imitate.

There is another aspect of the Eucharist that developed only slowly in the Church: namely, the devotional aspect. After the Eucharistic action, which is primary, the Eucharistic presence remains. Initially what remained after the meal was reserved to be taken to the sick. In the high middle ages the reserved presence became the object of private personal prayer and adoration. It was out of this devotional aspect of the Eucharist that the feast of Corpus Christi came into existence. First celebrated in 1274, it became a feast of the universal Church in 1317. Thus, if you had gone to St. Augustine in 5th century and told him you wanted to make a visit to the Blessed Sacrament, he wouldn't have the slightest notion of what you were talking about.

Once again, when we talk about the reserved sacrament, we need to remember that we are dealing with mystery. We call this feast the Solemnity of the Body and Blood of Christ. Again we need to realize that it is not a piece of flesh or a vial of blood that we venerate. What we encounter in the reserved sacrament is the person of Jesus. We don't pray to flesh and blood. We pray to what they signify, namely, the Lord Jesus truly present among us, wrapped in mystery: mystery before which we bow in awe and wonder, as we meet in the sacrament where God become one of us in Jesus.

I'd like to end with a personal experience that happened in June 1954 (more than half a century ago). I was in Switzerland and visited Zermatt, a tiny town 6000 feet above sea level, at the foot of the Matterhorn which rises another 5 or 6 000 feet. The village was very quiet then, as it is a skiing resort. I met an American couple, with whom I went one day to visit the local pastor to arrange for Mass. Zermatt is German-speaking. I couldn't handle German conversation, he couldn't handle English. So much to the amazement of my two friends, we managed to converse *in Latin.* It was just two days till Corpus Christi. He invited me to carry the Blessed Sacrament through the streets of the village. But I had planned to go on to Lucerne. There was a splendid Corpus Christi procession there. The whole city turned out for it. I found it a wonderful experience, as the procession of hundreds of people made its way through the city — at one point going through the famous covered bridge over the river.

But I have always regretted that I did not stay at Zermatt *to* carry the Blessed Sacrament through the streets of this wonderful little village way up in the sky.

THE TENTH SUNDAY IN ORDINARY TIME

Hosea 6:3-6
Psalm 50: 1, 8, 12-13, 14-15
Romans 4:18-25
Matthew 9: 9-13

The Gospel highlights in rapid succession three events: Matthew's call to discipleship, Jesus' table-fellowship with sinners, the scandal taken by the Pharisees at the company Jesus kept. Evidently Jesus was accustomed to hang out with the friends of his disciples, not a few of whom, it would seem, were unsavory characters. At least Jesus' enemies thought they were. The point of the Gospel – Jesus' statement that he came to call not the righteous but sinners – is supported by a text from the prophet Hosea (which is in our first reading), where the prophet says: "It is love I desire, not sacrifice, knowledge of God rather than holocausts." Jesus repeats these words: "I desire mercy, not sacrifice."

By choosing this text Jesus puts himself in the company of the Old Testament prophets who continually assert that love and mercy are more important than religious ritual. The prophets are not saying that ritual is unimportant, but that it has meaning only when it has to do with our everyday life.

Liturgy, the prophets assert, in no uncertain terms, means nothing to God (in fact, is loathsome to God), unless it intersects with our daily effort to find God in our lives and do God's will in our everyday responsibilities. In other words, *Liturgy is about life, not just about correct ritual.* The worship of God is not a garment we put on on Sunday and then carefully put away until Sunday comes around again. Liturgy is an expression of who we are, of who we are trying to become.

It is important that we do everything we can to make Sunday celebrations of liturgy good celebrations: good music, good homilies, good participation. But it is what happens *before* liturgy and *after* liturgy that makes for that deep encounter with the mystery of God which is at the heart of authentic worship.

Reflecting on the meaning of Eucharist faces us with two questions. First, what do we bring to the Eucharist when we come to celebrate? Second what do we take from the Eucharist when we leave the celebration?

What we are *called to bring* to Eucharist are the faith experiences, the experiences of grace, the experiences of God's presence and action in our lives that took place during the week. This is to say that what we bring to Sunday Eucharist is the mystery of the dying and rising of the Lord, as we experience that mystery in the daily realities of our lives. What we are *invited to take from* Eucharist is the inspiration to go out and encounter the grace of God as we continue to experience the paschal mystery in the week that lies ahead.

For the Eucharist to mean all this for us we need a proper theological perspective that will clarify for us the way the grace of God operates in our lives. Too many of us were brought up on a faulty, indeed an erroneous, understanding of grace that severely diminished God's role in our daily lives. We were taught to see God's grace being infused into us in certain special places (the church building) and at certain special times (time of Mass). But the world, we were made to understand, was a place so profane and sinful that no one in his or her right mind could expect to find God's grace there.

Hence liturgy took on special importance, because it alone was the place and time for acquiring grace. It alone was the place and time where and when we encounter the wondrous mystery of God present in the Risen Jesus. It was at Mass, not in the world, that we experienced God's presence.

Thus the Mass brought us a measure of solace and peace: it gave us the courage to go out and face a world full of temptations and all sorts of enticements to evil. It strengthened us to go forth to do battle with the forces of evil arrayed against us on all sides in this vale of tears. It brightened our spirit, for it gave us an experience of transcendence that otherwise would be totally absent from our lives.

And so, for a few moments each week we encountered the sacred. We met God, not merely as making moral demands on us but also as sanctifying us by the gift of

God's grace. But once Eucharist was over, we were sent forth once again into the secularity of the world and the monotony of an everyday life: a life from which, at best, God seemed to be remote. To put it in the simplest terms: in this view of worship, Sunday was the day when we were able to encounter God; the other days of the week were not.

But there is another, and much more authentic, theological perspective that views God's relationship to us in a very different way. God's actions in us are not confined simply to sacred places and sacred moments. The grace of God's self-communication to us is always and everywhere present in the world.

God's grace is not an intervention "from the outside." For our God is an immanent God whose presence and grace are everywhere. God is continually calling us to conversion, to heartfelt communion with our sisters and brothers and to compassionate concern for the needy, the oppressed, the victims of injustice and prejudice.

And God does this in our everyday lives. *This means we do not have a relationship with God in addition to the relationships we have with others*. "Our relationship with God is *not inseparable from* every relationship we have. We experience God most completely by experiencing ourselves and other people, and whenever we experience ourselves and other people, we also experience God. The love of God is radically united to the love of self and the love of neighbor." (Skelley, 100)

All this is to say that the place where God acts is, not just the Church or even primarily the Church. It is the world. This means that if the experience of God is to be found at all, it will be found, first of all, in the joys and struggles of "real" life, not just or even primarily in religious ritual.

Or to put it the other way around: we will experience God's grace in ritual only if we are already experiencing it (or at least beginning to) in daily life. This is to say that the acts of worship which we call liturgy must not be seen as isolated, special interventions of grace into otherwise profane and graceless lives. Rather these acts of worship are symbolic expressions of what Karl Rahner has called "the liturgy of the world."

The liturgy of the Church is the symbolic manifestation of God's continual self-revelation to us and our free response to God, a process that takes place throughout our lives and our history. In Rahner's view, the Eucharist and indeed all the sacraments are "special outbursts" into history "of the innermost, ever-present gracious endowment of the world with God himself." (Rahner, TI, 19, 143)

In these "special outbursts" of the transcendent (which we call liturgy) we are obeying Jesus' call to remember him: "As often as you do this, remember me." What does it mean to remember him? It means remembering his death and resurrection, not as a past event of history, but as a transcendent event whose present reality is our experience as we celebrate Eucharist. And, let us not forget that we are not simply remembering an event that occurred among the disciples of Jesus.

We are remembering what Jesus is doing now in the midst of the Christian community, in the world that belongs to him. It is what God in Jesus is doing in our lives here and now that we enfold into the saving mystery of his death and resurrection.

We die to sin and selfishness. We rise to love and peace and justice. We die (or at least begin the process of dying) to a culture of consumerism and rise to a concern for the poor, the oppressed and the neglected members of our society. We strive in our individual and community lives to live out the challenge of the prophets. It's the challenge which Jesus makes his own, as he responds to the Pharisees who were unable to see that worship has meaning only if it is in touch with life.

Mitch Finley – a popular writer on things Catholic – once said that it was often true that experiencing God's presence in the context of his family life was at times more meaningful to him than what he experienced in liturgy.

THE ELEVENTH SUNDAY IN ORDINARY TIME

Exodus 19: 2-6
Psalm 100: 1-2, 5
Romans 5: 6-11
Matthew 9: 36-10:8

I remember some time ago being in a big bookstore in Louisville. I was looking at the religion section. Another man was doing the same thing. I said something to him about one of the books I was looking at: a book on Christology. He seemed like a pleasant man. Then he asked me: "Are you a born-again Christian?" "Oh, yes, (I said) I have been born again – and again and again." He was a bit puzzled. He asked another question: "Have you accepted Jesus as your personal savior?" I thought for a moment and then I said: "Oh, no, I not would dare even think of that. I accept Jesus? I'm just happy that Jesus accepts me." He looked even more puzzled and that was the end of our theological conversation.

I thought of this rather strange conversation, when I looked at this wonderful reading from Paul to the Romans. It's a reading that really forces one to ponder. Paul tells us, with a sense of wonderment that we have been reconciled to God through Jesus. The point he makes in this reading is that this shouldn't have happened. We are all sinners – some big, but mostly small. None of us would qualify as top-flight sinners. We are mostly the petty variety, selfish sinners, foolish sinners. But we *are* all sinners. As sinners we don't deserve reconciliation. We have absolutely no

212

claim on God's forgiveness. Paul shakes his head in disbelief. What God has done for us makes no sense whatever.

Then, in a puzzled sort of way, Paul says: "Well, I suppose, it might happen – though surely even this would be rare – that someone would be willing to give his or her life for a good person. But for sinners? Surely no one in her or his right mind would die for sinners." Yet the absurdity of what God did. Christ died for us *while we were still sinners!*

"While we were still sinners!" Paul is so astounded by this that he says it twice, and the second time he makes it more emphatic: *"while we were enemies."* It's as if Paul knows it to be true that we are reconciled and forgiven; yet equally he knows that, from a human point of view, it doesn't make any sense. It's as if he just can't believe it. It's too good to be true, as if he is saying "this is too much to ask of anyone, let alone of God." Yet God does reconcile us. In effect, Paul is saying: "We worship a God who does eccentric, preposterous things: things we would never think of doing, things that don't make sense to us. God's ways certainly are not our ways.

One thing we don't seem able to get through our heads is that God desires us more than we could even want anything at all. Think of something you want with all your might, something you must have. The intensity of your desire for that is nothing compared to God's burning desire for you and for me, for each of us.

There is a wonderful scene in Tolstoy's huge novel, *War and Peace.* Pierre, a likeable but eccentric character is speaking to the lovely and beautiful Natasha. He says to her: "If I were not myself but the handsomest, cleverest best man in the world and if I were free, I would at this moment ask on my knees for your hand and your love."

That is a kind of pale image of our God. He remakes us as a holy people, not from above but from below. He kneels to wash feet – a symbol that he washes alienation and pettiness and selfishness out of our hearts. He falls in our streets and lets his blood run into our soil.

Long ago you and I were baptized. In that moment of exquisite grace we were reborn, washed clean, made new. But the years have passed and it may be that we don't feel new anymore. There are times when we wonder: what happed to that white robe and that burning candle and that oil that long since has dried up on our foreheads.

What we need to realize is that they are all still there. Our baptism is not a single event that happened in a moment of time and is all over. Baptism is not an event at all, really. It is a process that *began* at the font. Our baptism is now. Right now God is washing the blood, healing the hurt, remaking us again – and again and again. And why? Because God's love always means mercy. As Pope John Paul II once put it: "Mercy is love's second name."

God's love is like the sea. Have you ever walked into the ocean or a lake and reveled in the water, got yourself thoroughly soaked in the process? As the waves dash against you, you are more and more penetrated, as it were, by the water.

The sea is God's love. Getting soaked in it is getting forgiven. It is receiving mercy. But we mustn't just shiver at the water's edge. We need to take the plunge and know – though it seems to make no sense – that we are forgiven. We are reconciled. We are awash in grace, soaked in it. We are God's holy people, his priestly people.

Yes, we are indeed born-again Christians – born again every moment of every day. Being remade, forgiven, reconciled. We are ever one with God and with one another. Our baptism means being swamped by these waters every day – if only we let it happen.

Recently I reread a wonderful article called: "The Priestliness of the Human Heart." The author makes the point that we must not think of God as separate from ourselves and from the world. "The Trinity," he says, "is the largest embrace in the universe. There is nothing outside that divine embrace." We all live within the circle of the Trinity. No person, no thing can ever fall out of that circle. For with God there is no outside. *Think of that: with God there is always and only an inside. There is no outside.* What a marvelous image of the Trinity – divine arms embracing lovingly every person, every thing. Nothing, nothing, is outside that embrace.

We all know what it means to be embraced by someone. The more important the person is in our lives, the more meaningful the embrace. What does it mean to be embraced by God who is "all" in our lives? It means that the world is "intense with the eternal." Beneath the outward appearances of our lives, God is at work. We need to open our hearts to the intensity of the divine activity going on within us. This is what it means to find the kingdom of God that is within.

THE TWELFTH SUNDAY IN ORDINARY TIME

Jeremiah 20: 10 – 13
Psalm 69:8-10, 14, 17, 33-35
Romans 5:12 -15
Matthew 10: 26-33

The first reading today is part of the autobiography of the prophet Jeremiah. Jeremiah is a lonely, tormented, tragic figure whose whole life seems to be a failure. Yet deep in his heart he knows that he will not fail, because he has the deep sense that God is with him and will vindicate him. But the vindication he dreams of takes the form of vengeance against his enemies. God will step in and destroy them – and at last Jeremiah will rejoice.

Jeremiah was a great man and a great prophet; yet he was a man of his own time. Jesus' message of forgiving enemies and praying for persecutors was completely foreign to him. To him such thinking would have made no sense whatsoever.

How very different is Jesus' way of dealing with enemies. He calls us to love them and truly be concerned for their good. For two thousand years that has been Jesus' message to us. Through the centuries Christians have not been spectacularly faithful to this revolutionary teaching of Jesus. In dealing with those who mistreat us, we have more often followed Jeremiah rather than Jesus. The pages of history are wet with the blood of enemies dispatched by Christian swords and arms.

Yet that is not the full story. The other side of the picture shows us countless women and men so fiercely committed to Christ and to the Gospel of peace and love that they have laid down their lives as Christian martyrs. In our own time we have the example of a Franz Jagerstatter, an Austrian peasant who went to his death in prison rather than join Hitler's unjust war. And there is Oscar Romero murdered at the altar, the women and the priests who were martyred in Latin America, seven Cistercians monks martyred in Algeria for the sake of the Gospel.

Yes, there have been Jeremiah-Christians who have sought revenge over their enemies and Jesus-Christians who have begged for their forgiveness. And must we not say that there is a bit of both in all of us? And that not only in our relationships with enemies but even with those we call friends.

There is a kind of perversity in us that wants to hurt when we get hurt; but there is also in us a grace that wants to forgive and love even when we are hurt. And that perversity and grace often struggle within us; and we aren't always sure which will win out. And sometimes we wonder why the struggle.

It is this very struggle that Paul is attempting to deal with in our second reading. In order to express the universality of sin and the radical helplessness of the human condition, Paul has recourse to the Adam typology, which was current in Jewish thought at the time. But it is important that we follow the movement of his thought. His emphasis is not on Adam, not even on comparing Adam and Jesus. His great concern is with the saving love of God that brings us forgiveness of sin. He is concerned with the grace that comes with Christ – a grace that is infinitely more powerful than sin. Paul would not even have thought of Adam except that he saw the human race – which once had its beginning in Adam – now having a new beginning with Christ. Christ, therefore, is the new Adam. It is this new beginning that takes place in history that reminds Paul of the mythical account of a first beginning that took place in paradise.

To put it another way, it is not Adam that leads Paul to Christ, but Christ who leads him to reflect on Adam. In other words, the weight of Paul's words is not on Adam and a kind of primordial sin that was thought to affect all of humanity; no, the weight of his argument is on Christ and his grace.

For Paul the sinful condition of humanity remains a mystery. What is important for him is the fact that Christ's grace and Christ's grace alone makes it possible for us to overcome that sinful condition that so mysteriously seems to affect us all. It's the mystery involved, as Paul writes later in Romans, in the strange phenomenon that so often I don't do what I really want to do or I do what I really don't want to do. Paul doesn't pretend to understand that perversity; it seems to have been part of the human condition as far back as one can go. Hence it is easy to link it with Adam. But what that link means we simply do not understand.

What we can understand – and this is all that matters – is that whatever explanation there is of that human perversity and how it began – the really important thing is to know that it can be brought to an end and overcome by the superabundant grace of God given to us in Jesus, God's incarnate Word.

There is, therefore, an essential optimism in Paul – an optimism that may have a bit of autobiography in it. No matter how steeped one may become in sin – and Paul may well have been thinking of his own persecution of Jesus' followers – the grace brought by Christ is ever so much more powerful than our sinfulness.

In baptism we are re-introduced into the paradise of God's intimate friendship and love – that humanity had in some mysterious way forfeited. Sadly, some rather unfortunate theories about the sin of Adam (and here I have in mind Augustine's teaching on original sin and the pessimistic twist it gave to our western faith tradition) have tended to obscure the profound and heartening theology that Paul is teaching us.

Yet his joyful message is there: we *can* overcome the Jeremiah traits in us that would seek revenge against those who persecute us. We *can* live the Gospel of unconditional love and non-violence that Jesus taught and lived. For He has communicated to us the grace-power to live and act in the same way as He did.

We live today in a world where violence seems to be all around us: violence on a global scale. The only way to deal with violence that so many world leaders seem to know is to make war. Yes, we sure know how to train people to make war. When will we awaken to the fact that people can be trained to make peace? There is enough evidence to show that people can be trained in non-violence, just as they can be trained in violence. When the revolution took place several years ago in the Philippines against the Marcos government, Richard Deats and Hildegard Goss-Mayr of the Fellowship of Reconciliation were there training people in non-violence. The revolution was a non-violent revolution.

We even have within our government the structures for training people in nonviolence. When Ronald Reagan was president, The United States Institute for Peace was set up. It had, I understand, a strange birth. Provisions for it were attached to the defense budget and Reagan had to accept it or veto the whole bill. So the USIP is something of a providential accident. As it presently exists, those who know about it, seems to see it mostly as a think-tank to explore *ideas* regarding conflict management and peace-making. Yet its mission statement suggests *action* also. The mission statement says that it was established by Congress to "support the development, transmission and *use* of knowledge to promote peace and curb violent international conflict." It offers training, peace information services about ways "to promote international peace and the resolution of conflicts among nations and peoples of the world without recourse to violence." The USIP does indeed exists. But who ever hears about it?

Did our government consult with it before going to war in Iraq? Has it consulted the USIP about how we should now be proceeding in Iraq? I strongly doubt it. Yet this institute could provide significant ways of teaching people how to make peace instead of how to make war. It just may be that the USIP is one of the present-day secrets which our Gospel says must be and will be revealed.

Joan Baez, a peacemaker who realized, from her own experience, that the practice of nonviolence makes great demands on a person, once said: "Nonviolence is a flop. The only bigger flop is violence." The deaths of some 4000 of our wonderful young people serving in Iraq as well as thousands of Iraqi soldiers and citizens is a frightening indication of the fact that violence simply doesn't work. It only produces more violence. When will we learn that lesson? Our world and our country would be well advised to look for a better alternative. And soon.

THE THIRTEENTH SUNDAY OF ORDINARY TIME

2 Kings 4:8-11
Psalm 89: 2-3, 16-17, 18-19
Romans 6:3-4, 8-11
Matthew 10: 37-42

Today's readings are about "letting in" and "letting go." Or, to substitute nouns for verbs, the readings speak about hospitality and about detachment. Hospitality means "letting people into" our lives. That is the first reading's story: a woman extends hospitality to one of God's prophets. The climax of the gospel is likewise about hospitality: whether it be extended to a prophet or a righteous person or to the least significant of people who come to us. The Gospel presents a concrete picture of a simple act of hospitality: giving a cup of cold water to someone who is thirsty. Note it is not just a cup of water, but a cup of cold water. These warm summer days help us to appreciate the hospitality of a cup of cold water.

One could make a case, I think, for saying that the virtue most extolled in the New Testament is hospitality.
You might want to object and say: "No, the most extolled virtue in the New Testament is love: our love for God and our love for our sisters and brothers." And the objection would be a valid one except for the fact that hospitality is really love – indeed a very special kind of love.

It is love extended to the guest and often the guest who is a stranger. The Greek word for hospitality is *philoxenia*.

Philia means love and xenos means guest, but often it refers to a stranger who becomes guest when we offer hospitality. The Olive Tree, a Greek restaurant on Monroe Avenue, had on its window the words: *Kaire Xene* which mean: "Welcome Guest" or "Welcome Stranger." Thus, offering hospitality means extending care and food to "guests," "friends," "relatives." But it also frequently means the care and the meal extended to the stranger: the person we do not know.

Hospitality, especially when extended to strangers, involves both risk and mystery. The risk of course is that the stranger might take advantage of you, murder you in your sleep or rob you of your possessions. The mystery of hospitality is that the stranger may turn out to be, not the lowly person you thought you were caring for, but a person of great importance. Indeed, the stranger may be Christ himself.

That is why, both in Scripture and in Christian lore, the theme of hospitality is often linked with the theme of "mistaken identity." St. Martin of Tours gives half his cloak to a poor beggar and afterwards saw that the beggar was Christ. And the greatest example of the combination of these two themes (Hospitality and Mistaken Identity) is that moving picture in Matthew 25 of people who give hospitality to the hungry, the thirsty, the naked, the imprisoned only to learn at the judgment that the unknown stranger to whom they offered hospitality was none other than Jesus himself. "Since you did it to the least of my sisters and brothers, you did it to me."

There was a time when America was seen as a place of gracious hospitality for people who came from many places seeking a better life. Most of us here in this chapel, I suspect, trace our roots back to immigrants who came to this country seeking to build a new life in peace and freedom. Lady Liberty welcomed them at New York harbor. On the pedestal on which the Statue of Liberty stands, there is engraved the famous poem of Emma Lazarus: it is titled "The New Colossus":

Not like the brazen giant of Greek fame
With conquering limbs astride from land to land;
Here at our sea-washed, sunset gates shall stand
A mighty woman with a torch, whose flame
Is the imprisoned lightning and her name
Mother of exiles. From her beacon-hand
Glows world-wide welcome: her mild eyes command
The air-bridged harbor that twin cities frame.
"Keep ancient lands, your stories pomp," cries she
With silent lips. "Give me your tired, your poor,
Your huddled masses yearning to breathe free,
The wretched refuse of your teeming shore.
Send these, the homeless, tempest-tost to me,
I lift my lamp beside the golden door!

"The mighty woman with the torch," the Mother of exiles" – can it still be said that "From her beaconed-hand glows world-wide welcome?" Has the glowing welcome in her hand grown dim? Has her voice of hospitality been muted? These are questions we have to ask in the light of the law

225

that was passed so hastily under a cloak of fear after 9/11? The Patriot Act of 2002 allows the imprisonment of those who are suspected of being "terrorists" or "a threat to national security" without a court order and without due process. Moreover, it severely curtails the constitutional rights of American citizens, mixing foreign intelligence with domestic spying, allowing the FBI to spy on Americans whom no court has determined have done anything wrong.

There is an interesting precedent for this law in our history, namely the Alien and Sedition Act of 1798 which, among other things, allowed the President of the United States to arrest and deport aliens when he considered public safety required it. Many French immigrants who sought refuge from the atrocities of the French revolution had to leave the United Sates, often with nowhere to go. Fortunately, saner minds soon prevailed and when Jefferson was elected president in 1800, the law was repealed.

Still it is difficult not to see the parallel. We have to ask the question: "Is *xenophilia* (the love of the stranger) being replaced by *xenophobia* (the fear of the stranger)?" True, we must be concerned about terrorism. We must do all that we can reasonably to protect national security. But can we allow fears to deprive us of our constitutional freedoms? Can we allow mere suspicions to trump human hospitality?

Besides this theme of "letting in" to our lives: the other, the stranger, especially the helpless stranger, there is, also in today's readings, the other theme of "letting go" or, if you will, the theme of detachment. The two are closely linked: I can let others into my life only if I have truly learned to "let go" of myself.

This "letting go," to which the gospel calls us, is expressed in a startling way that is easily misunderstood. It is really about detachment: our duty to look into our lives to locate the things which are "precious" to us which we may have to let go of (or at least take a hard look at), if they seem to be impeding the totality of our commitment to the Lord Jesus and to the Kingdom.

This is the meaning of "detachment." It is unfortunate that "attachment" has been, in so much literature on spirituality, a no-no word. It is quite natural for us to be attached to family, friends, things, places. Even John of the Cross, with his insistence on total freedom from created things: *nada, nada, nada* (*nothing, nothing, nothing*) had at least one attachment. He was a poet, perhaps one of Spain's greatest. He absolutely refused to write bad poetry. In other words, he refused to give up his attachment to good writing. Nor would it have been right for him to do so. The real question we have to ask about attachments is: are they reasonable or are they crippling? Do they help me to be a true disciple of Jesus or do they interfere?

Jesus makes clear that "letting go" for the kingdom is going to cost. It is going to mean shedding blood, figuratively for most of us, literally for some. We don't sufficiently realize – and I don't think this an exaggeration – that our sisters in Brazil live continually with the possibility of martyrdom. For in Latin America, those who position themselves on the side of the poor and the oppressed not infrequently face death: not figuratively but quite literally.

All of us committed to discipleship for the sake of the kingdom must realize that we have to face death too: death to a false self, death to selfishness and self-seeking, death to the many illusions we so easily let ourselves live by. This kind of death always means resurrection, new life. When we "let go," we are more easily able "to let in."

THE FOURTEENTH SUNDAY OF ORDINARY TIME

Zechariah 9:9-10
Psalm 145:1-2, 8-9, 10-11, 13-14
Romans 8: 9, 11-13
Matthew 11:25-30

If a glass is filled to the brim with water, you cannot put any more water into it. But if it is empty you can fill it with water. I don't imagine anyone would have any inclination to dispute this fairly obvious fact. I mention it because it seems to me that one way of reflecting on today's liturgy is to see that it is about emptiness.

The Gospel is an unusual one. The first part is a prayer that Jesus addresses to his Father. It is a prayer which soars: it takes us into the heights of divinity. The second part is made up of words addressed by Jesus to us and brings us back from the very heights of divinity to the cares and burdens of everyday existence.

Though they seem to be very different (this soaring into divine life and then this plunging back to earth) there is, I think, a close link that can be made between them. I suggest that each of them can shed light on what it means to be empty.

In the prayer we are told that God reveals himself to the little ones: those who are not puffed up with a sense of their own importance, but rather realize that they are nothing without God and that they can do nothing without

God. What this means is that they are empty and because they are empty, God can fill them. Hence Jesus thanks God for revealing to the littlest children what God has hidden from the learned and the clever.

It is this experience which we have – namely, that it is the simple and the humble who are more open to reality than the proud and the self-satisfied (an experience which we have at the human level) – which Matthew uses to give us a peek, as it were, into the life of God.

There is a sense in which we can say that Jesus is the Emptiness of God. As he puts it: "Everything has been given over to me by my Father." He is only what the Father gives him and of course the Father gives him all. It is the receiving of everything from the Father that is the very being of the Son.

At the same time, it is the Father's total giving of himself to the Son that constitutes Him as Father. The Father is only what he gives. The Son is only what he receives. That which IS in the Father is the same as that which IS in the Son. This is what we mean by the Unity of God.

Another way of putting this is to say that in God there is a rich giving of self that never ends and is never stopped. It is a Love received only to be given: a Love perfectly shared and perfectly returned, a Circulation of Love which never finds a Self that halts that circulation.

Thus it can be said that each person of the Trinity is at once total Emptiness (i.e., always Giving) and total Fullness (i.e., always Receiving). To the degree that we empty ourselves --of selfishness, of a false self --to that degree we shall find ourselves inserted into that Circulation of Love which is the Life of God. If we are empty, as God's little ones, then divine love and the wisdom it begets, can flow into us, and through us into one another and to the neighbor.

When we become a community in which love is continually circulating and never finding a self that stops that circulation, we become a kind of human trinity, imaging the divine Trinity. For we are unique and different from one another, as are the Persons of the Trinity, yet everything we have we have as received: received ultimately from God, but also received from one another. In the human community, as in the divine Trinity, emptiness is fullness.

It is in this context that we can understand what Jesus says about his yoke being easy. Matthew is consciously contrasting Jesus' yoke with what the scribes called the "yoke of the Law." Jesus' yoke is easy; the yoke imposed by the scribes is burdensome. This should not be taken to mean that Jesus' challenge to us is less demanding than the stipulations of the law.

The difference between the two yokes is that the Pharisee imposed burdens on people but made little effort to help them carry those burdens. Jesus, on the other hand, is a fellow-yoke-bearer. The demands he makes on us are not

231

for his benefit but for ours. He asks no emptying of us that he has not experienced himself. He demands that we empty ourselves, because only then can we be filled. His yoke is easy, because it prepares us to receive, as little ones, the revelation of God's Love.

If Jesus asks us to empty ourselves it is because he understands, from his own experience, what true emptiness means and where it leads. For he emptied himself and took the form of a slave. It was because of that emptiness that God was able to fill him with divinity and give him the name that is above all names. In that wonderful hymn in Philippians, Paul sets up a causal relationship between Jesus' emptying of himself and God's exalting him. It is not simply that his exaltation follows after his self-emptying. It follows because of that self-emptying.

Only the little ones – who are empty and poor – can enter into that circulation of Love which constitutes the divine Reality. When I am empty and poor, this circulation of Love penetrates my whole being: feeding me when I am hungry and nourishing me at a deeper level of the spirit.

It is the Love that sends the winter's frost that makes me cold and the summer's heat that makes me sweat. It is the Love that speaks to me in the song of the birds and the noise of the city. It is the Love that seeks, through us, to become incarnate again in the world, especially when oppression and violence and alienation block Love's flow.

Our world yearns for peace. To seek peace, we must let that love circulate. To seek peace is to remove the dams of pride and self-will that try to hold back the flow of that love. Perhaps it is only when the human community enters, through emptiness and poverty, into this divine circulation of love that the picture described by Zechariah in our first reading can become a reality: the picture of the humble Messiah-King who comes in triumph, but who rides not on a war-horse or a war-chariot, but on a lowly ass.

He comes in triumph, because he brings peace. He banishes the instruments of war (the horse, the chariot, the bow and arrow) and he proclaims peace to all the nations.

We celebrated Independence Day. I remember a Roger Rosenblatt essay in which he said: "I love you America. But where are you? I can't find you anymore. You seem to be lost."

I wonder how many of us can no longer find the America we were taught to love. Is America today too full? Too full of itself, of its own pride, of its own conceit, of its own arrogance, its own seemingly relentless need to dominate. Do we need to think today of the emptying of America?

What are the things, the attitudes, the false loves, the false sense of self-righteousness, the false values that America has to let go of? It may be that to find America today we have to look, not to the politicians or the generals or the CEOs of corporate America, but to the little ones, the lowly, the poor, the seemingly insignificant, those to whom Jesus tells us God reveals himself. There it may be we shall find the America we love, the America that we seem to have lost.

THE FIFTEENTH SUNDAY IN ORDINARY TIME

Isaiah 55:10 -11
Psalm 65: 10, 11, 12-13, 14
Romans 8:18-23
Matthew 13:1-23

I must begin by confessing that the Gospel passage chosen for today is not one of my favorites. My problem with this Gospel is not with the parable of Jesus — which surely is challenging enough. My problem is with the interpretation of the parable which comes at the end of the reading. Almost certainly this explanation of the parable comes not from the lips of Jesus, but from the preaching of the early Church.

My reason for saying this is that Jesus was clearly an outstanding teacher. Too good a teacher to misuse a parable. Jesus understood well (as so many of his parables show) that a teacher does not tell a parable in order to present some eternal truth that people can store away for future reference. One tells a parable to challenge people to action – here and now. A listener's reaction to hearing a parable should not be: "Yes, now I understand," but "Yes, now I see something I must do."

The point that needs to be stressed is that it is the parable itself, and not some explanation of it, that challenges the hearers to action. An explanation added to a parable limits the power of the parable. It channels a person's thinking. It dispenses us from the need to reflect on the parable in order to see what it is calling us to do. It closes the parable by restricting it to a particular meaning, whereas the real power of a parable is that it is open-ended: it can challenge different people to different courses of action. It can challenge people to different actions at different times in their lives.

So, let's ignore the explanation given by the early Church in its preaching (though this is a legitimate approach if one wants to follow it. It is a part of our living tradition.) But let's set it aside and take a fresh approach to the parable to see what it can mean for us here and now.

To deal with the parable anew, it is helpful to know something of the agricultural practices of the time. In Jesus' day the seed was sown before the ground was plowed. That is why there was no need for the sower to exercise any special care about where he tossed the seed. He could throw it anywhere, for instance, in places where the ground was hard because people had worn a footpath across the field or in places where thorns and weeds were growing. He could sow in this indiscriminate way, because all the ground was going to be plowed anyway. The plowing would soften the hard ground and uproot the thorn bushes and the weeds.

Once the seeds began to grow, some of them would wither and die, because even after plowing, some of the soil would remain hard because there was rock beneath a shallow layer of good soil. Other seed would manage to grow up in the midst of some of the thorn bushes and weeds that managed to survive the plowing; but they would be overpowered and choked by the thorns and the weeds. But there would be much seed that would produce fruit: some a hundredfold, some sixty, some thirty. Since a twelve to one yield was considered good, a hundred to one would be a superb yield and even thirty would be well beyond the average yield. Against this background of agricultural information, we can face the parable and ask what is it challenging us to do? First, it is worth noting that the parable is more about the soil than the seed. What kind of soil are we when God plants in us the seeds that must be brought to fruition?

As I am sure you know, Thomas Merton sees these seeds as the "seeds of contemplation" which God sows in us: the seeds of prayer and the seeds of that total awareness of God which makes God's presence in our lives no longer just a matter of speculative knowledge, but a reality of personal experience. But these seeds will grow only if we offer the proper soil. It would be worth reflecting: what is the proper soil that we must be for contemplation to become a part of our lives?

Perhaps we could also see the parable calling us to a deeper experience of community. God plants the seeds of community in us; but for community to become a reality, we need to become actively and dynamically the good soil in which these seeds are sown. Perhaps we could reflect what are the qualities of good soil that would enable the seeds of community which God sows to flower in our midst. And we can think of community at various levels: the family community, the community of the Church, of the world, religious community.

Perhaps each of us would have slightly different thoughts about the seeds that must grow in the soil of community, if that community is to be a viable and healthy one. I would suggest three: freedom, dialogue and love. By freedom, I mean the right to be myself: to think my own thoughts, to make my own decisions. Freedom enables me to stand on my own feet and to be my own person before God. But freedom in community does not mean isolation or separation. I must exercise my freedom in the context of the freedoms of other persons which I must respect and which I must safeguard as much as my own. This intermingling of many individual freedoms can exist only where there is true dialogue.

Dialogue has as its goal a sharing of the truth. It is not just that I want to share my truth with another. I also want to share the truth which the other has that I do not have. Dialogue is a kind of opening up of what had been closed frontiers. Dialogue calls for listening -- real listening, not just a waiting till the other is through so that you can straighten them out. You don't try to win a dialogue. You do hope to be enriched by it because of the mutual sharing. Catholics are not generally very good at dialogue. We need to learn to do it better. It is so essential if we wish to move from "living together in isolation" to true community.

A third seed of community which I would suggest is love, non-violent love.

There are times when our relationships bring out the worst in people. The whole point of non-violent love is to bring out the best in people. Non-violent love is love that doesn't lay down conditions. It does not say "I love you if you do this or if you avoid that." It simply says, not so much in words, but in action: "I love you regardless of what you say or do. I love you because you are the image of God. More than that, you and I are one in God."

This oneness is at a level of perception that unfortunately we don't always achieve, but it is there. And, since we are one, I love you as my other self. There are no strings attached to my love for you. This kind of love means respect for the uniqueness of each person. Another person's uniqueness may not be to my liking, but I must love people as who they are, not as we would wish them to be.

I remember seeing a wonderful example of this kind of love at a Sister's funeral. I saw it in the Sister's niece: the niece, in her gentle loving attention to the young man sitting next to her in chapel. He was clearly physically and mentally handicapped. He was very restless, grabbing her hand or putting his hand around her neck.

She made no effort to scold him or tell him how he must behave. She responded to him with gentle tenderness. In fact, I was so mesmerized by their interaction that I almost forgot the Mass that was going on.

I had a moment to speak with her after the service. I said to her: "You are a wonderful caregiver." With a smile on her face and the hint of a tear in her eye, she said: "He's my son."

THE SIXTEENTH SUNDAY IN ORDINARY TIME

Wisdom 12:13, 16-19
Psalm 86: 5-6, 9-10, 15-16
Romans 8:26-27
Matthew 13:24-43

The Gospel is one of several parables Jesus told about something he must have seen often in the lush fields of Galilee: the sowing of seed. The parable is about a problem posed to a farmer by his servants and the twofold solution to the problem given by the farmer.

Today's Gospel continues last week's with another parable about a sower and the seed. Once more an explanation is appended which probably comes, not from Jesus, but from the early Church. This parable differs from last Sunday's wherein, you will remember, the emphasis was on the good soil. Here the emphasis is on the good seed that is sown and the rather odd question put to the owner by the slaves: "If you sowed good seed, how come there are weeds growing up in the field?" A rather silly question. If you have ever tried to raise a garden, you know that weeds grow up unbidden. Hardly a surprise. The owner's sinister remark is equally strange (that an enemy has done this). What seems to have happened here is that the original parable has been retold to fit the later explanation.

The problem is this: the servants noticed that considerable weeds had grown up in the midst of the wheat they had

241

planted. The servants evidently wanted to have a perfect wheat field. So they pose the problem: shall we pull up the weeds?

The farmer, however, has a clearer vision and a deeper perception. He gives a twofold solution to the problem posed by his servants. The first and immediate solution: let the weeds and wheat grow side by side. He also gives them the ultimate solution, namely, the separation of the wheat from the weeds. This solution, however, is not to be carried out till the end — till the time of the harvest. The emphasis in the parable seems to be on the immediate solution rather than the ultimate one.

What meaning does this parable have for us? Let's do what we did last week: ignore the explanation that got attached to the parable and seek out the meaning and the challenge the parable may have for us now.

One way of reflecting on the parable is to see it as symbol of the Patience of God, namely, God's willingness to wait and see how things turn out, as women and men exercise their freedom and prove themselves worthy or unworthy of God's blessing. If you recall last Sunday's parable — about the different kinds of soil in which the seed was planted — you might have reflected then that soil is soil and can only be what it is. We, by contrast, are not destined by our nature to be a particular kind of soil without any possibility of change. If now we are poor soil, we can change and by our own free choice, and with the aid of God's grace, become a better kind of soil that produces good fruit and produces it in abundance.

So, too, we can read today's parable in a similar way. Wheat is wheat and weeds are weeds. They cannot change from one to the other. The good seed is capable of producing good fruit; the darnel, which is the specific weed spoken of in the parable, simply cannot produce anything but more weeds.

But what is true of the good seed and the darnel is not true of us. For God has gifted us with free will. We have the power, therefore, to change. We are able to go through a process of conversion, whereby we can become what we are not yet; whereby we can grow from where we are now into a much deeper intimacy with God – something to which we are called. That is the heart of the Christian Gospel message: the call to change and conversion. Sometimes our progress is slow. But our God is patient: when God sees that we seem to be lagging, God cheers us on, encouraging us to make the changes we need to make, if we are to become the person God wills us to be. But he is patient. God is willing to wait. (Doesn't the parable of the prodigal son show us that patience so vividly?)

Perhaps we might also see the parable, not just as a symbol of God's loving patience but also we can see it as a call to us to be patient with ourselves, precisely in order that we may have the time to undergo change, the time to grow. We have to be able to "forgive" ourselves for

243

yesterday's hasty action or the thoughtless word we uttered - actions and words that were hurtful to another person.

Notice I say "forgive." I do not say "excuse" or "justify." We have to accept responsibility for our actions. But we must not be so paralyzed by guilt that we fail to see the possibilities of growth even in the wrongful things we do. We have to be patient with ourselves for broken resolutions made in the past. To put it simply, we have to believe in our own basic and fundamental goodness. We must not yield to the depressing conviction that we certainly are the ornery person we appear to be and it's hopeless to think that we can change.

What I am saying is that we must not give up on ourselves. And the basic reason for that is that God, who is mild and patient with us, never gives up on us. And in the long run, it is the grace of God, not simply our initiative, that enables us to change and become better persons.

This view of the parable – that places our call to change in the context of a patient, mild God who treats us with great leniency – is borne out by our first reading, where God is described as one whose care is for all and whose mastery over all things makes him lenient with all: with both wheat and weeds. You have filled your children with good grounds for hope because you forgive their sins.

One way, then, of thinking of this parable is to see the wisdom of bringing our failings before the Lord, as the slaves brought the master the news of the weeds invasion of the wheat field. We need to believe in God's infinite Care and Patience. We need to have the certitude that, however discouraged we may be with ourselves at times, God has not given up on us and never will.

Then perhaps we shall experience God's power in our lives in ways we had never dreamed of, as God leads us to wondrous growth. God can help us turn difficult situations and agonizing questions into new insights. God's grace can show us new opportunities that may lie hidden in what seem to be our failures.

God is great. God may bring what we mistakenly thought were only weeds in our lives into a ripe and fruitful harvest of good fruit.

THE SEVENTEENTH SUNDAY IN ORDINARY TIME

1 Kings 3:5, 7-12
Psalm 119: 57, 72, 76-77 127-128, 129-130
Romans 8: 28-30
Matthew 13:44-52

Today is another parable Sunday — four in fact. They are so brief and succinct, though, that one has to hang on to every word to get their full import. The first two tell about two men - one poor, the other rich —each of whom unexpectedly finds something of such inestimable value that he joyfully gives up *everything* he has to possess it.

The first parable is about a peasant — a poor man – who has hired himself out to plow another man's field. While plowing, he suddenly and unexpectedly strikes something solid in the ground. He digs around it and finds to his amazement and delight that it is a treasure chest someone had buried. In Jesus' day, remember, there were no Chase Manhattan banks with funds guaranteed by the Roman government. It was not uncommon, therefore, for people to bury their valuables for safekeeping. At times this might be done in a hurry; for instance, if someone were in flight in time of war. Many treasures were buried and their owners never lived to return to claim them. However this treasure got there, the peasant was so overwhelmed by this unexpected surprise, the buried treasure. He knows he must possess it. So he buries it again. He sells everything he has: his donkey, his plow, his home, and buys the field. He is so excited that, no matter what the cost, he must have that treasure. [In passing, let me suggest that you not get hung up on the question of whether the peasant was being unjust to the owner of the field in not telling him about the hidden treasure. Parables are told to make one point, in this case the man's willingness to give up everything to possess that field. Whether he acted unjustly or not has nothing to do with the reason for which the parable was told. So don't bother sympathizing with the land owner.]

Parable number two makes the same point as the first. The main character, in contrast with the first parable, is a rich man: a merchant who came upon a very precious pearl. Whereas in the first parable the peasant came upon the treasure quite by chance, the merchant is a deliberate seeker: his life is dedicated to the search for fine pearls. He wants to get as many pearls as he can. Then one day he finds, not just a beautiful pearl, but — to his amazing gaze —a pearl more beautiful than he could ever imagine. The Greek word (polutimon) which describes this pearl is impossible to do justice to in translation. It is so valuable that you simply cannot put a price on it.

When the pearl merchant sees this pearl of inestimable beauty and value, he knows he must have it. It is costly. He has to sell his ship, his caravan, all the other pearls that he has gathered over the years. He gives up everything. He actually becomes poor in order to possess this one pearl. He knows that it is worth it. The greatest of riches is to possess this pearl. Compared to it, nothing else matters.

These two parables are intended to say something very important about discipleship in the kingdom. It is a treasure so great that no price tag is too high to put on it. It is a pearl so precious that you will never discover anything like it.

This treasure, this priceless pearl, is not something that can be achieved by half measures. This is the challenge of the two parables. Christian discipleship demands total commitment. A half-hearted disciple is no disciple at all. The question these parables force us to face is: What does total commitment mean for me at this moment in my life, at this moment in the life of the Church, at this moment in the life of our nation? It will not necessarily mean the same thing for each of us. It may not mean for us now what it meant in the past.

As we look back over our lives, we can see that there have been times — perhaps many times – when we have come upon the hidden treasure, the precious pearl: times when God calls us to an insight, a mission, what is often wondrous and precious, but almost always unexpected. We didn't know that it happened until it happened. In my own life I remember such an experience. It was October 23, 1983. I had just returned from Mass at St. Joseph's Convent Infirmary. As I came into the Motherhouse, I met a sister who said: "Something terrible has happened in Beirut: 250 marines were killed by a suicide terrorist attack." My reaction was immediate. Strangely, it was not first of all compassion or distress or anger. No, the thought that flashed into my mind seemed to have no connection with the heinous crime that happened in Beirut. What came to my mind was the realization: "I shall never smoke again." I had been a moderately heavy smoker for forty years. Where that reaction to the Beirut atrocity came from I cannot explain. It was as if intuitively I had gone through a process of reasoning: "Here is a terrible crime of violence. I must do something nonviolent at once. I shall stop doing violence to my body by ceasing to smoke." That was more than twenty years ago. At the time I was clearly addicted to smoking; yet, after that experience, I never once had the desire to smoke.

But that is not all. At that moment I knew as clearly as I knew my own name that I had to commit myself to a posture of nonviolence in the totality of my life. That this was a moment of grace, a discovery of the hidden treasure, the finding of the precious pearl – of that I have no doubt. How faithful I have been to that treasure is something I have to live with and need frequently to reflect upon. But that it was a huge grace of God calling me to a life of nonviolence — that I can never doubt.

For me that was a spectacular moment of grace. Yet I believe that all of us – as we look over our lives – can see that there have been "hidden treasure" moments in our lives: moments when God calls us to what is often wondrous and precious, but almost always unexpected. But we have to be alert. God is near us. For God is everywhere. We have to be attentive lest we miss that treasure hidden in the field. Boris Pasternak has said so wisely: "When a great moment knocks on the door of your life, it is often no louder than the beating of your heart, and it is very easy to miss it."

In a striking, oft-quoted poem called "The Bright Field," R. S. Thomas links our two parables with the experience that Moses had which changed his life – his experience of the bush in the desert that burned, yet was not consumed.

> *I have seen the sun break through*
> *to illuminate a small field*
> *for a while, and gone my way*
> *and forgotten it. But that was the pearl*
> *of great price, the one field that had*
> *that treasure in it. I realize now*
> *that I must give all I have*
> *to possess it. Life is not hurrying*
> *on to a receding future, nor hankering after*
> *an imagined past. It is the turning*
> *aside like Moses to the miracle*
> *of the lit bush, to a brightness*
> *that seemed as transitory as your youth*
> *once, but is the eternity that awaits you.*

THE EIGHTEENTH SUNDAY IN ORDINARY TIME

Isaiah 55:1-3
Psalm 145: 8-9. 15-16, 17-18
Romans 8:35, 37-39
Matthew 14:13-21

The early Church considered the event narrated in today's Gospel as of special significance. That is why it is one of the few events common to all four of the Gospels. The importance of the story is to be sought in its symbolic meaning. The feeding miracle is a symbolic action.

Do I need to clarify what I mean by a symbolic action? I think I do. Many people when they think of "symbol," think of it as the opposite of "real." Quite the contrary. Far from meaning "not real," symbol means "more real." A symbolic action expresses more reality than an act that is not a "symbolic action." Put it this way: a symbolic action has "surplus meaning."

Consider today's Gospel: You can read it as a simple event in which Jesus relieves the hunger of a large group of people for one evening. The surface meaning of the event is surely significant, but short-lived. Most of the people in the story probably were living on a very simple, maybe even starvation diet. Most families lived on the daily wage of the family wage-earner. Which means that Jesus' action didn't really change anything. So they got plenty of food at this one meal. But this did not answer for them the pressing question; where would their next meal

251

come from? How would they provide food for their families the next day and the next? Peoples' needs taken care of for one day —that is the only kind of meaning this story yields when you see it simply as an event.

But now look at this event as a "symbolic action." In satisfying this momentary need of these people, Jesus is saying much more to them. He sees people faced not only with hunger, but with sorrow, sickness, poverty, oppression. In this action Jesus is expressing his on-going care and aching concern for these people in all their needs and concerns. He is telling them that he is the source of life for all of them, that he has come that they may have abundant life.

Thus, what Jesus intends to say by this feeding miracle goes far beyond the obvious, namely, simply feeding hungry people at one meal. He wants them to realize that it is abundant life, eternal life that he comes to bring them in all its fullness.

This feeding miracle has also been understood by the Church as a symbolic action in yet another way. In fact, for the Church, this event is a symbol of a symbol. I say this because it is clearly intended by the Gospel-writers to be viewed as a symbol of the Eucharist. The story is told in terms of Eucharistic gestures. Jesus takes the bread, breaks it, gives it: the very words the Church uses in celebrating the Eucharist.

Hence part of the "surplus meaning" of the feeding miracle is that it is a symbol of the Eucharist. Now since the Eucharist is the Church's greatest symbol, the feeding miracle may well be said to be a symbol of a Symbol.

At this point it may happen that my words suddenly become uncomfortable. You may want to question me: "How can you say that the Eucharist is only a symbol? We remember the arguments we used to have with Protestants. We said Jesus was *really present* in the Eucharist, whereas Protestants said Jesus was *only symbolically present in* the Eucharist. You're confusing us, even upsetting us."

The southern novelist, Flannery O'Connor, once said: "If the Eucharist is only a symbol, then the hell with it."

If that is the way you feel, let me try to clarify. First of all, I did not say that the Eucharist is *only* a symbol. Placing "only" before symbol deprives it of its true meaning. So I did not say the Eucharist is *only* symbol, but rather that it is *truly* symbol. When I refer to the Eucharist as symbol I mean it has a rich fullness of meaning.

What we must understand is that "Real Presence" can be very REAL indeed and at the same time have that surplus of meaning that makes it at the same time a symbol. Our understanding of the Eucharist *is* truly enriched when we say Real Presence *and* Symbol.

Jesus is not present in the Eucharist just to be there. He becomes dynamically present in our midst. He is there to he the source of true life for all of us, as individuals and as a community. The Eucharist also means that inter-personal presence that unites us with all who are one with him. The Eucharist is, therefore, a potent symbol of our care and concern for our sisters and brothers, especially those who are poor and sick and oppressed, those who are needy in any way.

We come to Sunday Eucharist. If we come simply because we are supposed to, probably nothing happens in our lives. It's just another event for us. Or we may come because we want to enter into a deeper personal relationship with Jesus. This is fine, yet we have not plumbed the real depths of the of the symbolism of the Eucharist, until we realize that the Eucharist is indeed about Jesus' presence *to* us, but it is equally about our sisters and brothers and the life of Jesus that we must all share – not just at the Eucharist, but at all times. Excluding our sisters and brothers from our understanding of real presence is effectively to exclude Jesus.

When we allow the full symbolic dimensions of the Eucharist to unfold in our lives and hearts, it can be an exhilarating experience. It will raise to the level of conscious awareness that deep union with God and with our sisters and brothers that is always a reality, but not always adverted to by us. All of this can begin to happen in our lives, when we begin to understand what it means to say of the Eucharist: Real Presence is also Symbol.

THE NINETEENTH SUNDAY IN ORDINARY TIME

1 Kings 19:9a, 11-13a
Psalm 85: 9, 10, 11-12, 13-14
Romans 9: 1-5
Matthew 14:22-33

The first reading and the Gospel both narrate an elemental human experience: the experience of a terrifying and crippling fear. But the fear is overcome by a deep awareness of God: an awareness that brings quiet, calmness and reassurance.

The first reading is actually part two in a thrilling episode in the life of the prophet Elijah. In part one he had entered into a contest with the 400 priests of the god Baal on Mt. Carmel. In a mighty show of power he vanquishes them; and in an equally mighty display of terrible vengeance he slits their throats.

His bloody action rouses the ire of Queen Jezebel, who is the real power behind the throne in Israel. She will have her revenge and the prophet's life. The tables are reversed. Elijah fears for his life. This man of power and bravado is suddenly turned into a whimpering, depressed person fleeing in fear. And he flees to the traditional place of refuge: the desert. But he does not go just anywhere in the desert. He goes to God's mountain, here called Horeb, elsewhere and more commonly, Mt. Sinai. He goes to the place where Moses and the people of Israel had experienced God in fire and storm and earthquake.

At God's mountain, Elijah too had an experience of God, very different from the one experienced by Moses and the people of Israel. Indeed, it was different from any experience he could have dreamed of. [So often it is true that our God comes to us in ways that we never anticipate or expect!] Elijah who had always thought of God as a God of power--and indeed a power that was often destructive--comes to know God in a whole new way. The story has great narrative strength. We are told that God was not in the wind, not in the earthquake, not in the fire. In other words, God is no longer to be sought primarily in those terrifying natural manifestations that accompanied God's appearance to Moses.

Instead Elijah experiences God "in a tiny whispering sound" or, as a more literal translation of the Hebrew would have it, "in the sound of silence." This episode marks a giant leap forward in the human understanding of what it means when we talk about God and where we should search if we wish to find God. The first place to search for God is in the quiet silence of our inner selves, in the depths of our own hearts, where there is that bit of God that we call the image of God.

God's greatest power is to be located, not primarily in the works God accomplishes in nature, but in the works of persuasive love that God exercises over the hearts of women and men. True, we can find God in what God does in nature and what God does in our sisters and brothers.

But we cannot really do this unless we first find God in the quietness of our own hearts. We cannot understand the God of power till we have met the God of gentleness.

The Gospel also is a scene of fear: frightened men huddled together in their small boat, fearing for their survival. They bob about on an enraged sea, all the more fearful because for Semitic peoples, the sea was looked upon as a symbol of evil. At any moment it threatened to engulf the land. The only thing that held it back from overwhelming all things was the power of God – which in the beginning had imposed limits on the sea. In the Hebrew Scriptures God's power was often celebrated as power over the sea. In Job we read: "God walks on the crest of the waves." In psalm 77: "Through the sea was your way, your path through the deep waters."

If the sea summed up for the disciples all that they feared, Jesus coming to them "on the crest of the waves, making a path through the deep waters" is an epiphany for them, far more concrete than the disembodied voice heard by Elijah. It is a familiar Voice which they hear, a gentle Voice announcing his presence, calming their fears and calling them to trust: "Take courage! It is I. Do not be afraid."

It is significant that this is the first time in Matthew that Jesus is called "Son of God." Like God, he can calm troubled waters. He can also calm frightened hearts and bring them peace.

Yet this is not the whole story. Matthew adds an episode – the Peter story – that has no parallel in this story in Mark's Gospel. The Peter-episode is important for us. For it makes clear that Jesus does not remove our fears once and for all. We are all too aware that the fears and the doubts come back. We find God in our lives, but then times come when we ask again: Where is God?

What this Peter-episode is intended to tell us is that our acceptance of Jesus' assurance – that He is with us – is not a once-for-all experience that settles everything, so that fears and troubles are gone forever. Quite the contrary our acceptance of His Presence in our lives, soothing our fears and bringing calm to our hearts, is a process that must go on continually in our lives.

Peter is the type of the Christian disciple: a person of faith. He steps confidently out onto the water and begins to walk on it. He forgets himself. He forgets what the sea symbolizes. He has eyes only for Jesus. But then the old fear of the sea takes over. Whereas at first he had thought only of Jesus, now he thinks only of himself. He sees the flimsiness of what supports him. Because his thoughts are on himself, he forgets the Presence of the Lord. Filled with fear, faith fading, he begins to sink. Jesus rebukes him for failing to have faith. But Jesus also raises him up. And somehow we know that the Peter who is raised up is a new Peter: a different person from the proud man who with such bravado had stepped onto the sea.

Faith needs to face trials. They are in a sense the condition of faith's growth. Every experience of faith passes through fear and doubt and then acceptance of the outstretched hand of the Lord Jesus. It's all part of a seemingly unending process of growth. A process that increasingly brings us to a new and deeper understanding of God (even when we don't always realize that it does). Many times we step out and try to walk on the waters *by ourselves* (There is that strong Pelagian strain in all of us: the sense that we can do it all by ourselves); and when we begin to sink in sudden fear, his strong arm lifts us up. And each time we feel his touch in our own seeming failure in faith, our faith becomes deeper and stronger.

One day the time will come --though not yet --when He will bid us to come to Him walking on the waters. And we shall at last find that we can do so. For His power holding us up will no longer seem to be a power outside us. We will experience it as what in reality it always was (even when we did not understand), a power that dwells within us -- that bit of God in us which is God's image. Then, because we are aware that we are in God and can confidently forget ourselves, then, we shall walk on the crest of the waves. We shall make our path through the sea.

THE TWENTIETH SUNDAY IN ORDINARY TIME

Isaiah 56: 1, 6-7
Psalm 67: 2-3, 5, 6, 8
Romans 11:13-15, 29-32
Matthew 15:21-28

I want to point out that a key word in the first reading, in the psalm and in the second reading is the word "ALL." The first reading is from an anonymous author called Third Isaiah, who wrote after the return of the exiles from Babylon. He sees foreigners, Gentiles, coming to the Jerusalem Temple and being accepted equally with the Jews. God's house, he says, is a house of prayer for all peoples. He was the first biblical writer to say that word: All. This is one of the great "Catholic" pages of the Old Testament.

The psalm also makes use of the word ALL. "O God, let all the peoples praise you." In the second reading, Paul speaks of the mystery of the Jewish people and shows how God wills to extend his mercy to Jew and Gentile alike. God, Paul tells us, wants to have mercy on ALL.

All is a difficult word to say. Let's reflect on some of the situation in which we find it difficult to say ALL. Think of discipleship. If we read the Gospels, we cannot miss the point that Jesus asks for ALL. We find it hard to respond to this kind of a call. Often our situation is: we are ready to give SOME; and indeed there are times when we are prepared to give A GREAT DEAL. But to give ALL: this we find scary. We don't like to go quite that far. We don't like to say ALL to the demands of Christian discipleship.

There are other situations where we find it difficult to say ALL. When the Roman Catholic Church talks about eligibility for ordained ministry, she finds herself more comfortable in saying SOME rather than ALL.

But perhaps the area in which we find it most difficult to say ALL is when we are talking about God's plan of salvation. In this situation we tend to think and speak in exclusive language that is even more harmful than exclusive gender language. For, in thinking about God's salvific will, we tend to distinguish US from THE OTHERS. We are the objects of the divine salvific will; "The Others" are outside that salvific will.

Those whom we designate as "The Others" have been different people at different times in the history of the church. In the earliest period – about which we read in the New Testament, "The Others" were the Gentiles. Salvation, the Jewish Christians thought, was for US, not for them. Later, when the Church became largely a Gentile Church, the groups of people designated as the others changed radically. And, if we move quickly to our own time, we can all admit that 40 years or so ago, "The Others" were probably Protestants. We called them "heretics." We did not really believe – many of us at least – that their religious commitment was in any way a means of reaching God and achieving salvation.

The ecumenical movement has to a great extent begun to break down the barriers between Catholics and Protestants and we are more and more using the more inclusive term "Christian."

But the exclusive language continues and we go on distinguishing US and THE OTHERS. Now THE OTHERS would be Hindus, Buddhists, etc. – all those who are not Christians.

Yet we must remind ourselves that the Church cannot be true to her fundamental nature, if she continues to make this division in speaking of the saving purposes of God. We have to learn to say, not US and OTHERS, but ALL.

When I say this I do not mean that the Church must claim that all are somehow within her parameters. But she must say that God's saving hand reaches out to all. God uses the Church to save some. But His salvific will extends beyond the Church --to all who are ready to respond in faith. The Church must say this, if she is to be true to herself and to the Gospel. All of which brings us to today's impressive Gospel – a rapier-sharp dialogue between Jesus and this Gentile woman who comes from the area of Tyre and Sidon. On the one side of this dialogue is the Jewish rabbi, Jesus of Nazareth, and on the other side this Canaanite woman (Mark calls her a Syro-Phoenican woman, a more proper designation of where she came from). It is Matthew who uses the term "Canaanite" to describe her - a term had lost its geographical meaning and had come to mean the enemies of the Jews, in other words the outsiders, the others. The story surprises us, for Jesus confronts the woman with what can only be called the typical exclusive attitude of the Jews of the time. Salvation, he tells her, belongs to the Jews. But the woman refuses to abide by the exclusive language which Jesus uses. There is a battle of wits and, in the only incident of its kind, Jesus is outmaneuvered by this clever woman. But there is more than cleverness here. There is what many of Jesus' co-religionists of the time thought could belong only to Jews, namely, strong faith in God.

So undauntable is her faith that it wins, not only Jesus' admiration, but also what seems to be a reluctant but moving exercise of his healing power.

How are we to understand this strange story? Does Matthew mean to say that Jesus knew all the time that he would grant her request, but was putting her faith to trial? This is surely a possible interpretation, though it seems a bit contrived. There is another way of looking at this story which seems to fit its details better. Was Matthew telling us that this was a learning experience for Jesus: an experience that broke Him out of the exclusive mentality that so strongly characterized the Jews of His day? Was it an experience which made him realize that God always says: ALL? After all, if we say that Jesus was truly human, we must believe that His human understanding could and had to grow. Did Jesus originally consider his ministry as only to the Jews and was this the moment when He experienced God blowing His mind and bringing him to the realization that FAITH can blossom anywhere - in Jew or

Gentile? And, where FAITH is, there is God. Or does Matthew have this intent? Is he perhaps using this story as a kind of parable to teach the Church of his time that the Good News we call the Gospel is for all and that any exclusive claim to that Gospel meant infidelity to its very message?

We live in a time in human history in which – perhaps more than any other time – it is dangerous to distinguish between US and The Others. Whether we like it or not, our world has become one family, at least in the sense that our security and safety are bound up with the security and safety of the rest of the world. It may seem almost naive to talk about world unity, at a time when terrorism and ethnicity seem almost to force us to draw a line in the sand to separate US and the OTHERS. Yet, naive or not, it may be that not only in terms of salvation, but also in terms of world survival, we need more and more to think and speak in inclusive terms. We must learn to say ALL.

We live in troubled times in our Church, but we also live in troubled times in our country. There are times when our government in the past seemed to be adopting policies that were isolating us from the rest of the world. More and more we seem to be heading toward a policy of "doing it alone." After all we are the one super-power. The others need to listen to us. This is a very dangerous attitude to adopt in the world in which we live. Both as Church and as Country we can no longer afford to distinguish US from THEM. The very condition of our salvation, both in this life and in the next is our learning to say ALL, our learning to see One Humanity loved by God. To refuse to say ALL is to fail to live the fullness of discipleship.

THE TWENTY FIRST SUNDAY IN ORDINARY TIME

Isaiah 22: 19-23
Psalm 138:1-2, 2-3, 6, 8
Romans 11:33-36
Matthew 16:13-20

Quite a number of years ago Mortimer Adler wrote a book called: "How *to* Read a Book." Most people, until they read his book, felt quite certain that they knew how to read a book. They found there was more to it than they had realized. Some day — maybe when I arrive at old age — I would like to think about writing a hook on "How to Read the Gospels." I was a priest for quite a few years before I learned how to read the Gospels.

We used to read them as four historical and biographical writings, all four of them telling the same story in the same way. When we detected what seemed to be differences, we were quick to find some way — at times rather torturous ways -- of harmonizing them. Today this patchwork approach to reading the Gospels together — namely trying to put them together to make one harmonious story out of all four — is very much out of favor.

We have learned to recognize the uniqueness and the richness of each of the Gospels. They all communicate the same fundamental Good News about Jesus, but each does so with *its* own distinctive approach.

What we must state emphatically is that they are not biographies or histories. This is not to deny that they do contain biographical and historical information. They certainly do. But their primary intent is theological. The Gospels are documents which express the faith of the early Church. Sometimes they rearrange historical narratives, not necessarily in the order in which they happened, but in a way that suits their theological intent and the needs of the particular community for which each Gospel was written.

I make this point because it is crucially important when we read the Gospels to know what kind of question we should put to the text. The primary question is not: "What happened?" but *"What does it mean?"* Today's Gospel is a good example of what I am saying. All three synoptic Gospels relate the two questions Jesus put to his disciples: "Who do they say that I am?" and "Who do you say that I am?" All three also narrate that Peter spoke in the name of all and professed their faith in Jesus as Messiah. They all have Peter's statement: "You are the Messiah." Then at this point, there is a divergence in the narratives.

In Mark and Luke this confession of Peter becomes the occasion for Jesus to clarify the kind of Messiah he will be, namely a suffering Messiah and a Messiah whose followers must also take up the cross. Matthew also has this clarification about the suffering Messiah, but unlike the other two, he inserts a statement between Peter's profession that Jesus is the Messiah and Jesus' words about the sufferings that the Messiah and his followers must endure. The insertion has to do with the crucial and central role that Jesus intends Peter to play in "the community of God's people."

I say "the community of God's people" and I am using this phrase as a substitute for the Greek word which usually gets translated as "Church." The Greek word I am referring to is the word ekklesia. This word derives from the Greek word kalein which means "to call" and the preposition ek which, when added to kaleo, gives it the meaning: "to call together."

This is the precise meaning of "Church." Its references to a building is only secondary. Its primary meaning is "people gathered together by God." That is why a church building ought to look empty, until "the Church," – namely the people – arrive. All the people — readers, servers, communion ministers, the presiding priest and the rest of the participating congregation -- are the "Church."

I want to stress this because so often the Church seems to be an abstraction for people: something outside of them, something existing far away (like in Rome, for instance, or at a pastoral center on Buffalo Road in Rochester, NY). It would help us keep our perspectives straight if every time we heard or read the word "Church," we would add in our minds a parenthesis that would say: "This means people, people called by God;" or, you could vary this and on occasion say "Church. Yes, this means us – all of us bishops, priests, laity."

Why does Matthew speak here of a conferral of power on Peter over this community of God's people, when Mark and Luke say nothing about it? Is he perhaps transposing the conferral of power on Peter that in the 4th Gospel takes place after the resurrection, when Jesus calls Peter to feed his lambs and feed his sheep?

Now if you have followed the point I made earlier, you will understand that when we read this text of Jesus' words to Peter, the important question about this scene is not the historical question *when did it happen?* but the theological question: *what does it mean?* What is the meaning of the role, the power that Jesus has given to Peter? What kind of leadership is he called on to exercise in the community of God's people?

Part of the answer to these questions is to be found in history, namely, in the way in which the Petrine office has been exercised over time. Especially important is the way it was exercised in the early centuries of the Church that were closest to the Christ-event.

Obviously we would expect that there would be development in the way this office has been exercised through the course of history. But whether these developments are judged good or bad, this text from Matthew cannot be used to justify all these developments.

The only sound way of evaluating them is to ask whether they help or hinder the proper function of the successor of Peter as the center of unity in the Church, though not the source of that unity. All the local churches throughout the world contribute to that unity. The Pope acts best as the center of the Church's unity when he speaks for the Church rather than *to* the Church.

Thus, when the Pope gives a talk to a group meeting in Rome, this isn't necessarily the last word on that subject. Actions or pronouncements from various curial officials may or may not reflect the considered position of the pope or the belief of the community of God's people. The voice of the successor of St. Peter may sometimes be muffled in the statements made by those who are in his employ, but do not share the mandate he received from the Lord Jesus.

Today's Gospel is only one of two places in all the four Gospels in which the word "Church" is used. The word that is most often on the lips of Jesus is the word Kingdom. Note how Peter, who is made the rock-foundation of the Church, is given the keys of the kingdom. This must not lead us to make the mistake of identifying the Church and the Kingdom.

The Kingdom means the reign of God over the hearts and lives of God's people. The task of Peter and indeed of all ministers in the Church is to strive to lead people ever more fully into that personal acceptance of God's reign which constitutes the Kingdom.

But we must be clear that membership in the Church cannot simply be equated with membership in the Kingdom. We must keep a proper perspective on the relationship of the Church and the Kingdom. We need to see the Church not as an end in itself, but as the instrument of the Kingdom.

This is to say that what is ultimate for human life is not the Church but the Kingdom, namely, that full acceptance of God's reign over our hearts and our lives. What this means is that the Church exists ultimately in order to disappear. When the Kingdom of God is achieved in all its fullness, the Church will cease to be; for it will have achieved the purpose for which it exists.

Ultimacy belongs to the Kingdom, not to the Church. There was a time when we used to describe as the Church Triumphant those who had entered through death into the fullness of God and God's kingdom. That was at best a metaphor – and probably not a very good one at that. For in heaven there is no Church, only people.

THE TWENTY SECOND SUNDAY IN ORDINARY TIME

Jeremiah 20:7-9
Psalm 63: 2, 3-4, 5-6, 8-9
Romans 12:1-2
Matthew 16:21-27

I recently heard someone described as a truly "authentic" person. That is a high compliment. An authentic person is one who is in touch with her own inner truth, with her own center, where she finds her true self and also finds God. So often our lives can be inauthentic, because we fail to be ourselves before others. So often our prayer can be inauthentic, because we fail to be ourselves before God.

The first reading of today's liturgy puts before us one of the most authentic persons in the whole Bible. This reading is one of a series of prayers that biblical scholars refer to as "the confessions of Jeremiah." Hearing it enables us to enter into the very heart of Jeremiah and see how truly authentically human he is. There is no pretense in his prayer. It comes straight from the heart; and it's a heart that is broken. He has preached God's word, done God's work. What happens? All he meets with is opposition, suffering failure. In his despair he asks God: "What have you got against me that you let all this happen?"

He feels that God has let him down. He rails against God with outrageous boldness. "You have duped me, O Lord! Yet I know you are stronger than I." In effect, he is saying:

"God, you're a great Bully. And frankly I have had it up to my neck. I have been unflinchingly faithful in your service. And you haven't helped a bit. You've let me down."

Jeremiah's prayer sounds almost like blasphemy; yet it's anything but that: it's the authentic outpouring of a heart broken by a weight it seems unable to bear. It's Jeremiah being desperately honest with himself and with God, as he faces the temptation to pack up his bags and let God handle things alone. He faces the temptation to give up his call to be a prophet. "I will not mention God any more. I will speak in God's name no more."

Yet this is only half the picture – and only half the prayer. There is something else in Jeremiah's heart, just as genuine as its brokenness. It is God's word burning there, demanding to be spoken. And Jeremiah realizes he cannot rid himself of that Word. In spite of himself he must speak it, whatever the cost. And with that realization, the broken heart is somehow mended. And the prophet becomes whole again.

This prayer is surely one of the most moving passages in scripture: a man's honest grappling with his own inner truth, facing the desperateness of his own feelings and emotions and at the same time finding the depths of his commitment to God. And it is only when he reached the bottom of his despair that he realized the depths of that commitment.

Jeremiah's struggle for his own authenticity verifies Jesus' question in the Gospel: "What profit would there be to gain the whole world and forfeit one's life?"

In one sense Jeremiah gained nothing from his struggle with God; God did not change his situation; people continued to oppose and revile and persecute him. Yet in another sense, he gained everything: for he found his true self and he found God.

Jeremiah's struggle is proof – if proof be needed – that struggle with one's vocation and within one's vocation – far from being a death blow to that vocation, may be the very condition of its vitality.

Few of us are called to face the gigantic kind of struggle that was visited upon Jeremiah. But each of us experiences in one way or another, the reality of the Cross that Jesus speaks about to his uncomprehending disciples. There come times when we feel the sense of frustration and uselessness, the sense of wondering where we are going, the sense of being let down by others, even by God.

There are three ways of confronting the cross. (1) One is to fight it, as Peter so vainly tried to do in the Gospel reading. (2) Another way is to pretend it isn't there and to choose to live in a world of illusion and unreality. (3) Or one can come to grips with her or his genuine feelings, as Jeremiah did.

This last way is especially important in our prayer – if our prayer is to remain related to our lives, if it is to be authentic. In prayer we should never pretend to be what we are not or to feel what we do not feel.

It was the honesty of Jeremiah's prayer that put him on the road to true conversion and an understanding of his true identity.

Honesty in prayer can serve the same purpose for us too. For honesty in our contact with God puts us in touch with our own inner truth. And it is only in fidelity to our own inner truth that we can become authentic persons: knowing who we are and accepting God's plans for us, even when we don't understand. It is only in fidelity to our inner truth that we can begin to find the fulfillment in our own lives of the beautiful prayer of St. Augustine: *"Noverim Te, noverim me."* ("May I know You, O God. May I know myself.")

THE TWENTY THIRD SUNDAY IN ORDINARY TIME

Ezekiel 33:7-9
Psalm 95: 1-2, 6-7, 8-9
Romans 13: 8-10
Matthew 18-15-20

Some time ago I remember hearing on the News Hour with Jim Lehrer a distressing story. It was about a serious crime committed on the campus of the University of California at Berkeley. I don't recall the details, but the crime was the rape and beating of a young woman. The story centered about a young man who witnessed the crime and felt no responsibility to report it to the authorities.

There was a strong uproar from the other students, who demanded that he leave Berkeley. He was very defensive. "I didn't do anything wrong," he maintained." Berkeley has the best department in my field and I have no intention of leaving."

Our first reading, from Ezekiel, presupposes a society in which tribal unity was very strong and, therefore, it was a society in which people took it for granted that there is a responsibility to correct someone who is guilty of a crime.

That responsibility was more easily understood in Ezekiel's time precisely because the tribal morality that dominated society in his day saw people not as separate individuals, but as members of the tribe. What hurt one of them became the responsibility of all.

We live in a society where privacy has a much higher value than it had in Ezekiel's time. His was a society where the interdependence of individuals on one another was more obvious.

In our society there is much discussion that wants to suggest that a person's private morals are his or her own affair. If people want to do things that will shatter their lives, they are free to do so. Legislators, seeing this as a problem, want to make laws to oblige people to take responsibility for what others do, because what others do can affect the whole community.

So at times there have been calls for a Good Samaritan law that would oblige a person to report a crime that she or he may have witnessed. This is not an uncommon effort today: to try to enforce morality by legislation. It hardly ever works.

Today's Gospel calls us to do something that is not easy. To correct a brother or sister face-to-face is a difficult assignment to have. Most of us would prefer to duck it, maybe wanting to say, like the young Berkeley student: "It's not my affair. I didn't do anything wrong." (Though I suppose I ought to add that there are some few people who rather enjoy the responsibility of correcting others and even do it in some instances where no such responsibility exists).

But clearly the majority of people don't like to assume this responsibility; first, because it's hard to do and, second, because it seems to conflict with another responsibility we have, namely, the responsibility to respect the uniqueness of every person we meet and to allow them to be themselves.

We have to face the fact that there is a thin line between imposing my ideas on another and correcting her in such a way that helps her to become more fully her unique self; a thin line between sitting in judgment on another (which we must never do) and admonishing her against a course of action that clearly is going to bring harm to her and to others; a thin line between rash judgment and genuine concern.

Correcting a sister or brother is honest and authentic, only if somehow I make clear that it proceeds from a deep sense of caring, the kind of caring Paul calls for in our second reading: a caring that is so profound that I am willing to risk the loss of friendship, if my concrete expression of caring is rebuffed.

Yet, unless I am grossly misreading Jesus' words, he is telling us that we must walk that thin line. He is saying that we need to correct one another – because we care. And we care because we are a community in Jesus Christ.

And we are a community, not principally because we have built community, but because Jesus has drawn us into the circle of his friends, the circle of his love. Indeed, I must see them as a part of a wider family to which we all belong and for whose needs we must respond as to our own.

Thus when you begin to reflect upon it, loving our neighbor as ourselves takes on a rich meaning: a meaning that we may never have thought about before or perhaps didn't want to think about.

Yes, we are all one human community: a community to which Jesus forever belongs, because he became one of us. In becoming one of us he drew all humanity into the embrace of that circle of Love that is the life of the Blessed Trinity. In the opening prayer of the Mass, we prayed:
Lord, our God,
in you justice and mercy meet.
With unparalleled love
you have saved us from death
and drawn us into the circle of your life.

What a joy for us to be drawn into the circle of the friends of God. In that circle of friends, we are responsible for the good of all in that wonderful circle.

And in talking about responsibility to correct, we must not overlook the real possibility that there may be times when we ourselves (surprising as this may seem to us!) need to be corrected.

It requires courage and a lot of love to correct another. It takes humility, as well as a good sense of oneself, to be able to accept correction. This courage (to correct) and this humility (to accept correction) probably only make sense, when we live in that encircling Love that is the very life of God. That wonderful circle of friends of God – a circle that never confines - for it is always expanding.

THE TWENTY FOURTH SUNDAY IN ORDINARY TIME

Sirach 27: 30 – 28: 9
Psalm 103: 1-2, 3-4, 9-10, 11-12
Romans 14: 7-9
Matthew 18: 21-35

Dom James Fox, who had been Thomas Merton's abbot, became a hermit after he retired as abbot. One day two young men came to his hermitage looking for money. Money! They searched and found no money. They beat him and then made off with the few things they thought might be of value. As they were running out the door, he cried out: "Boys, come back." They turned around. Then he said: "I give you everything you have taken, so that you will not have the sin of stealing on your soul. And I forgive you what you have done." A foolhardy, unbelievable story of forgiveness. Not something to imitate. But it surely highlights the message of today's readings, which call us to an important but difficult virtue: forgiveness. Sirach tells us "Forgive your neighbor's injustice; then when you pray your sins will be forgiven."

These readings – all about forgiveness – we are hearing them on 9/11: a day that is no longer a date on our calendar, but a time to remember a terrible national disaster – and today at a time when we are suffering through an even worse disaster. At such a time what does it mean to forgive? Who is it that needs to be forgiven? Or better, perhaps, who is there that yet has the right to forgiveness? Forgiveness calls for an admission of guilt, an acceptance of the need to be forgiven. Forgiveness calls for actions that will show that forgiveness can rightfully be given. Before we can talk about forgiveness on the huge scale required by these events, we have to continue asking questions. We have to continue to make demands for accountability.

We simply cannot not handle the issue of forgiveness at this huge level of responsibility. Yet we have these readings today. Perhaps the best we can do is to reflect on them in terms of what goes on at a more personal level – in our own daily lives, where forgiveness is often called for in our interpersonal relationships.

Think of Jesus' words to Peter. Peter had heard Jesus speak about forgiveness before. He assumed he was being very generous when he set his forgiving limit at seven times. Jesus answers: "Not only seven times, but seventy times seven times."

You can, of course, give a literalist meaning to Jesus' words and conclude that he means 490 times. Then you might say: "So far this month I have forgiven so-and-so 489 times. So she is entitled to only one more time of forgiveness. After that I can really clobber her and still be a good Christian." But of course that would be a complete misreading of Jesus' words. What he says so clearly is that our forgiveness must have no limits. We must be ready to offer the hand of forgiveness to everyone and at all times.

We might ask the question: "Why must I forgive? What's the point?" I recall one time discussing this text in a scripture course I was teaching at Nazareth College. Even though this was some years ago, I have always remembered a very perceptive question put by one of the students. She said: "For me it's not enough to be told that Jesus wants me to forgive. I need to have some human basis for forgiving. I need to experience that forgiving will make some difference in my life. I don't want to sound selfish, but I do feel the need to ask: 'Is there some human good that I will experience in forgiving?'"

The question showed remarkable insight. After all Christian Faith is not about drawing up a list of things (one of them being to forgive) and saying: "If you want to be a follower of Jesus, you must do this and this; and you must do these things because Jesus commands them." No, Jesus respects our humanness. He wants what he commands to find some resonance in our human experience. He does not command us to do certain things, simply because he commands them. Rather he commands certain things because they are good for us. Forgiveness is good for us in a number of ways – and again I am talking about it at this personal level.

First of all, in forgiving another we expand our horizons. When we forgive we build community. We gain a friend. We break down barriers; and this is a good experience for us. It is not good for us to live with walls separating us from others. Second, when we forgive, we expand our lives not only horizontally, but vertically too. By that I mean that in forgiving others we prepare ourselves to receive God's forgiveness for our faults. That is the precise point of the parable of today's Gospel. The text of the parable speaks in terms of ancient Roman currency. The amount that the servant was owed by his fellow-servant was 100 denarii. Now a denarius was a normal day's pay for a worker. Hence the debt owed by the fellow-servant was not enormous: the equivalent of a hundred days' pay. But the debt which the first servant owed to his master was so large that he would never have been able to pay it back.

We are told that he owed his master "ten thousand talents." Now a "talent" was the largest unit of money known in the Near East and ten thousand would be the highest number they would use in counting. I suppose a talent might be likened to a million-dollar bill, if there is such a thing. To Palestinian peasants, ten thousand talents would be an amount of money that they would not even be able to imagine. It would be something like our trying to imagine our skyrocketing national debt. You get to a certain point in figures with zeros being added and added that the sum is quite beyond the capability of our imagination to grasp.

This contrast between a relatively small sum (100 denarii) and an enormous sum (10,000 talents) is at the heart of the point that the parable intends to make. The point is that the amount owed to the master by the first servant was so great that he could never in a million years repay it. We are expected to notice the naiveté of his plea: "Be patient with me and I will pay you back in full." Surely he knew better: that it was not within the possibility of his resources to be able ever to fulfill that promise.

On the other hand, in the case of the second servant, it was quite within the range of possibility for him to pay back the hundred denarii he owed. By saving a bit here and there – for instance buying generic foods instead of name brands at the Capernaum super-market – he could have gradually paid off his debt.

What the parable is asking of us is to do is put ourselves in the shoes of a fellow who has received what amounts to infinite mercy and who refuses to show the slightest mercy to a fellow-servant. It would be a misread of the story if one were to think that our God is a God of retaliation who says to us: "If you don't forgive, I'll show you: I won't forgive you either." This would be a misunderstanding of the God Jesus revealed to us: a God who always forgives.

The point of the parable is much more profound. It isn't saying that God doesn't want to forgive us, if we don't forgive. Rather the point is that God cannot forgive us unless we forgive. For unforgiving hearts are hardened hearts: because they refuse to impart forgiveness, they are incapable of receiving it. Suppose a friend asked you to plant a flower for her in a huge block of concrete. You might very much want to do this, because you love your friend. But you are unable to do so. For concrete is too hard a material to be able to receive the roots of the flower. In a similar manner forgiveness cannot be received into an unforgiving heart. Such a heart is a hardened heart.

There are times when spiritually we need "open heart" surgery. We need to have our sometimes hardened hearts opened by God's grace, so that His love may flow into us and through us to others.

We say the Lord's Prayer each day. We need to reflect on it often. When we ask for our daily bread, we speak for the millions of people in our world who go to bed hungry and accept our responsibilities toward them. When we ask for forgiveness for our trespasses, we oblige ourselves to be generous with our forgiveness. Be careful: The Lord's Prayer is a very dangerous prayer to say.

THE TWENTY FIFTH SUNDAY IN ORDINARY TIME

Isaiah 55:6-9
Psalm 145:2-3, 8-9, 17-18
Philippians: 1: 20c-24, 27a
Matthew 20: 1-16

The parable of today's Gospel is probably not your favorite Gospel parable. Almost instinctively our sympathies seem to go out to the wrong people. Yet it is an important parable. It offers a challenge we need to face. As parables go, too, there is a stroke of genius in the way it is told. There is a key-sentence that makes this parable both forceful and puzzling. It's that curious command that the vineyard owner gives to his foreman: "Pay the last first and the first to come last." This command sets the stage (one might almost say "sets the trap") for the challenge the parable is intended to convey.

Were it not for this command, the full-time workers would not have seen the pay given to those who worked only part of the day. They would have gone home happy that they had obtained work and earned a full-day's pay. The part-time workers would have gone away happy too, impressed by the generosity of the vineyard owner who had the insight and the compassion to realize that these workers, just as much as the full-time ones, needed a full-day's pay in order to feed their families.

The point is, if there had not been this command to reverse the order of payment, everyone would have been happy. But because there was this reversal, the full-time workers, as they are forced to wait and see what the others receive, only find that they receive the same amount. Immediately they are overwhelmed by unhealthy emotions. They do not share in the broad-minded generosity of the vineyard owner. They don't rejoice with their fellow-workers. They suddenly begin to feel that they have been unjustly treated: not because they did not receive the wage they had agreed upon, but because the other workers received the same as they did. What this really means is that, when they see the part-time workers receiving more than they deserve, suddenly they are no longer satisfied with the bargain they had entered into; they think they too should receive more than they deserve. They put themselves in a contradictory position: they begin to feel that they deserve more than they deserve. They simply cannot understand or appreciate the ways of the vineyard owner.

Just as these full-time workers cannot understand the ways of the vineyard owner, so Isaiah tells us in the first reading, we cannot fathom God's ways. His thoughts are not our thoughts, our ways are not his ways. The trouble with our God is that God continually refuses to fit into the stereo-type roles we try to cast God in. We believe in the principle of fairness: people ought to be treated in the same way. The difficulty is that God puts God's own twist on this principle. Our God is a God who loves people when they seem to deserve it – and this is something we can understand. But God also loves people even when they are not deserving. This we find difficult to accept, especially if we happen to believe ourselves to be among the deserving ones.

The real problem which this parable bumps us into is the mystery of a creature – who is all too often capable of not loving and not caring and indeed who frequently demands reasons why he or she should love or care – the mystery of this kind of creature trying to fathom the ways of a God who is all-loving and all-caring. You and I are quite capable of "not loving," of "not caring." What we find so hard to understand is that God can't do what we can: God can't not love. God can't not care. Because of this huge difference between God and us, we just don't understand. The result is that we tend to judge God as if sometimes God loves and other times God does not. Isn't this the reason why the question is so often on our lips: "Why does God allow things to happen the way they do?" Or, when our plans go awry or we face some unexpected suffering, we feel the need to implicate God: "Why does God allow this to happen to me?"

But we go even farther. We can, like those full-time workers make comparisons. We see people who, to all appearances at least, are less generous, less kindly (and therefore, we conclude, less deserving) than we are. Yet their lives seem to be smooth-sailing. We experience the cross in ways they seemingly do not. And we are left with the question: "Why?" "Why me?" The supreme example in the Bible of a person who kept asking "Why" is Job. He thunders out his questions about the strange ways of Providence and decries the unfairness of it all. Job doesn't get an answer. But he does get something

289

infinitely more important than an answer to his self-centered question. He gets the wisdom to know that there are times when we need to let go of the question "why" and put it in the hands of a God who is at once all-mystery and all-love.

Yet when I say that, I am reading Job in the light of the Gospel. I probably ought to say Job learned to leave the question "Why" in the hands of a God who is unfathomable Mystery. Period. That this One Who is All-Mystery is also All-Love, this is a revelation that had to wait the proclamation of the Gospel. We have this immense advantage over Job. For we know that our God loves us with a love beyond all calculating. We know – what Job could not know or at most could know only obscurely – that when God says: "My thoughts are not your thoughts and my ways are not your ways," that God is talking about the ways of divine Love. The Ways of One who loves us when we deserve it, but – surely the greatest mystery of all – who loves us even when we are most undeserving.

Wanting an answer to the question "Why," especially about the deep issues of human life, is perfectly understandable. The terrible events of September 11, 2001 moved us almost irresistibly to ask: "Why did this happen? Why did God allow this to happen?"

We should not ignore the need we have to put such questions. We should not try to suppress them. They serve a purpose. They are stages along the journey of the human spirit, yet we need to understand - speculatively at first perhaps, but more experientially as we get on with that journey – that one day we shall reach a point when we shall be able to let go of the need for explanations. When this time comes – and we can't hurry its coming – we shall stop asking God the question: "Why?" Then we shall have only one question to put to God and that question will be: "What?" When we reach the point where we really are grasped by the truth that God is ALL-LOVE, we shall be quite content to say: "What do you ask of me?"

At that point of self-surrender to Love, we shall be in good company: in the company of the one completely human person who made the journey best. We shall be with her who was content simply to say: "What do you ask of me? Be it done to me according to your word."

THE TWENTY SIXTH SUNDAY IN ORDINARY TIME

Ezekiel 18: 25-28
Psalm 25: 4-5, 6-7, 8-9
Philippians 2:1-11
Matthew 21: 28-32

There is a bit of subtle psychology in the deceptively simple parable of today's Gospel. It is about relationships – whether with God or with one another. It suggests that relationships, for us, always involve a struggle between saying "Yes" and saying "No." One of the baffling elements of human relationships is that people at times say one thing, when they really mean quite the opposite.

In human relationships we can affirm the other in his/her gifts or we can lessen their sense of self-worth by continually singling out their faults. A relationship grows toward maturity when more and more we are able to forget ourselves in the relationship and say a resounding "Yes" to the other in terms of who she is and who she can become.

Yet we need to realize that not infrequently self-seeking enters into our relationships, so that there is often an ambiguity in the "Yes" we say to others. It may be a "Yes" that is so half-hearted that eventually it becomes a "No."

But it is also true that there are times when for the moment we seem to say "No" to the other, but somehow there is a repentance in our "No" that moves us to reconsider, so that what began as "No" to the other actually becomes "Yes." In terms of our relationship with God, the Christian life is a process whereby – living in the midst of conflicting "No's" and "Yes's"—we learn increasingly and often slowly to make our response to God an irrevocable "Yes." We achieve perfection in the Christian life when we become a "total Yes" to God in every aspect of our lives. When we reach this point we are truly "in Christ." It is no longer we who live, but Christ lives in us.

There is a moving passage in the first chapter of 2nd Corinthians, in which Paul speaks of his relationship to the Christians at Corinth and defends himself against the charge of fickleness. He writes to them: "As God keeps his word, I declare that my word to you is not 'Yes' one minute and 'No' the next." Then he goes on to speak of Jesus and describes Him as One who is always YES. "Jesus Christ whom I preached to you as Son of God, he tells them, "was not alternately "Yes" and "No"; he was never anything but "Yes."

These are striking words. Paul is telling us that Jesus' real name is "YES." YES to God and YES to God's creation, and especially His human creation. Jesus is YES to God because He always does the will of God.

Jesus is YES to humanity because He identifies with us. But most especially He is YES to us because he identifies with the lowliest among us: the poor, the outcasts, the sinners. *By choice* Jesus associated with tax-collectors and those who were considered public sinners. He affirmed them, not in their sinfulness, but in the beauty and truth of their humanness that not even their sin could touch. Jesus said "Yes" to them, in order that they might be able to say "Yes" to the finer instincts in themselves and ultimately say "Yes" to God.

In the Gospel parable we are confronted with the son who says "Yes" with his lips, but "No" in his actions and the other son who says "No" in his words, but regrets his words and eventually says "Yes" by his actions.

What the parable tells us is that the first son who had initially said "No" underwent a change. He experienced repentance. But the genius of the parable consists in its calculated ambiguity. Did the "Yes" that he finally spoke mark a real and permanent change in him; or was it simply an isolated act of momentary repentance followed by a return to his customary self-centeredness? Was his "Yes" strong enough to see him through further and more difficult choices?

The answer is: we do not know. The parable deliberately gives us no hint of the answer. What it does is to leave us to reflect on the nature and quality of our own repentance. Is our "Yes" to God precarious, a "Yes" hovering hesitantly on the brink of "No"? Is it weak or strong, firm or shaky? And yet further, what is the "Yes" we say to one another, to our sisters and brothers in the human community?

In the Introduction to the Japanese edition of *The Seven Storey Mountain*, Thomas Merton describes the "No's" and "Yes's" of his life:

> *It is my intention to make my entire life a rejection of, a protest against, the crimes and injustices of war and political tyranny...By my monastic life and vows I am saying NO to all the concentration camps, the aerial bombardments, the staged political trials, the judicial murders, the racial injustices, the economic tyrannies and the whole socio-economic apparatus which seems geared for nothing but global destruction in spite of all its fair words in favor of peace. I make monastic silence a protest against the lies of politicians, propagandists and agitators...*
>
> *If I say NO to all these secular forces, I also say YES to all that is good in the world and in men and women...I say YES to all that is beautiful in nature...I say YES to all the men and women who are my brothers and sisters in the world.*

We have to ask ourselves: is our "YES" to our fellow-men and women a firm reaching out to all in our society who have been victimized by power-politics, by multi-national corporations, by imperialistic attitudes.

Today, as we hear this parable, we need to reflect on the "Yes's" and No's" that the Gospel calls us to say and to live. Do we continually say "YES" to life and do we make our own lives a protest against all those things that demean and violate personal dignity, freedom and equality? Do we oppose such violations of the human spirit, whether they occur in our country, in our world or in our Church? Do we say "NO" to war and all the preparations for war, because we insist on saying "YES" to life? And do we affirm all life-issues in a consistent life-ethic?

Recently I was asked to write a blurb for a new – and I think, important – book. It's a biography of a woman that you may or may not have heard about. Her name is Hildegard Goss-Mayr. The title is *Marked for Life*. The event that marked her for life refers to an action she performed when she was only ten years old. She lives in Vienna. When the Nazis invaded Austria, people were forced to stand on the sidewalks and give the Nazi salute as Hitler and his entourage passed by. This ten-year-old girl stood in the crowd with her hands at her side. She refused to greet Hitler and thus say "Yes" to the terrible acts of violence of a ruthless dictator. Hands at her side was her way of saying "No." It was indeed an action that "marked her for life." From then on this gracious woman has given her life to the practice and teaching of non-violence as the only way to achieve a global world where peace and compassion replace war and violence as the news of the world.

In spite of all the violence and terrorism, non-violence is going to win out. Hildegard Goss-Mayr models in herself the new world consciousness that is in process of being born: a heightened consciousness of human solidarity and oneness.

To return to the parable, the deliberate ambiguities in the parable of today's Gospel invite us to look at what may be ambiguities in our own lives. Jesus Christ was never anything but "YES." What did that "YES" mean to Him? What must "YES" mean to us, his disciples?

THE TWENTY SEVENTH SUNDAY IN ORDINARY TIME

Isaiah 5: 1-7
Psalm 80: 9, 12, 13-14, 15-16, 19-20
Philippians 4: 6-9
Matthew 21: 33-43

The parable of today's Gospel is an exegetical nightmare. It begins as a simple parable about a vineyard owner claiming his share of the fruits of his vineyard. The parable reminds us of Isaiah's well known song about God's vineyard. Matthew writes in such a way that clearly indicates he has that song in mind.

Yet the Isaiah song was about a vineyard that yielded a poor crop of grapes, despite the loving care of the vineyard owner. Matthew's parable, on the other hand, makes a completely different point: the vineyard produces *good* fruit, but the tenant farmers refuse to hand any of it over to the owner. The brutality of the tenants is surely exaggerated, when we are told that they murdered the owner's representative rather than hand over to the owner what was his due. The wisdom of the vineyard owner is surely called into question by his foolhardiness in sending his son, unprotected, to wicked farmers who had not scrupled at murder. The inconsistency of the parable is also seen in the unwarranted assumption by the tenants that, if the son and heir is gone, they will automatically inherit the land. In sum, I guess the best we can say is that this parable, whose original meaning is probably lost to us, has been turned into an allegory that has more to do with

298

the antagonism that existed between Jews and Christians at the time that Matthew's Gospel was written than anything said by Jesus during his ministry.

It is probably impossible for us to recover the original meaning intended by Jesus. Perhaps the simplest thing to do is to reflect on God's people as his vineyard and God's desire that that vineyard produce good fruit for God.

When the scriptures speak of God's vineyard, they picture God as a God with a green thumb: God knows how to lavish care and attention on the vineyard. But the scriptures also make plain that, when the vineyard fails to respond to this care and attention, God will either uproot it (as in the case of the Isaian song) or God looks for another vineyard: one that will produce the fruit God expects.

In the Fourth Gospel, as you know, the vineyard image is further refined: Jesus becomes the vine and we are the branches engrafted into the vine in Baptism. For Baptism inserts us into the life-stream that flows through the Vine. It calls us to live in Christ, as He lives in the Father. Since we are joined to God's son, God has high expectations of us. God expects us to be like the Vine to which we are joined, that is, God expects us to be fruitful. God lavishes love and tender care on us. But God truly wants us to respond.

What does it mean to respond to God? What does God expect of us? Actually, more than we are able to do by ourselves. God wants us to realize that we cannot live as isolated branches: we can only live by the life of the Vine. Only when we are joined to the Vine are we able to do more than we are able to do.

To put it another way, to respond to God is to reach beyond ourselves (beyond our pettiness, our self-centeredness), so that in the very act of transcending ourselves we are able to find our true identity and the identity of one another in Christ Jesus our Lord.

Did you notice the two things we asked of God in the opening prayer? We asked, first, that God "lead us to seek beyond our reach," and, second, we asked: "Give us the strength to stand before Your Truth." It might be helpful to reflect briefly on these two rather extraordinary petitions.

What do we mean when we ask to be led "to seek beyond our reach?" Quite simply what we have just been reflecting about, namely, that transcending of ourselves that will enable us to do what, alone and unaided, we cannot do. "To seek beyond our reach" is to seek to do the impossible. It's to dream the impossible dream.

And that impossible dream that Jesus dares us to dream is a community, and indeed, a world in which in which everyone cares for the other more than for self; a community, a world, in which the basic needs of others become more important than our own, often superfluous, needs. It is to dream about a world in which there will be no more war, no more killing, no more exploitation, no more manipulating of people for profit and money.

To be able to dream this impossible dream, requires of us that we cleanse our imagination. Our imagination has been crippled by so much evil that we have almost lost the capacity of imagining what it would be like to live in peace and harmony, in a world where life is not threatened, where air and water are not polluted, and where people are genuinely concerned for the true welfare of their sisters and brothers. As Denise Levertov has written:

The poet must give us
imagination of peace to oust the intense familiar
imagination of disaster.

Reaching beyond what is in our immediate grasp means more than dreaming and imagining, it calls for activity, for involvement. In earlier ages most people had neither the education, nor the communication skills, nor the political savvy to strive to make the world a better and safer world. We are perhaps the first age of women and men who do have all these assets of education, communication and the power to influence public action and moral behavior. We have the awesome responsibility to make use of the power we have as a people. The stakes are high. We dare not shirk the accountability we have before God and before our world.

There is also in the prayer for today the petition: "Give us courage to stand before your Truth." To stand with courage before God's truth is to see reality as it truly is — perhaps for the first time. It is to stand like Moses before a Burning Bush that at once reveals and also consumes our frailty, our weakness, our isolation, in such a way that there is nothing left in us of significance except Christ.

To stand before God's Truth is to stand before a mirror and to see in that mirror only the features of Christ. For the Truth of God is a revelation of our identity. It is a call to experience the oneness of all reality. It's the call of the vinedresser to produce fruit. That fruit today is especially the fruit of peace based on justice and forgiveness in a world in danger of losing its own sanity because its hubris, pride, and arrogance refuse to see that we all belong to one world and that it's everybody's world and not just ours. The fruit today is the fruit of plenty that will not tolerate a world of hunger and poverty and that commits itself to overcome these terrible evils that demean and dehumanize so many wonderful people.

Oscar Romero was chosen as archbishop of San Salvador because he was thought to be a safe choice who would stir the waters of political unrest. But one day he heard the true call of the Gospel: he saw the plight of the poor and finally had the courage to stand before God's truth and proclaimed it — till his life was taken one fateful day as he raised the chalice at Mass. Oscar Romero once wrote:

A Gospel that does not unsettle,
a Word of God that does not get under anyone's skin,

a Word of God that does not touch the real sin of the society in which it is being proclaimed, what Gospel is that?

What Gospel indeed.

THE TWENTY EIGHTH SUNDAY IN ORDINARY TIME

Isaiah 25: 6-10
Psalm 23: 1-4, 5-6
Philippians 4:12-14, 19-20
Matthew 22:1-14

The Gospel and the first reading are allegories rather than parables. The starting point of each is a frequent biblical theme: the banquet to which God invites God's people. And not just any banquet: it is a wedding banquet celebrating God's marriage with God's people. In the Isaiah reading God is the bridegroom and Israel, God's bride. The Gospel reading has the same theme, but with a significant modification. The Gospel banquet celebrates the wedding of God's people to God's Son. Here the Son has become the bridegroom. God is the Father who sends out invitations to the marriage of God's Son.

An interesting feature of the Gospel narrative is that there is a father of the groom. There is a groom. There are the invited guests. But strangely there is no mention of the bride. Why this omission? What has happened is that there is a fusion of the bride and the invited guests. What the Gospel story is telling us is that those invited to the banquet were not only guests; they were at the same time the bride of the banquet. What the story is saying in a rather cryptic way is that the bride, in effect, has refused to come to her own wedding.

What this allegory is actually wrestling with is a mystery: the mystery of a people called by God to be God's spouse and who reject that invitation. And it is important to realize that the early Christians had no doubts as to who were the *dramatis personae* of this drama of salvation. They identified Israel of old as the people who were called, and who, in the harshest way possible, said: "No." At the same time, they identified themselves with the people brought in from the streets to share the wedding feast. Thus, they saw themselves as the true guests, because at God's call, they came. Or, at a deeper level, they saw themselves as the new Bride who accepted the call of the Bridegroom.

We need to note the obvious smugness in this attitude, as the early Christians, while rejoicing that they had been called and had responded positively to the call, puzzled – perhaps more than they should have – over the mystery of Israel's refusal to accept Jesus. It is difficult for us to understand how perplexing this problem was for the early Christians. Paul labors through three chapters (9-11) in his epistle to the Romans, puzzling – one might almost say, agonizing – over the fate of his people. He cannot see God going back on the election of Israel as God's chosen people. The only solution he can think of is that in the end somehow all will work out as God wills. In God is the final resolution of the mystery.

As time went on, Christians tended, more and more, not just to puzzle over the mystery of Israel's failure to accept Christ, as Paul did. They resolved the mystery simply by asserting the culpability of Israel and seeing their rejection as a just act of God. This helps to account for the antagonism between Jews and Christians in the last part of the first century: an antagonism that clearly surfaces in the Gospel of Matthew, and specifically in last Sunday's Gospel and this Sunday's too. It also helps to explain why, when Christians achieved a position of prominence in society, anti-Semitism reared its ugly head and the persecution of Jews persisted in Christendom for centuries and indeed down to our own times. The Holocaust has to be seen as the culmination of centuries of anti-Semitism. There are still many questions being asked today about the Church and the attitude it took toward the terrible persecution of the Jews under the Nazis.

In 1963 Rolf Hotchhuch's play, *The Deputy,* treats Pope Pius XII as a renegade for not having openly protested against the mass murder of Jews by Hitler. True, the play may be partially faulted by failing to mention the Jews whom the Pope saved by opening churches and religious houses to hide them. Still the question remains. It does not go away. It comes up periodically. Several years ago John Cornwell had published a book called: *Hitler's Pope: The Secret History of Pius XII* which accused the Pope of not speaking out against the Nazis, and of suppressing an encyclical of his predecessor, Pius XI, that strongly condemned Nazism. Recently, James Carroll in his book *The Sword of Constantine: The Church and the Jews: A History* repeated similar charges.

Today we Christians should be in a better position to understand the Jewish people who, despite all sorts of hardships, have clung to their identity. Perhaps we need to see in that never-lost identity a Sign that, though they have not accepted Christ as the Bridegroom, they are still – in a mysterious way we may not be able to understand – the Bride of God who entered into covenant with them and who is a God who does not renege on promises made. Israel is still the Israel of God.

This may well mean that our reflection on the Gospel should highlight, not Israel's refusal to accept Jesus that so puzzled the early Church, but rather the implications that flow from the fact that we maintain that we *have* accepted Christ. As individuals and as Church we are the Bride of Christ. Our focus should not be 'why didn't Israel respond to Jesus?', but how ought we to respond?

First, we can take a hint from Isaiah and realize that as God's people we are not working to achieve salvation, but that as God's people, salvation is already God's gift to us. Hear Isaiah: "Let us rejoice and be glad that God has saved us." And the reference is to the present, not the future. It does not mean: "some day we will get to heaven." It means salvation is a reality of the present moment.

To say that salvation is a reality of the present moment means, among other things, that we have at our disposal not only our own gifts and talents, but the hidden strength of God acting in us. This is what Paul is talking about when he says, with a confidence born not of pride but of faith, "I can do all things in him who strengthens me." That's the real thing. We can really believe it.

Perhaps one final point about the Gospel. We are not only the invited guests and the Bride. We fit another role in the Gospel story: we are also the messengers of God's invitation. God sends us with the good news of salvation to all, and especially to the poor and the needy. Perhaps the most important message we are called to bring to our country and our world today is the promise of God's peace.

At the same time, we need to believe that God never goes back on God's promises. The Jewish people still remain – in a way we cannot yet full understand – God's chosen people.

THE TWENTY-NINTH SUNDAY IN ORDINARY TIME

Isaiah 45: 1, 4-6
Psalm 96: 1, 3, 4-5, 7-8, 9-10
1 Thessalonians: 1: 1-5b
Matthew 22:15-21

Whereas the first reading speaks of a surprising harmony between state and religion (as Isaiah sees a Persian Emperor becoming, unwittingly, the instrument of God's plans) the Gospel poses the problem of the possibility of conflict rather than harmony.

Jesus' questioners are clearly trying to force him into a political blunder. The question: "Is it lawful to pay the census tax to Caesar or not?" puts Jesus on the horns of a dilemma. If he answers "Yes," he will lose favor with the majority of the people and be branded as a traitor to Jewish independence. If he said "No," he risked getting in trouble with Roman authority as a fomenter of rebellion.

Jesus deftly evades the trap. He asks to see the coin with which the tax would be paid. They show him a denarius, a Roman coin. Unwittingly, they are caught in their own trap. For, by using Roman coins, they are accepting the imperial system and obligating themselves to pay tax within that system.

Jesus, pressing his advantage, asks for the name of the person whose image is on the coin. They have to acknowledge that it is Caesar's. Then he asks them to read the inscription on the coin. The Gospel doesn't tell us what they read. But we know from coins of the period that the inscription would have been five Latin words: "Tiberius Caesar, divi Augusti filius." Translated this means: "Tiberius Caesar, Son of the god Augustus."

There was not sufficient room on the coin to spell these five words out in full. So all are abbreviated except, significantly, the words "Caesar" and "God." And it is these two words -"Caesar" and "God" – that Jesus picks up in his memorable answer. Using the first word "Caesar," he answers their question about paying taxes to Caesar." "Give to Caesar the things that are Caesar's." But he doesn't stop there. Picking up the other word fully spelled out on the Roman coin ("God"), he enunciates another principle that lifts the dialogue to a new level: "Give to God the things that are God's."

It would be a misunderstanding to think that Jesus is setting forth two parallel and equally binding principles. The principle about Caesar was the answer to a question. The second was the enunciating of an absolute principle that relativizes the first. For our duty to Caesar is conditioned by the preemptive duty to give to God what is God's due. Caesar's claim to our allegiance disappears when Caesar claims what belongs only to God. Thus the words on the Roman coin – the denarius – yield two principles which are of fundamental importance.

The first principle – about Caesar – must always yield to the one about God. Yet it is important to say that, while the principle about God relativizes the principle about Caesar, it does not nullify it. It remains a command of Jesus that we give to Caesar the things that are Caesar's.

These principles, like so many in the Gospel, are not immediately translatable into concrete directives that will enable us to know easily what we owe to Caesar and what we owe to God.

The early Christians had to struggle with the concrete application of these principles to their life-situation; and we have to do the same in ours. For them, Caesar meant the imperial power that was despotic and often oppressive. For them, Caesar was embodied in a person, that of the emperor. For us, Caesar is not someone outside of us. In a democracy like ours Caesar is not independent of the people. Caesar is embodied in people. In many ways "Caesar" is (or ought to be) the creation of the people. We create Caesar by our vote, by our efforts to involve ourselves critically in the actions of our government. We create Caesar when we assume our share of responsibility for what our government does, as well as our responsibility to do all we can to change the course of government when it appears to be moving in directions that harm rather than enhance the common good of people.

We are finally reaching the end of a terribly enervating couple of years of political campaigns that have been tiresome and – frankly – boring. In a few weeks we shall be going to the polling places to cast our vote. And we shall be going as Catholics. Richard R. Gaillardetz has written: "I would challenge the position of some Catholic politicians who contend that, although they personally support Catholic teaching on issues like abortion, euthanasia or stem cell research, they do not wish to impose their private religious beliefs on others." Those who hold such a position seem to be saying that the moral beliefs they hold as Catholics are somehow something outside of them. Hence when they are acting in a political context, those moral commitments remain at home. They are not carried into the public arena.

This is an untenable position. It raises the question: may a Catholic ever accept legislation, like Roe vs. Wade? To answer this question, one must make an important distinction. We must distinguish *the moral principles* we hold from *the practical application* of those principles. Catholics may agree on certain moral principles, while at the same time disagreeing on the way in which those principles are best implemented. Thus, Catholic social teaching calls Catholics to a "preferential option for the poor." We are not free to dismiss the plight of the poor as somebody else's problem. Yet we can disagree on what Catholic social teaching obligates us to do as the most effective way of dealing with poverty.

The issue that probably raises the most difficult questions for Catholics is abortion. Catholic social teaching demands of a conscientious Catholic the commitment to oppose abortion not just privately, but publicly as well. But, if we keep in mind the difference between a moral principle and its implementation, "might not conscientious Catholics, precisely because of their convictions regarding abortion, pursue alternate strategies that in their judgment might be more effective in reducing the number of abortions in our country than criminalizing them?" (Gaillardetz)

In other words, could one make the judgment that it will be more fruitful to change the culture than to change the law?

Some years ago a Catholic diocese in England issued a statement asserting that in that diocese no woman with an unwanted pregnancy need have recourse to abortion. The diocese agreed to support the woman and her child – financially and psychologically. This support would continue till the child came of age.

In 2004 Mark Roche, then dean of Notre Dame Law School, pointed out that "the world's lowest abortion rates are in Belgium and the Netherlands, where abortion is legal but where the welfare state is strong."

Many Americans are unhappy with their country today. Patriotism is at a low ebb. In America today we need a patriotism that is prophetic. Prophetic patriots are like the prophets of old. They were called "the troublers of Israel," continually calling an erring people to turn back to God and to follow God's will. Prophetic patriotism is perhaps the patriotism of a few: people like Mohandas Gandhi, Martin Luther King, Jr., Dorothy Day, Thomas Merton and hosts of people less well-known. These are the people who refuse to remain silent and passive when they perceive that their country was (or is) moving in directions that are risky and morally questionable. *Silence in the face of evil is the betrayal of patriotism.*

THE THIRTIETH SUNDAY IN ORDINARY TIME

Exodus 22:20-26
Psalm 18: 2-3, 3-4, 47, 51
1 Thessalonians 1: 5c-10
Matthew 22: 34-40

After we have reached a certain age, we don't really learn anything new (at least anything of real significance). But what we do learn, if we are truly alert, is new connections, new contexts in which to place what we already know.

Keep this reflection in mind as we try to grasp the meaning of Jesus' words in today's Gospel. It is important to note that, when Jesus gives his answer to the lawyer's question, he was not telling this man or his companions anything new. He was quoting a familiar passage from Deuteronomy – one that every Jew would know. In fact, it is a bit of scripture which devout Jews recite every day, expressing their obligation to love God above all things. Nor was his coupling of this passage with a passage from Leviticus (which speaks of "neighbor" love) foreign to their way of thinking.

What *was* new about Jesus' statement was the connection he made and the context into which he put these scripture passages. The lawyer's question is about "the greatest commandment of the law." What he is thinking about was the body of 613 laws which the rabbis agreed were binding on all Jews.

The lawyer's question, therefore, was: "Which of these 613 laws, which Jewish scholars accept as binding, is the one that gives unity to all the rest?"

Is there any parallel in our Christian tradition that would enable someone to put a similar question to Jesus? Actually there is. We have a code of canon law that has almost three times as many laws as the body of Jewish laws. In it are 1752 laws that, like the 613, tell us how we are supposed to act in given situations. (I say 1752, though I think John Paul II added a few more). Jesus' answer to the lawyer in our Gospel reading could also be given to a canon lawyer who might ask which law in canon law is the greatest.

The genius of Jesus' answer is that he says, in effect, "None." What he insists is that no one of these 613 laws (or no one of our 1752 canons in our Canon Law) is most important. No one of these laws can give unity to them all. What he is telling his hearers and us is that, if you want to find the fundamental obligation that directs and unifies the whole life of a person who wants to serve God, you have to go outside these laws (whether Jewish laws or Christian laws). You cannot find the unity of the laws in a legal principle. You can only find it in a theological principle, namely, a principle that is specifically about God.

Another way of putting this is to say that Jesus distinguishes between the laws and the Law. There is no law among the laws that is fundamental and unifying. The one reality that is fundamental and unifying is The Law.

What I am suggesting is that we may use the word "law" in two different senses. Law may be used to indicate a rule of action which prescribes *what you are to do* in some particular kind of situation. But "law" may also be used to tell you, not so much what you must do in some particular situation, but what you must do in any situation. Or to put it another way and maybe more clearly, Law tells you *what you must be and what you must become.*

Law in the first sense (prescribing what to do) is always in the plural. For we are faced with a multitude of totally different situations on which we must act. Hence there must be laws to give us direction in this situation and that.

But Law, understood in the second sense (as indicating what we must be or at least try to become) is always in the singular. For it tells us how we are to live our lives in all situations and at all times. It brings moral unity into our lives. It is in building this moral unity that we form our conscience.

In understanding today's Gospel, it is helpful to note that the lawyer was thinking of law in the first sense: law as a rule of action to be applied to specific situations, whereas Jesus has moved the dialogue to a whole new level. He is no longer talking about any one of the 613 Jewish laws or [we can add] the 1752 Christian laws. He is talking about the Law which is outside all specific laws. He has made new connections. He has placed the discussion in a new context. He has moved from a legal context to a theological one.

What then becomes clear is that the principle of unity of all laws turns out to be not really a law at all. It is the spirit that should motivate everything we do: both those things that are prescribed by particular laws and those many, many areas of life that do not seem to come under the direction of any particular law at all.

As a matter of fact, most of the things I do in my life – my actions, my relationships, my conversations – are not regulated by any particular law. How do you deal with misunderstandings that have come up with a dear friend? How do you break the news to someone that a child or a parent has died? No particular law can tell you what to do in these and countless other relational situations in our lives. But everything I do involves my response to God's goodness and my neighbor's needs. In other words, whatever I do involves me, in one way or another, in loving God and loving my neighbor.

To lead a good moral life, therefore, it is not sufficient for me to respond to those situations that are covered by some particular law. I have to respond to all situations in terms of the demands of God's love and the good of the neighbor.

If I live simply by the law, I will be quite satisfied with myself, if I keep the laws which obligate me. If, on the other hand, I live by love, I know that I shall never be satisfied with myself or with my actions. For there will always be "MORE" that love asks of me – for the service of God and the good of the neighbor. The Law does not abolish the particular laws, like the Ten Commandments, for instance; it simply places them in a new context, in which they take on new meaning. If we center our moral life around the mere carrying out of the various laws that bind us, it is all too easy to generate in oneself a smug sense of self-righteousness: I have kept the laws. Therefore, I have done all that I have to do.

On the other hand, following the Law, namely, the uncompromising demands of total love of God and continuous response to my neighbor's needs, leaves me with a salutary and healthy sense of self-discontent, for I know that I cannot really do all that I have to do. The task of total love is always unfinished business.

THE THIRTY-FIRST SUNDAY IN ORDINARY TIME

Malachi 1:14b-2:2b, 8-10
Psalm 131: 1, 2, 3
1 Thessalonians 2: 7b-9, 13
Matthew 23:1-12

A quick look at today's readings suggests that they are rough on religious leaders. The prophet Malachi, writing for the exiles who have returned from Babylon to Jerusalem, has only critical words for their religious leaders. He indicts them for partiality in the administration of justice and for their failure to give people the instruction in the Law. Yet the Malachi reading ends on an unusual note. After speaking of divisions, he says to the whole community of Israel: "Have we not all the one Father? Has not the one God created us?"

Both the criticism of religious leaders and at the same time the earnest call to realize that "only one is our Father" are probably the reason why this passage from Malachi was chosen to go with today's Gospel.

In the Gospel, Matthew has strong words of blame for the religious leaders of his time, the scribes and Pharisees. He chides them for their failure to give proper leadership to the people. He warns against their hypocrisy: "They do not practice what they preach." They lay heavy burdens on people instead of giving them help to carry their burdens. They are vain and ostentatious, always wanting positions of honor and honorific titles. They obviously want to be served rather than to serve their people.

So, if the Gospel picks up Malachi's message of being "rough on religious leaders," it seems that the religious leaders Matthew has in mind are the Jewish leaders in Jesus' life time. So at first reading it might seem that the religious leaders of Church community for which Matthew wrote, as well as the leaders of today's Church are off the hook. But unfortunately for those who would think this way, we need to realize that the Gospel of Matthew was written with a pastoral concern for the Church of his day and in fact for the Church of any age, including our own.

The perennial value of this Gospel passage is the perspective on church that it implies. The censures that Matthew directs against the Jewish leaders for the most part don't seem to be any big deal. So they weren't very kind or helpful. So they were vain and took joy in titles and positions of honor. Granted they ought to be above this sort of thing.

But the point that the Gospel is making is that it's the mentality behind these petty concerns that would be fatal to the health and well-being of the kind of community that Jesus intended the community of his followers to be. The Christian community must be absolutely egalitarian. There is no place for privilege, titles, honors, etc. There is a place for hierarchy. But the hierarchy that Matthew emphasizes turns out to be no hierarchy at all, at least not one that separates some in the community from others. The only human hierarchy Matthew recognizes is one that unites rather than separates; for it is a hierarchy of service. The greatest among you is the one who will be servant of the rest.

The Christian community, as Matthew conceives it in this passage, is a communion of sisters and brothers in which God is the Father and Jesus is the Teacher. The point is all of us, from the greatest among us to the least (however one defines these terms) are brothers and sisters.

Note Matthew's description of Christ as our one Teacher. You would expect that he would say: "You have One Teacher; and you are all students." After all, teachers relate to students. But that is not what the text says. It deliberately breaks this expected relationship. It puts it this way: "You have one Teacher; the rest of you are brothers and sisters." Why does Matthew use "brothers and sisters," where he might be expected to use "students"? His obvious intent is to lead us to the climax of the ecclesiology of this passage, where he says: "Do not call anyone among you 'father.' Only One is your Father, the One in heaven."

We might ask: "Does Matthew allow for any hierarchy among those who are called "brothers and sisters"? The answer is "Yes," but – as I have already pointed out – it is not a hierarchy of title or privilege or wealth or power. It is a hierarchy of service in which the only greatness that matters belongs to those who serve the rest.

If we look at history, we know that all too many times Church authority has rendered the Gospel ineffective by opting for a hierarchy of privilege and power rather than of service, of domination rather than empowerment. One day St. Thomas Aquinas was a not too willing guest of Pope Alexander IV in the Pope's palace. The Pope waved his hand about the palace and said: "Well, Peter can no longer say: 'Gold and silver I have not.'" (He was referring to the story in Acts where Peter sees a lame man near the temple and says: "Gold and silver I have not. But what I have I give." And he cured the man of his lameness). Thomas answered: "Yes, Peter has great wealth. He can no longer say: gold and silver, I have none. But neither can he any longer say: 'Arise and walk.'"

The Second Vatican Council was deeply conscious that hierarchy has all too often operated out of a position of privilege. Article 32 of *Lumen Gentium* captured something of the ecclesiology implicit in today's Gospel reading. They said: "The laity have Christ for their brother who, though he is Lord of all, came not to be served but to serve." The document continues: "They also have for their brothers those in the sacred ministry..." In these strong words the Council is saying that all in the Christian community, whatever their ministry, are brothers and sisters. Is this one way of understanding Jesus' words: "Do not call anyone among you father? You have only One Father: the One in heaven." Is this to remind us of the egalitarian nature of the Church, namely, that no matter what role we have in the Church – pope, bishop, priest, religious, laity – what is most basic is that we are all sisters and brothers?

Of the highest priority among the services that the Church leaders are obliged to provide for all their brothers and sisters is the celebration of the Eucharist. As you know a Synod of bishops of the world, met with the Pope several years ago to discuss the topic of the Eucharist. One of the issues they discussed in their final report is the primal importance of the Sunday Eucharist. They highlight a huge problem that exists in many places in the world. They said: "The lack of priests to celebrate the Sunday Eucharist worries us a great deal." Such a statement of concern would surely be followed, one might expect, by some creative ways of providing the necessary priests so that everywhere the celebration of Sunday Eucharist might again be a reality in the life of the Church. Yet this is what they said: "[This worry] invites us to pray and more actively promote priestly vocations."

A good enough approach, I suppose. After all, Jesus did tell us to pray for whatever we needed and he assures us that God will answer our prayers. It's true. God does indeed answer our prayers. But – and this is a big "but" – does God necessarily have to answer our prayers in the way we think God should answer them or even in the way we expect God to answer them?

In the context of intercessory prayer and the mystery of God's response, I want to tell you a story (one I wish I could tell to the bishops). It's about a man who was stranded on a house top in a flood. A group came by on a large raft and offered to take him along. He said: "No, thank you. I'm a man of prayer. God will take care of me." Then a helicopter hovered over the house; and again, with his certainty about divine assistance, he refused the invitation to get aboard the helicopter. Not long afterwards a couple in a row boat came along and called to him to join them. But again he said no, that he was waiting for God to help him. Finally, the flood covered the house completely and the man drowned. When he got to the next life, he reproached God: "Why didn't you help me? Why didn't you hear my prayer?" God gave him a stern look and answered: "I tried to help you. Why do you think I sent that raft and that helicopter and finally that rowboat?"

THE THIRTY-SECOND SUNDAY IN ORDINARY TIME

Wisdom 6:12-16
Psalm 63: 2, 3-4, 5-6, 7-8
1 Thessalonians 4:13-18
Matthew 25: 1-13

In a contemporary version of the Gospel parable the wise virgins would undoubtedly be those who used the long-lasting Duracell batteries; the foolish virgins, those who settled for the cheaper batteries that didn't last as long. But somehow the parable loses its picturesqueness when translated into today's way of providing portable light. Much more poetic to think of oil lamps, even though the number of people remembering them is becoming fewer and fewer.

I remember as a child visiting my grandparents' home and being fascinated by those marvelous brass lamps, with the big base filled with oil, and the key you turned to lengthen the wick and the glass shade that protected the flame, and the little opening in the base with a small top on it that you had to unscrew to replenish the supply of oil. My grandparents' house did not have electricity in all the rooms. I liked best being in the room with the oil lamps. There was something exciting about watching the flickering flame and the shadows it cast on the walls. It was a special thrill when I was allowed to turn the key that made the wick go up higher and make the flame bigger.

Twenty-five years ago last summer I was in Israel. In the shops in the old city of Jerusalem, one of the most plentiful articles for sale were replicas of ancient Palestinian clay lamps. I brought one home, but, alas, I don't remember what happened to it.

The remarkable thing about these clay lamps is that they all seemed to be about the same size and were all quite small: about three inches in length, maybe a couple of inches in width. They were quite shallow, barely an inch deep. They had two openings: a larger one at the center (into which you poured the oil) and a small one in the front where you would put the floating wick that would burn the oil.

You needed only one look at these clay lamps to realize that, if you expected to use them for any length of time, you had better carry an extra supply of oil. There were just too small to expect them to burn for very long. Today's parable centers about these little clay oil lamps. The wise virgins were those who brought an extra supply of oil with them; those who failed to do so were the foolish virgins. Jesus' intent in this parable is to express not only the need of being prepared for the Lord's coming, but also the need of proper foresight as an important element of that preparation. It is not enough to have the initial light. There is the continual need of renewing that light.

Each one of us, when we were baptized, was given a light -- a lighted candle as a symbol of faith. We were admonished to keep it burning bright. It is as if we were given little clay lamps, in which the light of faith had been lighted. But the initial lighting was not enough. The light of faith has to be continually renewed.

Keeping the light of faith burning means a number of things. First of all, it means deepening our perception of what faith is and what it is meant to do in our lives. Faith which is an obedient response to God's self-revelation is not primarily an answer to all of life's questions. A person of faith may well have as many unanswered questions as an unbeliever. Faith is the call to live by God's light, while often leaving many questions unanswered. Faith is surely a light for us, but it does not necessarily dispel all the darkness that so often envelops our lives. Faith gives us a place to stand, even if it's in the shadowlands. Faith lights the way through darkness. If it cannot avoid the valley of darkness, it can show us the way through the darkness with the confidence that the God of mystery is at our side.

To use another metaphor, faith may be likened to the center of a circle where light is the brightest. Faith roots us in that center. From that center we can go out to many points on the circumference, where there may be a great deal of darkness. But we need not fear. For, being rooted in the light that is at the center of the circle, we can return there, not always to get answers that will penetrate the darkness on the circumference, but to be assured that, as we walk through the darkness, our hand is in the hand of God.

Second, renewing faith not only means deepening our perception of what it means; it also widens the areas of our lives that we allow faith to touch. Thus, faith is not only a vertical experience in which we meet God. It is also a horizontal experience in which we meet one another in God. Faith not only leads us to the Heart of God. It draws us also into the hearts of our sisters and brothers.

Perhaps a third dimension of faith-renewal that is especially necessary today is the deepening of our grasp of the faith-symbols that we use to articulate our experience of God. One of the reasons many people find it difficult to experience God's power as love and tenderness is because we are limited by the traditional faith-symbols our tradition has tended to use in speaking about God.

All the language we use about God is analogical or metaphorical. They are symbols derived from human experience. These symbols drawn from human experience may enrich or they may impoverish the way we think about God.

The symbols of our western Christian tradition have been strongly male-derived and male-dominated. They have failed to give due attention to feminine symbols of God. Our tradition, in consequence, tends to conceive of God as a power that transforms by might and by force rather than a power that transforms by love and mercy.

References to feminine symbols of God do indeed abound in our tradition. The tradition has simply tended to ignore them or allow them to be overwhelmed by male images. Thus, all too readily the feminine side of God has been neglected. This is not just an affront to women. It is also an affront to God, a refusal to expand the way we think about God.

Today's first reading – from the Book of Wisdom expresses beautifully this neglected aspect of our experience of God. It speaks of Wisdom both as created and uncreated. Wisdom is a creature of God. Yet at a profounder level, Wisdom is God, making her rounds seeking those worthy of her and graciously appearing to them.

Read the Book of Wisdom or Proverbs and you will see that Wisdom, whether created or uncreated, is always She, not He. Holy Wisdom, Hagia Sophia is the feminine name of God. Julian of Norwich is entirely within the biblical tradition when she writes glowingly about her experience of God our Mother and of Jesus our Mother.

One final dimension of faith. Faith is deeply personal, yet it is not an individual experience. It is a community reality. I recall years ago making a retreat at Gethsemani in Merton's hermitage. One evening I sat on the porch. It was dusk and the fireflies began to light up the darkness of the valley. One would appear here, one there. Thousands of them flickering at different moments in different places. The thought came to me: what if they all lighted up at once? The brightness would be dazzling. It would dispel all the darkness in the valley. The valley would be full of light.

Your little clay lamp or mine can shed but a small bit of light, where there may be much darkness. But millions of clay lamps, continually replenished with oil, could fill the world with light: a light that could dissipate and burn away all the violence and anger and hatred that seem to be so strong in our world and so destructive of our society.

God who places the future in our hands will give us the resources to build the future that is not yet, but that can be. We must have the faith and the wisdom to hope.

THE THIRTY-THIRD SUNDAY IN ORDINARY TIME

Proverbs 31:10-13, 19-20, 30-31
Psalm 128:1-2, 3, 4-5
1 Thessalonians 5:1-6
John 15:4-5

To understand the parable, we need to clear our minds – for the moment at least – from the ordinary way in which we use the word "talents." For ordinarily we think of talents as "special gifts" people have from God, which they ought to use for God's glory and for the service of God's people. This is a derived meaning of the word. In its original meaning the word "talent" designated a piece of money.

In the Roman monetary system the basic bit of money was the denarius. It would, I suppose, be roughly equivalent to our one-dollar bill. The parable, however, is not about denarii, but about talents. By contrast with the denarius, a talent was the largest denomination of Roman currency. Roughly, a talent amounted to about 10,000 denarii. Now that was an enormous amount of money.

In the economic system of the time one denarius was the normal day's pay of an ordinary worker. Suppose a person were to work six days a week (with no time off other than the Sabbath), it would take him more than 30 years, at a denarius a day to earn ONE talent. To earn 5 talents, he would have to work, roughly, a hundred and fifty years at a denarius a day.

As I have mentioned, the parable's meaning has become obscured because of a transfer of meaning. The symbol used in the parable has come to designate that which it symbolizes. Hence "talents" have come to mean particular gifts, natural and spiritual, which we have received from God. Thus, the parable becomes one about the proper use of the gifts (i.e., the talents) God has given us.

The parable becomes significantly more powerful when we understand that Jesus is talking in the parable about money. When we understand the parable in this way, we see that the third fellow who received the one talent was receiving more than he would probably have made in his whole lifetime.

It is evident from the parable that the wealthy man who gave so prodigally of his money expected his servants to use the money to make more money for him when he returned. Using the money to make more money involved taking risks. The stakes were high. Hence the risks were big.

Simply put, the parable is about taking risks for the Kingdom of God. Jesus acted out this parable in his life. His life was one continual risk. He risked his good name and reputation by associating with the outcasts of society: not only those who were outcasts because they were poor, but also those who were outcasts because they were sinners. When Jesus' opponents accused him of spending time with drunkards, prostitutes and tax-collectors, they had plenty of evidence to back up their charge.

Jesus risked the anger of the religious establishment when he cured people on the Lord's Day. He drew their wrath upon himself when he refused to accept their narrow understanding of God. He risked his very life by openly challenging the legalism of the religious leaders and offering in its place a way of life that would give primacy, not to laws, but to persons, their worth, their dignity, their freedom.

You don't have to read very far into the gospels to realize that Jesus did not play it safe. Proclaiming the kingdom of God brought constant risks. He was not afraid to face them. All of which brings us to the parable about the three men. Two of them took risks with the money they had been given. We are not told what risks they took. But they must have taken the chance of losing their money in order to be able to return double the amount to their master.

We are told exactly what the third servant did: he took no risks. He buried the money in the ground. He was looking for security and he found it – in the ground. He wanted to make sure that he would be able to return exactly what he had received.

What he found out, but too late, was that that was not enough. Yes, the parable is about taking risks for the Kingdom of God as against seeking security at all costs. I don't mean to imply that the parable is about acting rashly or in a foolhardy way. In fact, there is in our moral tradition a special virtue that is concerned with risk-taking. It is the virtue of prudence, for which St. Thomas Aquinas had the highest regard. He saw it as regulating all the moral virtues.

But one thing St. Thomas is very clear about: *prudence is very much concerned with acting in a particular situation*, not with refusing to act. Prudence, he tells us, seeks for certitude, but not a certitude that is absolute. Prudence means weighing the issues at stake in a given situation and then being willing to take the risks involved in pursuing a particular course of action or making a particular decision. What must be stressed is that a prudent person is a person who ACTS – never precipitously or rashly, but nonetheless with the realization that we cannot go through life waiting for perfect certitude before we act.

We must not confuse prudence with cautiousness, which is no virtue at all. The cautious person is so paralyzed by the risks which prudence sees that he or she is afraid to act at all. The first two servants were prudent; the third was cautious. He wasn't going to take any risks. So he buried his talent and in a sense buried himself with it.

We have to learn to run the risks that are necessarily involved in contingent situations. Opening our hearts in friendship to another means running risks: the risk among other things of getting hurt.

Reading and learning and expanding our minds mean risk: we may have to change the way we have been thinking. Making decisions that are truly our own and taking responsibility for them, instead of standing in the shadow of someone else's decision, means taking risks. It also means becoming a more authentic person. Offering ourselves totally to God's will entails risks. He may ask too much of us! He asked Jesus to go to the cross.

Passing judgment on our state and national policies in the light of moral values when so many of our political leaders are talking simply about strategies and tactics; being ready – if we really believe it – to say that our national and state stances are all too often arrogant, pragmatic and unprincipled – means taking risks. For such judgments require that we act to make our positions known. It means putting ourselves and our integrity on the line.

Passing judgment on leadership in the Catholic Church is something we have – in the past at least – grown accustomed not to do. When certain teachings or policies come to us from the Vatican, we have been brought up to accept them, whether these policies or teachings make sense to us or not.

Much has happened in the Church in recent years that force us to challenge this unquestioning approach. The Second Vatican Council called for prudent dialogue in the Church between pastors (understood either as bishops or pastors of parishes) and the laity. The Council invites the laity to this dialogue by pointing out that the laity, by reason of the knowledge and competence they may enjoy, are permitted – even sometimes obliged – to speak up on matters that concern the good of the Church. Pastors, for their part, are called upon to promote the dignity as well as the responsibility of the laity in the Church. "Let them willingly make use of their *prudent* advice. They should confidently entrust to them offices in the service of the Church and leave them freedom and space to act. Indeed, they should encourage them to take up work on their own initiative" (art. 37 *Lumen Gentium*).

Note here a twofold call: one the call to a readiness to offer prudent advice, but also the call to a willingness to listen to that prudent advice. Note also that it is a call to act. Groups like "The Voice of the Faithful," "Call to Action," "Future Church," "The American Catholic" and other such groups are responding to this call. As they work for radical change in the Church's structure: change that will accept and value the *sensus fidelium*, that practical knowledge that belongs, not just to priests and bishops, but to the whole body of the faithful as they live out faith in response to the Holy Spirit.

Thus, prudently raising questions about current practices in the church is, the Council says, a right – maybe even a duty. It clearly involves risks. But it may be that at the present time prudent loyal opposition on some issues may well be the call of prudence. *"We have to make ourselves heard."* (Thomas Merton)

SOLEMNITY OF CHRIST THE KING

Ezekiel 34: 11-12, 15-17
Psalm 23: 1-2, 2-3, 5-6
1 Corinthians 15:20-26, 28
Matthew 25:31-46

One of the great classics of western literature – that probably few people read today – is St. Augustine's *City of God*. It is a huge book, both in length and in the breadth of its vision. He wrote it in the beginning of the fifth century when civilization as he knew it seemed about to collapse. He describes two cities: the city of God and the earthly city. "These two cities," Augustine writes, "were made by two loves: the earthly city by the love of self-unto the contempt of God, the heavenly city by the love of God unto the contempt of self." (Bk. 4, c. 28)

Augustine offers a sweeping view of human history – whose goal is to transform the earthly city, the world, into the heavenly city or the kingdom of God.

Today is the feast of Christ the King. It is fitting therefore that we reflect briefly on the kingdom of God. Since kings are pretty much "out" these days, we may find it difficult to get excited about this topic.

Yet the kingdom must have meant something exciting to Jesus. He was continuingly speaking about it. It's at the heart of his preaching. It's fair, then, to put the question:

what made Jesus so enthusiastic about the "kingdom of God"? What did he mean by the Kingdom of God?

In his preaching Jesus never offers one simple answer to that question. He did give lots of hints of what the kingdom of God meant to him. We should not be surprised that He never defines it. Jesus was not a philosopher proclaiming abstract truths. He was preeminently – and so marvelously – a story-teller. He describes the kingdom in stories taken from real life situations that his hearers would understand.

Have you ever noticed how his story-parables tell us, not what the kingdom is, but what it is "like"? It's like a sower who puts seed in the ground and watches and waits for it to grow. It's like a man coming upon a valuable treasure hidden in a field who sells everything he has to buy that field. It's like a pearl merchant finding the most exquisite of pearls who gives up all his pearls to have that one pearl. It is like a lowly mustard seed that grows into a big tree, a fishnet that catches good and bad fish, a banquet for which some turn up and others do not.

Every one of these stories – and so many others Jesus told – gives us some insight into what the kingdom meant to Jesus. It is a many-sided reality that can never be fully captured in words or any single story.

Some time ago I was asked to write an article on the kingdom of God. In the article I pointed out the different meanings of the Greek word for kingdom, Basileia. My editor graciously said she liked my article, but asked me if I could simplify it a bit. It was a bit on the heavy side. The editor was being very gentle.

So I looked for help. One day I asked Sister Catherine Teresa Martin what she thought Jesus meant by the kingdom. Her answer was this: "I think Jesus meant that the kingdom is the way God wants the world to be. The world is partially there (there are a lot of good people), but it is not yet fully there."

I thought to myself: "Great Scott! What it took Augustine some 900 pages to say, and Jesus a number of parables, Catherine put into one sentence!"

How does God want the world to be? God has given us an answer in Jesus. For in Jesus God entered into the world fully and completely. The Second Vatican Council has said: "By his incarnation the Son of God has identified himself in some fashion with every human being. He worked with human hands, he thought with a human mind...and loved with a human heart." *(Gaudium et Spes,* 22)

Over the centuries there have been times when the disciples of Jesus forgot this deepest meaning of the incarnation and looked upon the world with suspicion. They saw the sinfulness of the world and its failings (which are certainly there) and ignored the goodness that is also there; hence they fled from the world.

There have been entire spiritualities centering about this attitude of world denial. They have been spiritualities that have seen the human body and sexuality as evil. There have been spiritualities that have cultivated the mentality that if you enjoyed something it must be evil, and if you did something that was especially difficult for you it must be pleasing to God.

This simply does not fit with an understanding of a God who became part of the human situation, not viewing it from afar, but immersed in it in all its messiness, triviality, and pettiness. Jesus scandalized supposedly holy people because he was not afraid to be in touch with sinners, with the reprobates of the world.

Vatican II has said: "It is clear that Christians are not deterred by the Christian message from building up the world or impelled to neglect the well-being of their fellow men and women. They are rather more stringently bound to do these things." *(Gaudium et Spes, 32)*

Indeed, the Council begins its document on the Church and the world with these words: "The joys and hopes, the sorrows and anxieties of this age, especially those who are poor or in any way afflicted, these too are the joys and sorrows of the followers of Christ. Indeed, nothing genuinely human fails to raise an echo in their hearts." (Art. 1)

Today's Gospel reading makes very concrete and graphic this sharing in people's joys and sorrows, but especially the poor and deprived of our world. In fact, the Gospel is about as subtle as being hit over the head with a sledge hammer.

Christ is everywhere in the world, since "he has joined himself in some way with every human person." But he is particularly present, hidden – so often it is true – in those whose needs are greatest: he is in the hungry, the sick, the naked, the imprisoned, the exiled, the displaced. What the Gospel makes vividly clear is that these seem to be the places where Jesus so often goes unnoticed.

A loving, concerned Jesus moves about – so often unrecognized – where hurricanes and floods and earthquakes and racial discrimination and hunger and homelessness and poverty and all the things that oppress the poor are part of the landscape.

But one day we will hear: "I was hungry and you fed me, thirsty and you gave me to drink, imprisoned and you visited me." And we will ask in surprise, "When did we do these things"? And we will be told -- what we should have realized all along but seem so easily to forget: "What you did to the least of my brothers and sisters, you did to me."

Yet the Gospel suggests another possible scenario: "I was hungry and you took away my food stamps. I was sick and you deprived me of my health insurance. I was in school and you took away teachers and nurses. I was a detainee in prison and you abused and mistreated me." And once again the refrain: "Since you did it to the least of my sisters and brothers, you did it to me." And there will be surprise and disbelief and – eternal regrets.

APPENDIX 1

Biography of William H. Shannon

William H. Shannon was born December 6, 1917, in
Rochester, N.Y. He grew up in St. Salome Parish in
Irondequoit, N.Y., and was educated at the parish school,
St. Andrew's Seminary (Rochester), and St. Bernard's
Seminary (Rochester). He was ordained on June 5, 1943,
by Bishop James E. Kearney at Sacred Heart Cathedral and
was named a domestic prelate (monsignor) in 1966.

His sole parish assignment was as assistant pastor at
Sacred Heart Cathedral from 1943 to 1945. When he was
appointed professor of religion at Nazareth College of
Rochester in 1946, he began an association with Nazareth
and the Sisters of Saint Joseph that continued for the rest
of his life.

Msgr. Shannon earned a master's degree in history from
Canisius College in 1949 and a doctorate in history from
the University of Ottawa in 1953, and he completed post-
doctoral work at McMaster University. He was named full
professor at Nazareth College in 1958 and was honored as
professor emeritus upon his retirement in 1982.

While a faculty member and chair of the college's
Department of Theology, he became a widely known and
respected teacher of theology, Scripture, and Church
history. Committed to the spirit and reforms of the Second
Vatican Council, he wrote often about Biblical and
liturgical renewals, authority in the Church, and

interreligious dialogue. He served as chaplain of the college from 1949 to 1975, and as chaplain at the Motherhouse of the Sisters of Saint Joseph from 1980 until his death in 2012.

In the 1970s Monsignor Shannon developed a deep interest in the writing of Thomas Merton. His research and contacts with other Merton scholars led him to play a key role in organizing the International Thomas Merton Society (for which he served as founding president), and his extensive writing on the Cistercian monk's life and works established him as one of the world's foremost authorities on Merton. He authored and edited many books and articles including several volumes of Merton's letters and essays, The Thomas Merton Encyclopedia, and Silent Lamp, an acclaimed biography. He also wrote extensively on a range of topics including spirituality, non-violence, moral issues, liturgy, Scripture, and prayer.

After his retirement, Monsignor Shannon continued lecturing and attending conferences worldwide. His correspondence suggests the many associations he developed during his long and prolific career.   His distinctions include an endowed chair in Catholic studies and a lecture series at Nazareth College, both of which bear his name. He received honorary degrees from Nazareth College, St. Bernard's Institute of Theology and Ministry, and St. Bonaventure University.

In addition to his scholarship, Monsignor Shannon will be remembered for the spiritual guidance he offered to many, his commitment to non-violence, the depth and insight of his homilies, and his perspective on faith.

Kathleen Urbanic
Congregational Archivist for the Sisters of Saint Joseph of Rochester

APPENDIX 2

A Monumental Contribution:

The William H. Shannon Papers in the SSJ Rochester Archives

The files of a world-renowned scholar are a treasure for any archives, and that is certainly the case with the papers of Monsignor William H. Shannon.

Father Shannon, founding chairman of the Department of Religious Studies at Nazareth College and longtime chaplain at the Motherhouse of the Sisters Saint Joseph, left his papers to the SSJ Rochester Archives at the time of his death in 2012. His files, which fill 39 archival cartons and measure 18 linear feet, represent a career that spans more than six decades and touches on many aspects of religious studies including Scripture, Church history, the renewals of the Second Vatican Council, interreligious dialogue, contemplative prayer, and the writings of Thomas Merton. He wrote and lectured prolifically on these and other topics, becoming widely known and respected for his insight, his commitment to non-violence, and his perspective on faith.

Father Shannon, who often referred to himself as "a Sister of Saint Joseph in spirit," lived at the SSJ Motherhouse for 65 years and chose to leave his scholarly papers in the care of the Sisters' Archives. The task of sorting through his files and collection of books fell to three of his close friends and Nazareth College colleagues: Dr. Christine Bochen, Professor of Religious Studies, Dr. .Monica Weis, SSJ, Professor Emerita of English and. Dr. Barbara Staropoli, SSJ, Professor Emerita of Music. Following his wishes, they sent many of the books and his talks on Merton to the Thomas Merton Room in the library at Nazareth College, created with a generous endowment from Father Shannon in 1985.

The remaining material came to the SSJ Archives, where consulting archivist Diane Riley undertook the work of appraising the papers, arranging them according to archival standards, and organizing them into archival cartons. This careful process took several months and was supported by a grant from the SSJ Ministry Foundation. Diane also prepared a finding aid which provides researchers with detailed information about the collection. The finding aid has been posted on the SSJ Rochester website (www.ssjrochester.org) as well as the International Thomas Merton Society (www.merton.org) and the Catholic Theological Society of America.

The collection contains wonderful resources, including Father Shannon's published articles, lectures, and research files on an array of topics relating to Catholicism, spirituality, religious belief, moral issues, and Biblical studies. Because he was one of the world's foremost authorities on Thomas Merton, his Merton files – which fill nine cartons – are of special value.

A meticulous scholar, Father Shannon carefully saved his correspondence with friends of Merton and Merton researchers living in many parts of the world including North America, Europe, Russia, and Asia. He also saved his homilies, given over the course of several decades on Sundays as well as on feast days, holy days, and secular holidays such as Memorial Day and Thanksgiving.

Father Charles Curran, priest of the Diocese of Rochester, highly respected moral theologian and Professor Emeritus of Southern Methodist University in Dallas, noted that Bill Shannon "made a monumental contribution to Catholic scholarship and life in his writing, especially about Thomas Merton." Thanks to Father Shannon's foresight in leaving his papers to our archives, that contribution will continue as researchers use the Shannon collection and mine the riches there.

Kathleen Urbanic,

Congregational Archivist for the Sisters of Saint Joseph